CW00408023

# The other side of language

# The other side of language
## A philosophy of listening

Gemma Corradi Fiumara
Translated by Charles Lambert

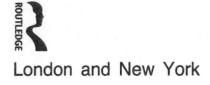

London and New York

First published 1990
by Routledge
11 New Fetter Lane, London EC4P 4EE

Simultaneously published in the USA and Canada
by Routledge
a division of Routledge, Chapman and Hall, Inc.
29 West 35th Street, New York, NY 10001

Set in 10/12pt Times by Input Typesetting Ltd, London
and printed in England by Clays Ltd, St Ives plc

*British Library Cataloguing in Publication Data*
Corradi Fiumara, Gemma
   The other side of language: a philosophy of
   listening.
   I. Title  II. Filsofia dell' ascotto. (Milan: Jaca Book)
   *English*
   195

ISBN 0–415–02621–0

*Library of Congress Cataloging-in-Publication Data*
Corradi Fiumara, Gemma.
   [Filosofia dell'ascolto. English]
   The other side of language: a philosophy of listening/Gemma
   Corradi Fiumara.
      p.    cm.
   Translation of: Filosofia dell'ascolto. (Milan: Jaca Book)
   Includes bibliographical references.
   ISBN 0–415–02621–0
   1. Listening (Philosophy) 2. Knowledge. Theory of. I. Title.
B105.L54C6713 1990
128'.3–dc20   89–10948

The publishers have made every effort to contact the copyright holders
for the jacket illustration 'Maquette of a Monument Symbolizing the
Liberation of the Spirit' by Antoine Pevsner. We will be pleased to
hear from anyone holding the copyright for this material.

195
Fi
(349)

In memory of Paola, Roca and Mirella

# Contents

# Chapter 1

# Towards a fuller understanding of *logos*

## 'SAYING' AND 'LISTENING' IN WESTERN TRADITION

Among the widespread meanings of the Greek term *logos*[1] there do not appear to be recognizable references to the notion and capacity of listening; in the tradition of western thought we are thus faced with a system of knowledge that tends to ignore listening processes. On the other hand, among the possible meanings of the verb *legein*[2] (besides the prevalent ones related to saying) there are meanings of a different nature, such as to 'shelter', 'gather', 'keep', 'receive', which would surely be more conducive to a cognitive attitude based on 'proper hearing'.[3]

Within the realm of practical activity that can be associated with a 'doing' word – the verb *legein* – we can identify relational propensities which seem to disappear entirely at the level of the substantive noun *logos*. As is well known, abstract nouns such as *logos* imply a level of linguistic achievement which surpasses practical matters; such terms require in fact a further stage in the skill for conceptual development.

We could therefore better render the meaning of the term *logos* if we also refer to the verb *legein*. Of course this verb means 'say', 'speak', 'enunciate', and if we begin from this well-known rendering and follow the same semantic path we come upon similar meanings, such as 'reason', 'account', 'expression', etc. There is a need, however, to look further into the possible ways of understanding such a pivotal word in the west as *logos*. Perhaps we could start out by admitting that there could be no saying without hearing, no speaking which is not also an integral part of listening, no speech which is not somehow received. In view of the problems and contentions which can be encountered in research into the phylogenesis and ontogenesis of language we are inclined to believe that an individual can speak only if he is listened to, rather than there being something he might say that one would subsequently attend to 'by means of' listening.[4]

The meaning the Greeks assigned to the word *logos* has gradually gained worldwide acceptance, and whatever might have been passed down through the action word *legein* has been disregarded. This moulding, ordering sense of 'saying', in fact, has become drastically detached from the semantic richness of *legein*. Elevated to an essential principle of our culture, such a ruling set of meanings appears to control and shape all of our rational pursuits, and it is amazing that our culture can develop in association with such a limited, reduced-by-half concept of language.

The tendency to constantly invoke dialogue in conjunction with this blind-spot on the issue of listening thus appears as a puzzling feature of our culture. As Heidegger points out:

> Language came to be represented – indeed first of all with the Greeks – as vocalisation, as sound and voice, hence phonetically . . . Language is a vocalisation which signifies something. This suggests that language attains at the outset that preponderant character which we designate with the name 'expression'. This correct but externally contrived representation of language as 'expression', remains definitive from now on. It is still so today. Language is taken to be expression, and vice versa.[5]

The search for a listening perspective would not require us to devise some way of drawing out our knowledge claims, starting from some hypothetical centre, or conceptual frame, and then seeing how far it unfolds, or is reproduced, in the details of our understanding. It would be perhaps more fruitful to tackle an upward-directed analysis of our rational pursuits starting from the original mechanisms, from the basic premises. At any moment in which reality is constructed we can identify an attitude which is able to say and not to listen – at that moment, in fact, a halved and overwhelming *logos* manifests itself. If we start out from this basic concern we can then perhaps go back into the cultural wire-netting and discover how the mechanism of 'saying without listening' has multiplied and spread, to finally constitute itself as a generalized form of domination and control.[6]

It is not merely a question of understanding the power shifts from one epistemology to another: the unavoidable philosophical problem lies in clarifying the preliminary interactions behind the functioning of control mechanisms. 'Logic, as the doctrine of *logos*, considers thinking to be the assertion of something about something. According to logic, such speech is the basic characteristic of thinking'.[7] A thinking primarily anchored to saying-without-listening.

Following this line of argument one should refer to Heidegger's etymological-philosophical study in which he attempts to reveal a more fundamental sense of *logos*. Starting out with Heraclitus' famous fragment – 'When you have listened, not to me but to the . . . *Logos*, it is wise to agree that all things are one'[8] – Heidegger goes on to remark:

> No-one would want to deny that in the language of the Greeks from early on *legein* means to talk, say or tell. However, just as early and even more originally, *legein* means what is expressed in the similar German word *legen:* to lay down, to lay before. In *legen* a 'bringing together' prevails, the Latin *legere* understood as *lesen*, in the sense of collecting and bringing together. *Legein* properly means the laying-down and laying-before which gathers itself and others.[9]

Perhaps this gathering of itself epitomizes the sort of concentrated listening that is required in intellectual midwifery – the maieutic method. It may be worth noticing that in another Heraclitean fragment the two terms 'listen' and 'speak' are, indeed, used together and, significantly enough, the first term *precedes* the other: 'Men who do not know how to listen or to speak.'[10]

In any case, the fact that in our western mother tongue *legein* mainly, though not exclusively, means 'say', 'speak', 'tell', is beyond question. At the same time we believe that it is essential for us not to neglect, or relinquish, our concern for any 'lesser' significance and not to be satisfied with the accepted, predominant meaning ascribed to *legein*. This is a tentative pursuit which keeps us linked with the complexity of humans; an effort to retrieve subordinate, minor dimensions and to explore those areas which provoke indifference or even repugnance in the clear logic of 'normal', established thinking.

A wider circulation of meanings which may safeguard the

lesser elements can only enhance our respect for the inexhaustible complexity of rationality.[11] It is difficult to imagine how we could possibly claim the right to neglect one of the possible thought formulations winding along the path towards hominization. Neither is there any reason for letting go, or allowing ourselves to lose, the sense of *legein* as laying down or keeping. As Heidegger puts it: 'Is it not finally time to engage ourselves with a question which probably decides many things? The question asks: How does the proper sense of *legein*, to lay, come to mean saying and talking?'[12] To carry forth this unavoidable question rather than attempt to devise any kind of acceptable answer to it, it may be fit time to follow Heidegger in his investigation into the meaning of *legein*. He eloquently says:

> To lay means to bring to lie. Thus to lay is at the same time to place one thing beside another, to lay them together. To lay is to gather (*lesen*). The *lesen* better known to us, namely, the *reading* of something written, remains but one sort of gathering, in the sense of bringing-together-into-lying-before, although it is indeed the predominant sort. The gleaning at harvest time gathers fruit from the soil. The gathering of the vintage involves picking grapes from the vine. Picking and gleaning are followed by the bringing together of the fruit. So long as we persist in the usual appearance we are inclined to take this bringing together as the gathering itself or even its termination. But gathering is more than mere amassing. To gathering belongs a collecting which brings under shelter. Accommodation governs the sheltering; accommodation is in turn governed by safekeeping. That 'something extra' which makes gathering more than a jumbling together that snatches things up is not something only added afterward. Even less is it the conclusion of the gathering, coming last. *The safekeeping that brings something in has already determined the first steps of the gathering and arranged everything that follows.* If we are blind to everything but the sequence of steps, then the collecting follows the picking and gleaning, the bringing under shelter follows the collecting, until finally everything is accommodated in bins and storage rooms. This gives rise to the illusion that preservation and safekeeping have nothing to do with gathering. Yet what would become of a vintage which has not been gathered with an eye to the fundamental matter

of its being sheltered? The sheltering comes first in the essential formation of the vintage.[13]

Here we have a vivid description of the basic doing engendered by listening; as such it brings forth into full bloom a *logos* no longer understood as mere 'saying' but also, and perhaps above all, as a capacity for cultivating proper hearing.

Heidegger further suggests that:

> *Lesen* (to gather) thought in this way does not simply stand near *legen* (to lay). Nor does the former simply accompany the latter. Rather, gathering is already included in laying. Every gathering is already a laying. Every laying is of itself gathering. Then what does 'to lay' mean? Laying brings to lie, in that it lets things lie together before us. All too readily we take this 'letting' in the sense of omitting or letting go. To lay, to bring to lie, to let lie, would then mean to concern ourselves no longer with what is laid down and lies before us – to ignore it. However, *legein* . . . means just this, that whatever lies before us involves us and therefore concerns us.[14]

*Legein*, therefore, is to lay: 'Laying is the letting-lie-before – which is gathered into itself – of that which comes together into presence.'[15] At this point, however, the question could once again be raised: 'How do we shift from the proper sense of *legein*, to lay, to its official meaning, to say, and to talk?' We believe that it is no longer a matter of elegant question-and-answer subtleties. A wider perspective would no longer justify the usual kind of investigation; through the concern for listening we are engaged in a pursuit of such scope that it can not simply be reduced to the question of how this Greek word, *legein*, shifts in meaning from 'lay' to 'say'. And its relevance lies not in the etymological vicissitudes of certain basic terms in our western mother tongue, but in recognizing that meanings may be other than mutually exclusive and that, in any case, *legein* in the sense of 'to lay' allows itself to be placed in a subordinate position by its more assertive meanings which thus acquire semantic predominance. No one would deny that talking necessarily implies listening, and yet no one bothers to point out, for example, that in our culture there has always been a vast profusion of scholarly works focussing on expressive activity and very few, almost none in comparison, devoted to the study of listening. And if cultural concerns lose the 'powerful eros'[16] of true *philo*-sophy then we may find ourselves within a culture that is increasingly separated from the cultivation of rational life.

## THE 'SECONDARY' ISSUE OF LISTENING

'The vulgar tongues', suggests Vico, 'should be the most weighty witnesses concerning the ancient customs of the people that were in use at the time the languages were formed.'[17] The practical sense of *legein* could perhaps be construed as the most 'weighty', reliable witness to the ancient customs of western civilization, when the term was able to unfold in its fuller meaning. With the advent and rule of concepts, the fullness of the word was reduced to mere 'saying' and it almost lost its sense of 'gathering'. This 'second' sense is fully borne out by the 'doing word' *legein* understood as an activity expressed in the germinal productivity of traditions, and in 'vulgar tongues'. The meaning of sheltering, then, although primordial, is not primary in our culture.

Adopting the superior conceptual functions of a coercive *logos* we may thus lose the secure foothold from which we could set up ways of life capable of 'letting-lie-together-before'.[18] 'Scientific' research seems to be the only cultural area in which progress (in the sense of success) can be achieved, since it revolves around such basic logical forms as asking questions, predicting and conditioning. The vital need to be listened to must coexist as a subordinate with the derivatives of an increasingly arrogant *logos*, ready even to ignore anything that does not properly fit in with a logocentric system of knowledge.[19]

Our fashionable language, for example, already resounds with worrisome expressions such as 'ozone layer', 'greenhouse effect', 'acid rain' – all sad news coming across from nature. And yet, it is difficult to perceive that we *hear* this news because these things begin to affect us and that in fact we hear *nothing* until the damage inflicted by our deaf logic only concerns the planet we inhabit. There must be some problem of listening if we only hear from earth when it is so seriously endangered that we cannot help paying heed.

Exploring the term 'logos' Heidegger repeatedly wonders: 'If such is the essence of speaking, then what is hearing?'[20] It may be worth pointing out how rarely this kind of question is engaged in throughout the vast parabola of western tradition – magnificent with philosophic-scientific achievements and perhaps rather opaque in the use of archaic mechanisms of paranoid, Manichaean, excommunicating 'rationality'. We are confronted by a way of thinking that is associated with only half the meaning of our *logos*, so that the simple connotation of *legein* as 'laying' and therefore as 'letting-lie-together-before' may sound banal or even incomprehensible.

Wittgenstein, for instance, recalls: 'In the course of our conversations Russell would often exclaim: "Logic's hell!" And this *perfectly* expresses the feeling we had when we were thinking about the problems of logic; that is to say, their immense difficulty, their hard or slippery texture.'[21] A hardness that might stifle the potential for listening and induce an unfavourable climate for dialogue, constraining it in the coils of restrictive arguments. Logical constructs, seen as 'hard' and slippery', do not appear to further an attitude of listening. And Wittgenstein goes on:

> I believe that the main reason for feeling like this was the following fact: that every time some new linguistic phenomenon occurred to us, it could retrospectively show that our previous explanation was unworkable. We felt that language could always make new, and impossible, demands; and that this made all explanations futile . . .

And further on: 'We say: but that *isn't* how it is! – *It is* like that, though! And all we can do is keep repeating these antitheses.'[22] And, of course, that is all we can do in a logocratic culture in which it is 'logical' for us to remain anchored to assertive discourse. In simple speaking all we can do is 'keep repeating these antitheses', thus uprooting language from a wider and deeper context in which the vast realm of listening could be included. Perhaps there is no justifiable reason why we should have to 'keep repeating' and could not decide, instead, to listen.

Recognizing a distortion in our conception of the *logos* underlying western culture, Heidegger argues: 'We *wrongly* think that the activation of the body's audio equipment is hearing proper. But then hearing in the sense of hearkening and heeding is supposed to be a transposition of hearing proper into the realm of the spiritual.'[23] Irreplaceable and yet ignored, the value of 'heeding' and of 'hearkening' is once again advocated: it is precisely this aspect of our culture that rationality has largely neglected; a culture that still toils with the monotony of so-called theoretical contrasts which perhaps only represent an archaic warlike strategy transposed into the realm of epistemology. The wearisome logomachies of our culture testify to a way of reasoning that is not sufficiently interested in 'heeding', and manages to express itself most of all in the deployment of controversies and invectives, often unaware that it is even trying to stir up contrasts.

Paradoxically, fomenting conflicts seems to be tragically liberating with respect to the crushing deafness produced by an assertive culture intoxicated by the effectiveness of its own 'saying' and increasingly incapable of paying 'heed'. 'Acumen in all areas of life, always driving them apart, and no acumen for bridging the chasms between them',[24] remarks Canetti. This cognitive 'acumen', in fact, appears to be inevitable as it derives from the premises of a *logos* aimed at 'saying' (which is practically equivalent to 'defining') and only occasionally prepared to glean the messages by means of which it could 'bridge chasms', or resolve the gaps that no one knows how to come to terms with any more.

'In human relations', Gadamer points out:

> the important thing is . . . to experience the 'Thou' truly as a 'Thou', i.e. not to overlook his claim and listen to what he has to say to us. To this end, openness is necessary. But this openness exists ultimately not only for the person to whom one listens, but rather *anyone who listens is fundamentally open. Without this kind of openness to one another there is no genuine human relationship*. Belonging together always also means being able to listen to one another.[25]

Well then, if in the absence of a radical reciprocal openness to listening 'no genuine human relationship' exists, we might wonder why listening has never been the focus of philosophical research, and why we should concern ourselves with less fundamental ways of 'openness' when there is an admission that it is possible to be '*fundamentally*' open.

In the light of what we have been discussing, a question like this seems almost futile. In fact, we believe that no one could be held responsible for failing to create a philosophy of listening since this neglect (or blind spot) could be better understood as the harbinger of a desperate, voiceless need, one of the most disturbing and 'secret' queries of our times. In the rapidly escalating self-affirmation of *logos*, very little 'logical' space is left for the tradition of *legein*, and it is therefore unthinkable (unheard-of) that listening could be accepted as a philosophical concern, having by now become too alienated from the assertive tradition of saying.

Vico argues that:

> It is another property of the human mind that whenever men can form no idea of distant and unknown things, they judge them by what is familiar and at hand. This axiom points to the inexhaustible source of all the errors about the principles of humanity that have been adopted by entire nations and by all the scholars. For when the former began to take notice of them and the latter to investigate them, it was on the basis of their own enlightened, cultivated and magnificent times that they judged the origins of humanity, which must nevertheless by the nature of things have been small, crude and quite obscure. *Under this head come two types of conceit, one of nations and the other of scholars.*[26]

'The inexhaustible source of all the errors', then, is to be found in the enlightened, cultivated and magnificent custom of evaluating the phylogenetic and ontogenetic origins of hominization as subordinate to the enlightened logical standpoint of its investigators, so that *any* attitude which is *not* magnificently dialectical and assertive – listening, for example – will 'by the nature of things' have to be small, crude and obscure. The tacit, ubiquitous belief that recent western logic represents the most reliable cognitive standpoint appears to characterize world-wide culture. 'To this conceit of nations is added that of scholars, who will have it that what they know is as old as the world.'[27] And if listening, instead, were an even more ancient 'art', a capacity that has gradually been lost in the noisy inflation of discourse or in the infestation of pseudo-symbolic language? Or conversely could it be the vital, eco-logical rationality of times to come?

And yet Heidegger asks again:

> 'Is all this no more than an arbitrary interpretation and an all-too-alien translation with respect to the usual understanding which takes *logos* as meaning and reason? At first it does

sound strange, and *it may remain so for a long time* – calling *logos* 'the laying that gathers'. But how can anyone decide whether what this translation implies concerning the essence of *logos* remains appropriate, if only in the most remote way, to what Heraclitus named and thought in the name of *logos*?[28]

But the most important query arising from what Heidegger has indicated is that not only does it seem 'strange' to think that *logos* means 'the laying that gathers', but that 'it may remain so for a long time'. For *how* long? Perhaps until the well-spring of western tradition has become exhausted in its overwhelming production of a talking that is not sufficiently interested in listening, and which is parasitic to a 'culture' which can not properly be such, since it is more involved in hunting than in cultivation. The intellectual heritage based on the generally accepted meanings of *logos* is then of primary importance compared to the tradition associated with the meanings of *legein*, which, in fact, remains subordinate and 'secondary'. 'The saying and the talking of mortals comes to pass from early on as *legein*', insists Heidegger. 'The original *legein*, laying, unfolds itself early and in a manner ruling everything unconcealed as saying and talking. *Legein* as laying lets itself be overpowered by the predominant sense . . .'[29] Moreover, as Feyerabend often suggests, the intellectual heritage of the west causes the conceptual connections of other traditions to disappear and thus gives rise to an idea of truth which is fitting for the vacuum it has produced. 'Intellectuals' (like Vico's 'scholars') appear to be comfortably intent on a logic that has little interest in diverse logical paths. And this attitude seems to tally with a partial sense of *logos* understood precisely as a capacity for ordering and explaining, detached from any propensity to receive and listen.[30]

The countless voices of our culture, in fact, always seem to propound wise and rational arguments, arousing in us a desire to appear as equally rational, and therefore to give assent by competing in that same style.

It might be more fruitful, however, to train ourselves in detecting those ways of thinking that are able to parody the values of hominization and yet are unable to develop them. We could thus remain indifferent to those 'rules of good manners'[31] set up by the all-powerful tradition as well as by any contrasting *avant-garde*: the more timorous we are, the more we can be intimidated by those 'rules' that codify the complex games pertaining to the use of a half *logos*. Rules that exclude any attempt to re-establish a fuller *logos* of listening and saying. It almost seems that 'culture' requires aspirants to participate according to their specific qualifications, to become adherents to an immense task of justifying a 'logic' that knows very well how to say practically everything and hardly knows how to listen.

As Kant points out:

> The proverbial saying, *'fiat iustitia, pereat mundus'* (i.e. 'Let justice reign, even if all the rogues in the world must perish') may sound somewhat inflated, but it is nonetheless true . . . But it must not be misunderstood, or taken, for example, as a permit to apply one's own rights with the utmost rigour . . .
> 32

It would appear that here the serious risks inherent in misunderstanding a sound principle of right and the 'permit to apply one's own rights with the utmost rigour' are held to be comparable. Both misunderstanding (in the sense of incorrectly using a message) and using one's own rights (not only civil rights but, above all, rational rights) 'with the utmost rigour' may derive not so much from a 'misleading' categorization or abuse of current logic as from the pre-established dismissal of listening. Both the misunderstanding and utmost rigour ('hard' and 'slippery') that Kant warns us about would appear to be the primary derivatives of a dominant thinking that can not and hence will not further comprehension. 'Rigour' and, conversely, misunderstanding are deeply rooted in the exclusion of listening, in a trend which brooks no argument, where everyone obeys without too much fuss. These interwoven kinds of 'reasoning' lead us into a vicious circle, as powerful as it is elusive, a circle that can only be evaded with a force of silence that does not arise from astonished dumbfoundedness, but from serious, unyielding attention.

## A DIVIDED *LOGOS* AND ITS RESTORATION

Paradoxically, it is the major theoretical trends that appear to be in search of that aspect of our *logos* which has been lost in western thought, namely the capacity for attentive listening. In fact, the more rigorous the knowledge claims are, the more 'greedily' they demand to be listened to. And the need becomes so impelling that even double-edged means are adopted by the adherents in order to ensure that central claims be heard and accepted. As we are not sufficiently conversant with the attitude of openness, acceptance is once again confused with indoctrination and standards of success and popularity are taken to be the conditions best suited to guarantee knowledge claims.

It is well known how highly praised is the flourishing of rational thinking in Greek civilization and how its philosophy has given impetus and direction to our culture. There is, moreover, a general tendency to consider the merging of the 'philosophical' traditions of the Near East in the conceptual thinking of the Greeks as an occurrence which deserves only praise.[33] We tend to regard this cultural merging as entirely beneficial and are inclined to consider only its positive and enlightening aspects; every available document is thus interpreted in the light of this exalted judgement without careful scrutiny of the underlying perspective. The tradition soaring to cultural dominance might, in fact, be constitutive of the judgement itself. As is well known recent contributions which in some way deviate from this position can be linked with the philosophy of Heidegger. 'The name "logic" ', he says, 'is an abbreviation of the complete title which in Greek runs . . . the understanding that concerns the *logos* . . . the noun to the verb *legein*. Logic understands *legein* in the sense of . . . saying something about something.'[34] In this assertive understanding of logic the richness of practice and heritage inherent in the word *legein* is inadvertently wasted; the semantic abundance of this word is reduced to 'saying', resulting in the loss of its other meanings, such as 'preserving', which is characteristic of a listening attitude. In this reductive view our *logos* can no longer be considered as an instrument which simply promotes the growth of rationality, but also as a means for rational suppression. The world-view that encompasses our logico-metaphysical tradition has been 'transformed' at the historical beginning of western rationalism. The characteristics of that transformation can be seen in the propensity to render concepts increasingly abstract, thus leading to the disappearance of the multiplicity of relationships which had previously tied them to particular circumstances, and to their substitution with generalized relationships. Feyerabend adds that this tendency seems to display a general validity: it is known that proto-Indo-European spoken tongues had a much more complex structure and indeed the same is true of the direct antecedents of current languages.[35] A philosophy of listening can be envisaged as an attempt to recover the neglected and perhaps deeper roots of what we call thinking, an activity which in some way gathers and synthesizes human endeavours. In his introduction to *What is Called Thinking?* Vattimo suggests that language could be called 'the house of being' rather than a system of 'simple signs' void of reality.[36] And thus, if our *logos* must function as 'the house of being', we should ask how we can possibly 'host being' in such a lessened house, that is, in a language that can speak but can not listen. In the light of Heidegger's house metaphor, we can discern an indication of the need to enlarge this 'house' even in the writings of Derrida. His own introduction to *Margins of Philosophy* begins with the thought-provoking words 'Tympanise – philosophy' and the introductory chapter is entitled 'The tympanum'.

> We know that the membrane of the tympanum, a thin and transparent partition separating the auditory canal from the middle ear (the cavity) is stretched obliquely (*loxos*). Obliquely from above to below, from outside to inside, and from the back to the front. Therefore it is not perpendicular to the axis of the canal. One of the effects of this obliqueness is to increase the surface of impression and hence the capacity of vibration. It has been observed particularly in birds, that the precision of hearing is in direct proportion to the obliqueness of the tympanum. The tympanum squints. Consequently, to luxate the philosophical ear, to set the *loxos* in *logos* to work, is to avoid frontal and symmetrical protest, opposition in all the forms of *anti* . . . [37]

The issue in question is both a re-interpretation of *logos* and also its restoration, inasmuch as we are no longer subordinately dependent on the power, or domination, of mere saying; it is an attempt to retrieve the functions of listening which may allow for truer forms of dialogue rather than for dialectical dismantlings which tend to repropose what has been demolished. The various trends in deconstruction do not, in fact, attack the structure from outside. According to Derrida deconstructive turns

> are only possible and useful if they live within the structure, as only from within can they deliver their blows. They live in these structures in a certain way, because one always resides,

and more so when our dwelling is ignored. Operating necessarily from within, borrowing from the old structure all the
strategic and economic resources of subversion, depending
upon them structurally, the process of deconstruction is always
in a certain sense determined by its own activity. And anyone
who has already begun the same work in another area of the
same household will readily concede this point. No other
practice is so popular today, and one should even be able to
formalize its rules.[38]

We may now reintroduce Heraclitus' fragment – 'When you have
listened, not to me but to the . . . *Logos*, it is wise to agree
that all things are one'[39] – as well as Heidegger's innovative
comment:

> What happens then, when such hearing occurs? When there
> is such proper hearing there is *omolegein* which can only be
> what it is as *legein*. Proper hearing belongs to the *logos* . . .
> Therefore this hearing is itself a *legein*. As such the proper
> hearing of mortals is in a certain way the same as the *logos*.[40]

And still further:

> When proper hearing as *omolegein, is*, then the fateful comes
> to pass, and mortal *legein* is . . . dispatched to what is appro-
> priate, to whatever rests in the assemblage of primordially
> gathering laying before, i.e. in that which the laying that
> gathers has sent. Thus it is indeed fateful when mortals
> accomplish proper hearing.[41]

According to his approach, therefore, no *logos* can be posited
apart from the ways of *legein*. No *logos* outside of proper
hearing; or perhaps only a logos reduced by half may unfold:
overwhelming in its manifold expressions and yet primitive and
lacking in other basic respects. And Heidegger again insists, as
if constantly needing to justify his central claim:

> Thus is *logos* named without qualifications . . . the laying . . .
> In this fashion *logos* occurs essentially as the pure laying which
> gathers and assembles. *Logos* is the original assemblage of the
> primordial gathering from the primordial laying. *Logos* is the
> laying that gathers and only this.[42]

Outside an open realm in which we may summon our inner resources for the purpose of receiving and keeping messages we may be constrained at the level of ever more complex derivatives of the assertive *logos*; confinement in this domain may give rise to a yearning for past 'mythical' ways of life embodying a fuller rationality – not reduced by half and restricted to simple assertion. And the proper hearing which completes any saying can thus be described as:

> a *legein* which lets lie before us whatever already lies together before us; which indeed lies there by virtue of a laying which concerns everything that lies together before us of itself. This exceptional saying is the *legein* which comes to pass as the *logos*.[43]

In its fuller sense, then, even our saying could be epitomized in a formulation indicating an attitude of undivided attention and holding, an attitude also capable of letting anything be in its entireness. And if this is the case regarding the essence of speaking, Heidegger goes on to question and juxtapose the nature of hearing. The 'answer' comes forth in unequivocal form. Should there still be uncertainty regarding the wisdom of conceiving *logos* as the 'laying-that-gathers', and not only as speaking and reasoning, it would suffice to invoke once again the recommendation that Heraclitus makes. He, in fact, tells us explicitly that we should not listen to him and that our capacity for paying heed should be aimed at *logos* itself. 'The hearing appropriate to it', however, 'can not proceed casually toward it, only to pass it by once again. If there is to be proper hearing, mortals must have already heard the *logos* with an attention which implies nothing less than their belonging to the *logos*.'[44]

There is a demand here for a relationship with thinking anchored to humility and faithfulness, an approach which is unheard-of in our current thinking, revolving around grasping, mastering, using.

This 'secondary' and yet unrenunciable philosophical perspective is characterized by the requirement that we dwell with, abide by, whatever we try to know; that we aim at coexistence-with, rather than knowledge-of. This approach is radically different from the sort of cognitive enterprises which result in further production of the very knowledge that warrants them.

Memory, in the sense of human thinking that recalls, dwells

where everything that gives food for thought is kept in safety.
We shall call it the 'keeping'. It harbours and conceals what
gives us food for thought. 'Keeping' alone *gives* freely what
is to-be-thought, what is most thought-provoking[45]

says Heidegger.

If we concede that keeping represents the essential quality of
authentic listening and of remembering, then the sort of hearing
that preserves may well be deserving of philosophical priority.
And Heidegger thus articulates the long-neglected function of
our *logos:* 'Saying is a letting-lie-together-before which gathers
and is gathered.'[46] In this understanding of the basic guidelines
of our thinking we can retrieve and restore the life-enhancing
role of listening. To the extent that we approach in an accepting
manner, or let ourselves be accosted, we allow the existence and
further articulation of whatever faces us. Otherwise there would
be no sense in 'gathering' as it would still be an archaic preying
approach transferred into the domain of knowledge.

The whole question hinges on the capacity of 'letting-lie-
together-before' and of freeing our thinking from its 'constitutive'
compulsion to submit to a *lysis* – analyse – scrutinize, delve into,
explore, exhaust, probe the famous 'object of knowledge' of our
research tradition. The notion of integration thus becomes linked
to a general idea of coexistence which is more ecological than
logical in that it requires 'belonging' to our *logos;* it is concerned
with domestic issues because there are no more foreign affairs.
The search for a fuller understanding motivates a commitment
to be more conversant with the very basic assumptions underlying
our knowledge claims and to free them from those boundaries
which determine a very circumscribed dimension of progress,
however unhalting and successful. A recovery of our *logos* may
be facilitated by a retrieval of a more 'circular' way of thinking,
as it were, entailing repeated confrontations which may eventually result in the rule of dwelling and coexistence.

Even though the logical genius of the Greeks is the basic
source of our culture it may still in some respects be alien to
us.

Quite generally, the familiar, just because it is familiar, is
not cognitively understood. The commonest way in which we
deceive either ourselves or others about understanding is by
assuming something is familiar, and accepting it on that

account; with all its pros and cons, such knowing never gets anywhere and it knows not why.[47]

And the assumption of a problem is not a simple return to an old question but perhaps a more consequential pursuit. Our concern with the logical pivot of our culture, our attention to the results of its development and the discovery of certain limits may be conducive to an evolutionary approach which surpasses a formal analysis of the topic.

If 'totality' were to be interpreted as 'togetherness', or as our ecosystem, then the philosophical relevance of thinking in domestic terms might become more apparent. The listening and keeping approach, in its concern for letting-lie-together, allows us to identify at least two of the blind-spots which occur in our halved logic. The social sciences which derive from our *logos* – maybe itself only a very powerful and long lasting (Kuhnian) paradigm – must come to terms with all kinds of abysmal irrationality. In the scientific domain, on the other hand, there is now a growing concern for the unfolding proliferation of context-less achievements; namely 'local scientific successes which precede even the remotest notion of how to deal with them ethically or how to integrate them into the needs of the totality'.[48] There is a whole world yet to be discovered, not of unsolved issues but of relationships among things we know, of ways in which they might fit together.

There seems to be the deployment of an underlying non-listening and curtailed *logos* which can not see and question the bearing of its own achievements on humans. Under the covering of our halved *logos* there is constant denial of any ecological totality in favour of obstinate attention to the parts. While an ever-increasing formalization of specialized languages conceals the problem of reciprocity between different fields of research, a restoration of our *logos* by means of a recovery of our potential propensity for listening aims at a possible conjugation of standpoints.

# Chapter 2

# The logocentric system of culture

## LOGOCENTRISM AND KNOWLEDGE

In the writings of Xenophanes of Colophon the traditional conception of the gods is criticized in this way: 'Aethiopians have gods with snub noses and black hair, Thracians have gods with grey eyes and red hair.'[1]

> But if oxen and horses . . . had hands or could draw with hands and create works of art like those made by men, horses would draw pictures of gods like horses, and oxen of gods like oxen, and they would make the bodies (of their gods) in accordance with the form that each species itself possesses.[2]

At the dawn of western rationalism, in fact, as new theories seem to be contraposing traditionally derived attitudes, Xenophanes thus describes divinity:

> There is one god, among gods and men the greatest, not at all like mortals in body or in mind. He sees as a whole, thinks as a whole, and hears as a whole. But without toil he sets everything in motion, by the thought of his mind.[3]

Next to this famous contrast we might put Feyerabend's epigraphic remark according to which Xenophanes has not reached 'objectivity' in any way, 'but *has simply replaced the tribal gods* of the Greeks, Thracians and Ethiopians *with the tribal god of intellectuals*'.[4] A simple turn over in the rule of an epistemic area.

Nor can this contraposition be resolved by our revealing the 'tribal' limits of rationalism which underlie western culture; the question is rather whether we are capable of accepting a philo-

sophical project which occupies no 'space' and that can, therefore, attempt to elude those territorial dynamics that 'inexplicably' set the various areas of the rationalist tradition against one
another. If one asks how a philosophy of listening can 'coexist'
with the 'multitude of languages that speak the language of the
West . . . the only language spoken on the earth . . . the most
expressive form reached by mortal language',[5] we could reply in
this way: the point at issue is probably the attempt to perform
an exercise whereby we can develop a capacity for genuine
listening, that is an attitude which occupies no space but which
in a paradoxical sense creates ever new spaces in the very 'place'
in which it is carried out. Whereas a logocentric tradition tends
to scoff benevolently at, or study in an objective fashion, the
'magical', 'absurd' or 'banal' attitudes stemming from other *Weltanschauungen*, listening opens up the possibility of a philosophical activity that is no less rigorous, but which neither opposes
the tradition of western logos nor excommunicates anything that
'normal' rationality is unable to grasp or systematize.

When western knowledge tries to frame the entire world and
its history by making use of the power that basically emanates
from the voice of our rationality then, perhaps, an excessively
logocentric culture emerges in which there is no longer any room
for listening. In fact there is one voice only as the accredited
source of knowledge. It is well known that the celebrated science-
power equation is revealed in the coincidence of technological
development and social-political hegemony. But whenever we
define the effects of such power in terms of control and
repression, we draw upon a formal, and, one might even say,
superficial notion of power, understood as a function that is
carried out through the acts of forbidding, restricting and distinguishing. If this were its only, or even its main, function there
would not be such a vast, almost planetary acceptance of the
dictates of classicity as bearers of productivity and clarity in
every field. And yet, for as long as we move in a noosphere
that is saturated with both scientific and intellectual discourses
constantly reaching out to inform, permeate and mould, the
process of listening can never be more than a minimal philosophical aspiration or the concern of a minority. Unless of course it
comes to be seen as a more valid point of departure, should the
biosphere turn out be uninhabitable, and a change of route
worth the attempt.

The inhabitant of a tradition possesses 'objectivity' and, therefore, the 'right' to not listen when he fails even to notice his logical heritage, or when he proposes it as a background in cognitive pursuits. In a 'naive' rationalism, in fact, the correctness of a deduction, the discovery of a contradiction or the improvement of experience is regarded as something that effectively possesses an 'objective' content inasmuch as it is constructed in terms of a rigorous methodology. And yet 'objectivity' may even at times appear more as the result of a lack of cognitive perspicacity than of an intrinsic quality of philosophical rigour. It is in the twists and turns of these one-sided knowledge claims that a world view is imperturbably elevated to the status of criterion whereby we can even evaluate comparatively the quality and the goals of life.

When, on the other hand, we try to follow a path rooted in listening we are constantly asking which are the main axes of our culture. It appears that we can identify in the development of western logos the founding principle of a culture expressing itself in a multiplicity of splendid languages that shape and steer the wide variety of events constituting an epoch. The cogent rationality of the west is the light in which events are considered insofar as they share identical features or are amenable to proper systematization. The linguistic games based on the class of metalanguages can in fact reach the highest levels of epistemological sophistication and thus enable us to express and correlate the results of a variety of disciplines; a splendid way of being able to deal and 'play' with all the values and contents of our culture.

There is the risk, however, of being 'turned to stone' by constantly reading the logocentric guide of our experiences, in the sense that it is a guide that reads us-as-we-read a peculiar, predetermined 'reality'. Wittgenstein remarks that 'People who are constantly asking "why" are like tourists in front of a building reading Baedecker and are so busy reading the history of its construction, etc., that they are prevented from *seeing* the building.'[6] The secret arrogance[7] of logocentrism has a possible echo in another one of his remarks: 'What a curious attitude scientists have -: "We still don't know that; but it is knowable and it is only a matter of time before we get to know it!" As if that went without saying.'[8]

The structures of logocratic 'domination' could be at least

partially revised where they are more deeply rooted, possibly in the interactive categories which rule our primal experience of the world. We might, as an example, mention that the new way of thinking advocated by Nietzsche could be understood as a mode of thinking suited to listening and being heard, to fathom the inexhaustible complexity of phenomena precisely because it is ready to listen to them – having detached them from a Platonistic view that makes them copies of an ideal prototype. An aversion – almost – towards listening to the rich multiplicity of 'reality' seems to be linked with a background of profound fears and to the resulting defensive postures that express themselves in a tendency to reduce knowledge in general to a set of principles from which nothing can escape. A relentless battle is waged as an attempt is made to organize everything in the light, or shadow, of the 'best' principles of knowledge: a chronic struggle of territorial conquest where the 'territory' is the set of notions and principles for constructing reality. Listening thus comes to be an essential function in the attempt to identify and monitor possible predatory aspects of our knowledge, no longer even capable of rememorizing or imagining the Parmenidean function of the 'shepherds of being'.

In a cognitive context centred on an attempt to lead every consideration back under the aegis of a few powerful explicative principles (the 'superstructure of classicity' in von Wright's language),[9] it is inevitable that the anxious search for a wider sphere of application for those principles will prevail, as will the search for greater expanses of territory; the project is implemented, possibly, by excluding any form whatever of listening (which would in fact include a different concern, inasmuch as the modes of relating based on colonization or territorial increase would be abandoned in favour of coexistential, connubial, interactive models). Listening as de-stitution of the defining, dictating nature of our encompassing logic is essential to the life of thought so that it may develop in a living syntax of reciprocities and can resist the temptation to produce articulations (however 'critical' or 'dialectical') that are likely to degrade into the sterility or monotony of power games.

According to Heidegger, for example, we do not pay sufficient attention to the 'strange' function carried out by the 'exact conceptions' of language. He points out that they remain everywhere masters of the field of the various sciences of language, almost as though they were unyielding. They go back to an ancient tradition and yet the particular characteristic of language that is 'most ancient' escapes their attention. And so it happens, in Heidegger's view, that in spite of their antiquity and clarity they never lead to 'language as language'.[10] The 'most ancient' characteristic probably refers to the function of listening, since it is the only one capable of sustaining language in its integrated wholeness of hearing and saying.

## PREDETERMINATION OF KNOWLEDGE

The expansion of a kind of knowledge that is capable of moulding but not of generative listening appears to be linked with an underlying strategy of *fac et excusa* (first do and then justify) transposed into the epistemic level. In his political writings Kant ironically remarks:

> Seize any favourable opportunity of arbitrarily expropriating a right which the state enjoys over its own or over a neighbouring people; the justification can be presented far more easily and elegantly and the use of violence can be glossed over far more readily *after the fact* than if one were to think out convincing reasons in advance and then wait for counterarguments to be offered.[11]

Once the basic metastructure of thought has been expressed and established, then our scientific-philosophical discourse has really taken possession, not so much of property belonging to others (in which it might subsequently become interested), as of its own cultural territory. As a consequence of this, it exercises a supreme legislative power that establishes correct ways of thinking, and presents its epistemic rule 'easily and elegantly'. Nor would 'questioning' be possible when the body of rationality is rooted in a logos, as the generator of a knowledge, to which the entire planetary community tends to adhere, at least in part, for its productivity. And if a 'question' is ever to be articulated it will have to conform to the style of a logos that does speak and hardly listens.

If it is not possible to imagine the experience of listening, nor even to attempt it, we should ask how the intellectual 'community' operates in the management of its knowledge. For many intellectuals the basic concern is probably that of articulating and spreading an aspect of the rationality at their disposal, namely a feature of the dominant tradition. It would not be realistic to expect a very different cognitive attitude from an intellectual community composed predominantly of thinkers who usually soar to the level of 'executives' of thought and 'administrators' of concepts.[12] Moreover, the image of man which is commonly used in the pursuits of intellectuals is well suited to their habitat inasmuch as our image of people corresponds to the actual human beings that we generally come across. In 'common' thinking, furthermore, there is a prevailing tendency to let ourselves be determined by whatever we believe might confirm the direction which we are already tuned into (and thus, automatically, the direction that 'our' rationality imposes upon 'reality') and we hear nothing else. But we hear nothing else also because, in spite of our having risen to high levels of cognitive awareness, we have little familiarity with what it means to listen; we are in fact imbued with a logocratic culture in which the bearers of the word are predominantly involved in speaking, moulding and informing. When a chance to listen arises, there is always a suspicion we might submit to a 'warlike' phenomenon of benumbment or of violence, in which 'listening' becomes an anti-philosophical acceptance of an invasive message.

More than once Vico states that:

> When men are ignorant of the natural causes producing things, and cannot even explain them by analogy with similar things, they attribute their own nature to them. The vulgar, for example, say the magnet loves the iron . . . *The human mind, because of its indefinite nature, wherever it is lost in ignorance makes itself the rule of the universe in respect of everything it does not know.*[13]

The human mind, possessed by a thought that expresses itself ceaselessly, 'makes itself the rule of the universe in respect of everything it does not know' and, incapable of listening, since it knows nothing of the practice, makes itself the rule of the cognitive universe as the uncontested territory of a logos that speaks, orders and moulds. Such thinking will no longer have any 'logical space' and, consequently, no time (to 'waste') to listen to those 'stories' that do not form part of its own history or, paradoxically, of its own dialectical overturning – assuming that whatever is contradicted or overturned ultimately results in, and duplicates, the previous story.

Furthermore, a specific form of our rationality might be consolidated by the increasing hegemony of information processing. This form necessarily assumes prescriptive resonances in that it represents the set of those enunciations that are accepted as enunciations of knowledge and that, as a result of this, *must* be accepted as such. If one wonders how this immense mechanism developed, whereby whatever is sufficiently affirmed produces a *dutifulness* corresponding to the affirmation, we come up against the fundamental question of symbol formation that underlies the construction or distortion of reality.[14] As we know, saying tends to impose 'being', as a result of which nothing is more seriously normative than verbal, written or figurative expression. Any act of speech whatever is potentially normative, even if it is 'unaware' of it, and the most simple, 'innocuous' utterance, in this kind of normative blindness, can ultimately result in constraint and epistemic control. The distinction between a cognitive and a normative function, according to Gadamer, for instance, opposes aspects and moments which basically constitute a single thing. He further argues that:

> Hermeneutics cannot have any problem of a beginning . . . Wherever it arises, the problem of the beginning is, in fact, the problem of the end, for it is with respect to an end that a beginning is defined as a beginning of an end.[15]

Once more it is suggested that the speech act selects *an aspect* of reality simply by speaking about it, and whatever is said is then transformed into the statutory basis for a discourse which ultimately predetermines its end. At this point the greatest risk is no longer that we go too far but that we do not go far enough to be able to clarify sufficiently the boundless implications of our discursive, logocratic system.

'Thus', according to Gadamer, 'the dialectic of question and answer always precedes the dialectic of interpretation.'[16] But then, if we begin with a question ('it is with respect to an end that a beginning is defined'), we shall end up with more of our own questions and shall never achieve a listening experience which might allow our interlocutor – be it text or person – an opportunity for its own expression.

A similar situation faces us if we turn our attention towards knowledge of the natural world. As Prigogine and Stengers[17] have suggested, the dialogues conducted with nature by modern science are codified by the experimental method: it is the basis of our science's originality and, at the same time, of its specificity and limits. It is obvious that when nature is questioned through experiment it becomes simplified, prepared in a specific way and, occasionally, even mutilated according to pre-existing hypotheses. This does not, however, deprive nature of its ability to belie most hypotheses. Einstein, as we know, has often pointed out that nature usually answers 'no' to the questions that are put to it, and only occasionally '*maybe*'. Nevertheless, '*whether nature answers yes or no, it will always answer in the frame of the theoretical language in which it is being addressed*'.[18] The issue is whether there should be only one language, namely that of the questioner.

## EPISTEMIC PREJUDICE

The blind spot on the paths of listening is neither casual nor inexplicable if only we remember that a rationally encoded 'listening' is conducive to any kind of interpretative attitude gravitating toward the area of a more or less shared hegemonous cultural structure. The problem, therefore, is that of creating sufficient silence to allow ourselves at least to hear the incessant rumbling of our cultural world – a machinery of thought that seems to have lost its original vitality as a result of its enormous success. No longer able to hear the noise it makes, we nevertheless recognize a desolation that is not so much the deprecated crisis of values as, possibly, their inert realization.

An unshaken faith in the validity of our own mother tongue – the rationalist tradition – prevents us from *seeing* any different logical tradition because it is believed that it cannot be 'logical'. On the contrary it must be, for example, simply 'magical' and, therefore, both unworthy of being listened to and only suitable for 'scientific' investigation which can be propounded with ever new terms connected to a celebrated suffix, -*logy*, through which the branches of our knowledge are multiplied. A logocentric rationalism primarily capable of organizing discourse and hardly suited for receptive listening, historically proceeds in such a way that the dominant orientations are bound to succeed, and the defeated ones are not simply forced to submit, but should cease to exist. It is also possible that the rationalism of the modern age is sustained by an unknowing *frenzy* in the sense that it is not limited to the pursuit of new ways of its thinking but also tends to deny that earlier, minor or unsuccessful traditions ever existed. And, in order to avoid the labour of listening – a labour comparable to the germination of any real dialogue – a single tradition is recognized in which everything alien is considered irrelevant: the product of intellectual blindness or of an unwillingness to evolve.

The tendencies that are opposed to listening include both an over-evaluation of the tradition that leads cultural games and a presentation of the real, or even imaginary, cognitive values of that tradition, so that, finally, differences in level are transformed into qualitative differences and qualitative differences are changed into ingenuous yes-no dichotomies that, in their turn, flow into the efficient decrees of 'rational' and 'irrational', 'coherent' and 'absurd'. Feyerabend has remarked that dichotomies are not only abstract schemes of order designed to organize complex phenomena; they become integrated into life itself in such a way that the presence of contradictory aspects not only creates a problem or an undesiderable state (with which one can, and probably must, come to terms), but is seen as a negation of the 'values' of life itself.[19] Any violation of the ruling dichotomies affects the conscience of 'believers'; it appears to them as if the historic and social world were shaken to its very foundations.

Our culture is sufficiently logical to criticize the paternalistic despotism of institutions, thinkers or subcultures, but perhaps not logical enough to make clear to what extent the despotic rule is inherent in any kind of discourse that is not rooted in listening. In Kant's political writings we read: 'No-one can compel me to be happy in accordance with his conception of the welfare of others, for each may seek his happiness in whatever way he sees fit.'[20] He is even more explicit in a later passage:

A government might be established on the principle of benevolence towards the people, like that of a father towards his children. Under such a *paternal government (imperium paternale)*, the subjects, as immature children who cannot distinguish what is truly useful or harmful to themselves, would be obliged to behave purely passively and to rely upon the judgement of the head of state as to how they *ought* to be happy, and upon his kindness in willing their happiness at all. Such a government is the greatest conceivable *despotism*, i.e. a constitution which suspends the entire freedom of its subjects, who henceforth have no rights whatsoever.[21]

But a scientific and philosophical culture which knows how to speak but not how to listen also establishes, in a tacit and cogent manner, the basic principles for differentiating what is useful and what is damaging. A philosophical and scientific 'logos' is, in the final summing up, whatever tells people 'how they *ought* to be happy'. We almost seem to be on the point of glimpsing the poor cunning of a tradition that maintains its enormous power in the same way as the internal cohesion of a group is sometimes enforced: by directing contempt towards external structures which are to be regarded as primitive or subrational.

The élitist character of academic knowledge is not necessarily an obstacle to the birth of a philosophy of listening since it does not seem correct to interpret official knowledge as a structure run in a caste-like or oligarchical way. In principle, at least, anyone can rise to the highest positions of knowledge. At this particular moment of our philosophical journey the crucial point is not so much the possibility or impossibility of reaching the highest ranks, as the need to renounce our own individual or community 'tradition' in order to gain entrance.[22] Looked at in this way the organizational character of our knowledge would seem to be free and egalitarian in the sense that it is accessible to everyone. But we are not talking about the gradual achievement of equality among 'traditions', so much as the equality of access to a *single*, well-defined tradition, that of the talking logos. 'White liberals', Feyerabend insists, 'have opened up the promised land, but it is a promised land that must be constructed according to their plans.'[23] In this 'promised land' it would be reasonably easy to devote oneself to the glossing of the expressions delivered by the current messengers of logos, just as it would be appropriate to elaborate yet another form of normal, rational expression. It would be far less easy and appropriate – although not competitive in any sense – to research and practise philosophical listening.

# Chapter 3

# A philosophy of listening within a tradition of questioning

## LISTENING AND THE QUESTION

Invoking Gadamer's salient claims we are confronted by an illuminating hermeneutical openness which is, nonetheless, impinged upon by those prejudicial elements in our philosophical tradition which overshadow the function of listening. 'The problem that we should face is *the logical structure of openness*, which characterizes hermeneutical consciousness',[1] he suggests. It is at this point that the preliminary problem of how to discuss the *logical structure of openness* arises; the term 'openness', that is, needs to be clarified further. Unless there is a reasonable certainty of being able to understand the answers, or even the questions which might be addressed to us, the possibilities of a 'logical structure of openness' will be slight. There remains, however, one more problem, touching directly on the question: the doubt, which can not be easily dispelled, as to whether any 'logical structure' can be at all open to listening when our traditional reasoning primarily generates moulding and discursive splendours, perhaps too distant from the latent dimension of authentic listening.

One of Gadamer's statements may thus become considerably more significant: 'Anyone who listens is *fundamentally* open. Without this kind of openness to one another there is no genuine human relationship. Belonging together always also means being able to listen to one another.'[2] And yet, if there is one *fundamental* way of being open, why is it that the philosopher must be concerned with those *less* fundamental ways (such as, for example, the question) which, in the final analysis, might constitute the object of other scientific pursuits? The fact that there is another openness that is *more* fundamental than the question – the openness of listening – seems to be noticed almost *en passant*. And yet there is an obstinate attempt to conceal or ignore the considerable relevance of listening without ever posing the question as to why the vast body of philosophical literature tends to neglect the problem. Moreover, the general opinion would appear to be that the *fundamental* openness of listening neither needs nor deserves more attention, as if we already possessed that vital capacity. The illusion that we can speak to others without being able to listen is, perhaps, one that we all share.

If it is true that 'no genuine human relationship' exists without the radical and reciprocal openness of listening, it is significant that listening – in spite of its entailing such a crucial issue – is either ignored by philosophical study or, at best, touched upon fortuitously. On the basis of the arguments articulated up to now, an inquiry into the reasons for this paradox would appear to be almost futile. We could, in fact, construe that the absence of a philosophical analysis of listening is not the culpability of any particular orientation, since the phenomenon might be considered as the peak of a desperate and silent need, an interrogative that is too disquieting for western culture as a whole. In the dizzy affirmation of our *logos* there is hardly any 'logical' space left for the 'hidden' but essential tradition of listening. It is, in any case, un-thinkable that listening be revealed as a philosophical dimension, since it is, by now, too alien to the tradition based on expressive language.

The 'question', then, might prove to be an unfortunate procedure, apparently *philo*-sophical but, effectively, simply logo-cratic. We might be able to learn more by stopping to listen, if we were only able to free ourselves from a logico-dialectical *furor* that drives us on to come up with ever more critical questions while tacitly opposing proper hearing – as the contemporary individual, increasingly impoverished by expanding and inexorable logomachies, knows only too well. Although the formative value of critical questioning is extolled, Tommaseo remarked one century ago that 'Even when many people *hear* criticism, few *listen* to it, very few *understand* it and even fewer *feel* it.'[3]

The problem of listening might thus be considered the shadow-dimension of the epochal development of our culture. We busy ourselves, for example, with textual analysis as an *innovation* intended to explore the possibility of 'collaboration' between the text and the reader: almost as though listening, as the far more basic and extended problem of the *spoken* text, proved too disquieting or 'obscene' in the sense that it seems prudent to relegate it to a space outside a cultural scenery based on logocratic guidelines. The problem of letting a text relate with us may seem rather circumscribed when compared to the vaster and more generalized problem of listening. At first sight one might point out that a text which has not been well-used neither deteriorates nor ceases to exist. At least it continues to exist as something tangible, available for more successful encounters in the future. This is not the case with human beings. We should also bear in mind that the 'auscultation' of a written work seems to be limited to those who live in the Gutenberg galaxy, as consumers of printed culture. The problem of listening, on the contrary, is not restricted in terms of time or space. Whenever hermeneutics is prepared to wed itself to the discipline of listening it can no longer be seen as a simple interpretative technique as will almost have to be proposed as a way into philosophical research itself. 'Hermeneutics', Ricoeur insists, 'will cease to be presented as a *technique* . . . and will become the epicentre of the general problem of understanding.'[4]

As far as language is concerned, therefore, knowing how to listen does not represent a 'further stage' that must be attained. In our view listening belongs to the very 'essence' of language. It represents an uncompromising potentiality that prevents the adoption of a defensive position based on insufficient conditions; such non-dialogic conditions determine a general 'philosophical' premise that is already in itself too abstract, devitalized or, at the very least, excessively limiting. Human beings are ever more trying to put into words whatever they believe is hidden or absent in their culture. At the same time they are attempting, as never before, to give voice to that which is inexpressible or blocked in their inner world. Humans are perhaps no more 'unhappy' now than they were in the past, even though one aspect of their condition does seem to be emerging: the fact that people are no longer prepared to accept in resigned 'silence' the many problems that living and surviving involve. A state of dumb resignation no longer seems to be suited to human beings, and when they are unable to express themselves effectively they feel swindled and cheated out of something that is rightfully theirs. In both individual and group protest the expectation of being able to express oneself and be understood is re-emerging, as is the conviction that one has the 'right' to achieve more listening than could previously be obtained. This multi-faceted problem in contemporary culture has, however, had no effect on the hard shell of western thought. It has failed to grasp the need to begin to understand and abide by the listening process, as a primary and indispensable requirement for coexistence. Heidegger remarks that: 'Perhaps only a little can be said concerning proper hearing, which nevertheless concerns everyone directly. Here it is not so much a matter for research, but rather of paying thoughtful attention to simple things.'[5] It might thus sound inappropriate to be concerned with a 'science', 'technique' or 'art' of listening. And yet, even though it is a 'simple thing', there is the problem of paying 'thoughtful attention'. And even if 'research' were involved, it is understandable that listening is never focused upon since it clearly has no remunerative value in our dominant culture. From one extreme to the other in the vast array of possible social interactions the stress inevitably falls on the irreplaceable value of the expressive capacity rather than on a propensity to listen. The 'attentive willingness' to listen is even perceived as an eminently 'futile' stance that need not even surface in our culture, in spite of the fact that it represents a vital and essential requisite for thought. 'God grant the philosopher insight into what lies in front of everyone's eyes',[6] is one of Wittgenstein's remarks. Perhaps the problem of listening is also in front of our eyes and we simply fail to see it.

At the point in which Gadamer concludes that 'We shall have to consider in greater depth what is the *essence of the question*, if we are to clarify the particular nature of the hermeneutical experience',[7] we are suddenly confronted with the unhalting advance of western thought, driven on and 'obsessed' by one of the most expressive and assertive 'figures' of our language: the question itself. In a language which pays such homage to *speech* we arrive at the point of concealing any culture of listening that might possibly be wedded to it. If we need to 'consider in greater depth what is the *essence of the question*' in order to clarify the prerequisites of hermeneutical experience we might observe that an inability to listen to the answer renders the question useless and, with it, any attempt at hermeneutical philosophy.

When we try to go beyond a situation that is too cramped for authentic philosophical endeavour, we can not avoid the suspicion that even in the most 'open' and dialogical of perspectives we are phylogenetically linked to those deaf mechanisms of the ancient reptilian brain that coexists with the more recent cognitive structures: even in the appearance of logic itself, dynamics based on simple territoriality and domination can be inserted. Gadamer adds:

> Hence the sense of the question is the direction in which alone the answer can be given . . . A question places that which is questioned within a particular perspective. The emergence of the question opens up, as it were, the being of the object. Hence the logos that sets out this opened-up being is already an answer.[8]

And yet, should the object of the question – hypothetically – express itself outside the limits imposed by the question, it might encompass and even surpass the scope which is inherent in the question itself. The object might perhaps take its distance from a question that 'places that which is questioned *within* a particular perspective' and that is able to 'open up the being of the object'. Who or what would ever choose to be 'placed within' or 'opened up'? And the presumed stupidity of the person who is listening – who is silent and does not speak – might be a tribute to a logocentric culture that artfully decrees the 'poverty' of the listener. It might be a beneficially defensive 'stupidity', with a function comparable to that of camouflage in the animal world, or a wise ostentation of stupidity and madness adopted as a means for socio-cultural survival and for the pursuit of ulterior purposes.

> In the comic confusion between question and answer . . . that Plato describes, there is the profound recognition of the priority of the question in all knowledge and discourse that really reveals something of an object. Discourse that is intended to reveal something requires that that thing be opened up by the question.[9]

The very image of 'opening up' the object conveys an idea of territorial invasion based on those paradigms to which we owe the splendours of knowledge and the triumph of technology.

The sense of every question is realised in passing through this state of indeterminacy, in which it becomes an open question. Every true question achieves this openness. If it lacks this, then it is basically no more than an apparent question.[10]

And yet, if 'placing within' and 'opening up' the object are essential to the question itself, it becomes difficult to reconcile the invocation of openness with this intention of opening-up and placing-within. But then it would seem that our recognition of these and other possible incongruities is far too simple. In fact it would be more philosophical to recognize that we are all in the same boat, that of a knowledge that pushes on in the direction of a questioning speech and that has lost its potential for listening. 'When man understands he extends his mind and *takes in* the things, but when he does not understand he makes the things out of himself', remarks Vico.[11]

## ON THE 'PRIMACY' OF POSING QUESTIONS

With regard to 'the primacy of posing questions', Gadamer insists that 'the problem that we should face is the *logical structure of openness*, which characterizes hermeneutical consciousness'.[12] He also considers it as 'an immediately evident fact' that every new experience presupposes the presence of a question:

We can not have experiences without asking questions. The recognition that an object is different and not as we first thought, obviously involves the question whether it was this or that. The openness that is part of experience is, from a logical point of view, precisely the openness of being this or that.[13]

It is in relation to this position that the thesis we are trying to develop may appear more clearly, in the sense that 'the openness that is part of experience' can not, in our opinion, be seen 'from a logical point of view'. This is because the sort of logic that underlies our culture does not seem to allow for the *more authentic* openness that may sustain a revealing dialogue. Even the 'question structure' as a model for hermeneutical philosophy can be perplexing since we can not be sure if, or how, we can understand an answer, if we can allow ourselves to be questioned back, or be questioned on our own claim to pose questions.

But, above all, the logic behind the question allows 'the recognition that an object is different and not as we first thought' only on condition that we do not move too far away from the assumptions, style and paradigms imposed by the question itself. There may not be a sufficient awareness of the extent to which the question secretly predetermines or circumscribes the answer it receives.

Lyotard writes that:

> The question of the social bond, insofar as it is a question, is itself a language game, the game of inquiry. It immediately positions the person who asks, as well as the addressee and the referent asked about: it is already the social bond.[14]

If the construction of social bonds is rooted in questioning, without even a glimpse of the innovatory and healing dimension of understanding, it is inevitable that any orientation in the adjudication of knowledge claims will result in a state of no exit. The only form or orientation possible will then be based on critical preferences, emotional inclinations or simple tolerance. If we, for instance, look at the development of psychiatry or psychology, we can easily isolate a number of doctrinal clusters which are not so much determined by their clinically objective contents, so to speak, as by the way in which the questions that direct research into the 'phenomenon' have been formulated. The way in which a problem is expressed, therefore, ultimately constitutes a most salient element in the research. The techniques used to probe and process any problem whatsoever are moreover linked back to cultural and cognitive dimensions that are either not immediately evident or escape us altogether. They underlie language itself, developing along with the various forms of human expression.

We can certainly agree with Gadamer's remark that the way in which we seek 'initial' access to a problem is frequently expressed in the form of a question. As we have already suggested, however, the way in which a question is posed limits and conditions the quality, and level, of any answer that can be possibly worked out – whether it be right or wrong. If we wonder, for instance: 'What is there *in the mind* of this man who has gone mad?', we might come up with answers connected to traumas, intoxication or genetic damage. But if we throw doubt on the nature of the question in a problem-inducing way and then reply that 'Maybe there is nothing ill *within the mind* at all', we will effectively have rejected the question and, therefore, refused to operate within a given cultural and epistemic level. We might perhaps decide to continue our questioning in a different way by asking: 'Then how did he *become* mad?' If, however, the 'reply' tells us that 'Maybe he has *never become mad*' or that 'One does not *become* mad', we can then see that a certain kind of answer is equivalent to refusing the interrogative structure of a certain kind of discourse as well as the fundamental assumptions that determine its path.

To the extent that language's inbuilt operational modes elude our awareness, an ignorance of the incessant linguistic games that are played means that we are often unaware of resting upon 'natural' assumptions that seem indisputable precisely because they are not commonly emphasized. With regard to these 'natural ways of thinking' Langer suggests that they

> are not avowed by the average man, but simply followed. He is not conscious of assuming any basic principles . . . They are deeper than facts he may note or propositions he may moot. But, though they are not stated, they find expression in the *forms of his questions*. A question is really an ambiguous proposition; the answer is its determination. There can be only a certain number of alternatives that will complete its sense. In this way *the intellectual treatment of any datum*, any experience, any subject, *is determined by the nature of our questions, and only carried out in the answers*.[15]

The development of the human sciences is usually characterized, therefore, more by the formulation of essential questions than by the solutions that are elaborated in answer to them. Although it is certainly true that the answers are the material from which the edifice is built, the structure of the edifice is determined by the type of questions that were asked – in the sense that the answer collaborates with the question and produces everything that is demanded of it, and *nothing else*. The possibility, however, that the answer eludes the restrictive nature of the question remains. When we ask ourselves, for example: 'Why does this person *want to do* things that hurt him?', we have already assumed that the person *wants* to do them and that *they hurt him*. But if we then reply that 'Maybe *he doesn't want* to do these things at all' and go on to say: 'Maybe they don't *hurt him* at all but, on the contrary, allow him to survive', then we might be able to neutralize the type of questioning and the interrogative procedure itself – always assuming the questioner is able to listen to and receive the complex significance of the interaction. The power and originality of questioning is actually capable of generating a hypertrophy of language: by increasing its own power 'beyond measure' it finally pays heed to nothing but itself.

An insistent search for the sort of inner gathering that permits listening might be traced to Heraclitus' famous phrase: 'Measureless pride needs to be extinguished sooner than a raging fire'. Or else: 'One should quench arrogance rather than a conflagration.'[16] Mistaking one linguistic feature, such as the question, for an entire array of functions might be an example of this 'measureless pride' which ultimately overshadows vital aspects of the hermeneutic endeavour such as, for instance, listening. This aspect is as rare as it is ignored. And 'before you play with fire,' comments Heidegger, 'whether it be to kindle or extinguish it, put out first the flames of presumption, which overestimates itself and takes poor measure because it forgets the essence of *legein*'[17] – the essence of listening. Heraclitus' metaphor is faithfully taken up by Heidegger who recommends that we extinguish 'arrogance' first of all, before even beginning to move towards the choreographic model, or marching rhythm, of western culture.

Gadamer also says that:

> The art of dialectic is not the art of being able to win every argument. On the contrary, it is possible that someone who is practising the art of dialectic, i.e. the art of questioning and seeking truth, comes off worse in the argument in the eyes of those listening to it. Dialectic, as the art of asking questions, proves itself only because the person who knows how to ask questions is able to persist in the questioning, which involves being able to preserve his *orientation towards openness*.[18]

If the salient aspect of the art of questioning can be seen in knowing how 'to preserve an *orientation towards openness*'[18] one might argue that the willingness to keep alive this orientation towards openness is the genuine basis for every question. The very notion of question is sustained by an openness – presumably an openness towards listening to the answer. This orientation towards openness, therefore, comes across as the essential moment of the question, almost as though the very essence of questioning were derived from a willingness for openness. The point at issue, however, is that it is not clear whether the openness indicated by the question is *authentically* open or not. And the *grave* contractual weight of the question is beginning to be felt more and more, even in the 'natural' sciences: Prigogine and Stengers have repeatedly pointed out that, whether nature answers yes or no, the answer will always form part of the theoretical language that is being used to address it.[19]

Furthermore, as Gadamer has pointed out: 'As against the solidity of opinions, questioning makes the object and all its possibilities fluid. A person who possesses the "art" of questioning is a person who is able to prevent the suppression of a question by the dominant opinion.'[20] And yet it might also be the case that the dominant role of the question can suppress any kind of understanding that goes beyond the limited amount it prepares us to receive. There are frequent examples in the human sciences of this type of profanation and distortion: we determine an increasing distance with the 'object' of knowledge, which seems to withdraw – or shrink away – when faced by the invasion of a question that, like the 'solidity of opinions', tends to expand, blur the horizon and become an end unto itself. 'The openness of the question', as Gadamer specifies:

is not boundless. It is limited by the horizon of the question. A question which lacks this is, so to speak, floating. It becomes a question only when the fluid indeterminacy of the direction in which it is pointing is overcome by a specific alternative being presented. In other words, the question has to be asked. The asking of it implies openness, but also limitation.[21]

This perspective, however, may accentuate the condition whereby 'the asking of the question' or the inquisitive (interrogative) approach so heavily predetermines the reply to the point where it may conceal those 'waste elements' or 'disturbing features' which might instead reveal something more enlightening but unfortunately inaudible. We are not permitted to believe that creative messages from *beyond* the – intended – conceptual scope of the question might appear. Even an extended theoretical propensity to a methodology of the question can be undermined by a 'logical' frame incapable of opening itself to a more radical mode of listening.

According to Gadamer the close relation that exists between question and understanding is what gives the hermeneutic experience its true dimension:

> The first thing is the question that the text presents us with . . .
> Thus the relation of question and answer is, in fact, reversed.
> The voice that speaks to us from the past – be it text, work, trace – itself poses a question . . . For the text must be understood as answer to a real question.[22]

And what conditions are needed to assure that we can listen to and understand this question? What 'logic' allows for or promotes this understanding? It is possible moreover that *we* may formulate questions that we subsequently attribute or project on to the text which might instead be addressing unpredictable (unheard-of) questions to the 'interpreter'. Our cognitive coordinates might not allow for any 'logical' space in which to listen to a question. Indeed, from this point of view there is possibly not much sense in wondering where we stand philosophically because we all seem to be on the same side, adhering to a position that allows for and enhances the 'dialectical' splendours of questioning while, at the same time, distancing us from the risks that would be created by the transforming experience of proper hearing. In the context of a 'logic of question and answer' we can follow Gadamer up to the point at which he asserts that 'the logic of the human sciences is, then, as appears from what we have said, a logic of the question'.[23] But if we were capable of listening only to what we are willing to receive, and formulated our questions accordingly, we might then consider only those evident and massive questions to which we could 'respond' while remaining within certain safety limits. Heidegger suggests that 'It . . . might be helpful to us to rid ourselves of the habit of only hearing what we already understand.' And adds:

> This my proposal is addressed not only to all those who listen;
> it is addressed still more to him who tries to speak of language,
> all the more when he does so with the sole intent to show possibilities that will allow us to become mindful of language and our relation to it.[24]

Alternatively one would establish a continuation of a mechanism, so to speak, of question and answer that was there to provide a sense of cognitive security: the perpetuation of something defined in terms of itself, and ultimately tautological.

Heidegger also says that 'the authentic attitude of thinking is not a putting of questions – rather it is listening to the grant, the promise of what is to be put in question.'[25] And also: 'In order to perceive a clue, we must first be listening ahead into the sphere from which the clue comes.'[26]

One of the urgent philosophical problems that can be confronted, therefore, is why it should be so difficult to listen to something without transforming it into nothing or transferring it into our own language. Heidegger asks: 'But how are we to hear without translating, translate without interpreting?'[27] And this induces us to consider an even more radical issue: how can we theorize about translation and interpretation when the notion of listening is so alien to us that generally we do not even consider it worthy of our philosophical attention? The possibility of exercising a dominant contractual power over the natural world and thus distinguishing oneself from other living beings is certainly appealing. But there is also an insidious, all-pervading risk: we can see from the ecological history of our coexistence upon earth that it consists of an uninterrupted series of acts of domination which have been performed by means of a symbolic superiority expressed through the cogent questions we know how to pose. These relations, however, based as they are on the possibility of symbolic control, are bursting with the immense power that lies within their jurisdiction; a linguistic power that in the long run becomes an end in itself and that ultimately stiffens and becomes inertial, thus impeding an equilibrium of survival and coexistence. In the absence of listening the symbolic function whereby we construct and interact with 'reality' may turn out to be dia-bolic.[28] As an extreme hypothesis, the value of our symbolic games and our most successful 'questions' lies precisely in the fervour with which we exact the most massive responses, whether positive or negative. A possibly greater value might be derived, however, by gravitating towards the object and allowing ourselves to listen more attentively to 'the promise of what is to be put into question'.

Phylogenetically, language has managed to be born and we are not to ask if the advantages outweigh the disadvantages, nor whether the current maturation of our symbolic life is 'sufficient'.

The birth of language has taken place and it is not important to know if we have instruments to attribute to it a sense of direction. And yet even the struggles for freedom of speech that, in the modern age, have enabled language to enjoy an effective liberty might seem disappointing: although language has freed itself of the authority of positive religions and social power it may not have found its own autonomy in its service to life. It might be more important, therefore, to search for a modesty and mildness of language that can exorcise the risk that it become an end in itself; language might thus become available for the patient labours of coexistence.

It is possible that a hermeneutics rooted in listening does not constitute at all an alternative mode of knowing comparable to the sort of understanding that is presented as an 'alternative' to the explicative and predictive modes of science. Perhaps it would be better to surrender all 'cognitive' claims and give up the notion of an alternative knowledge. Nor would we bother to struggle for the auspices of knowledge if it were not for a link with a Platonistic tradition according to which any action that was not based on verifiable knowledge would be ultimately 'irrational'. And yet even though a hermeneutics based on listening would not even partially coincide with 'real knowledge' as such, it might still be seen as a further way of interaction and coexistence.

## INTERPRETATIVE LISTENING AND EPISTEMOLOGY

The effort to be 'rational' in hermeneutics might consist in giving up the idea that there are basic terms in which *any* contribution inherent to the discussion must be made; searching for 'rationality' in hermeneutics might be comparable to taking over the language of the other rather than trying to translate or transmute it into one's own. In the domain of hermeneutics the pursuit of investigation may turn out to be a mild and persevering *continuation* of the conversation.[29] Generally speaking, in the philosophical scene two different orientations can be pointed out. Epistemology, on the one hand, is supposed to be occupied with 'real' cognitive problems of major significance, those problems in which our indissoluble bonds with 'rationality' are unfolded for examination; hermeneutics, on the other hand, should be concerned with everything that is left. As Rorty suggests, whatever can not be rendered commensurable with such logically accepted standards seems to end up by being relegated into the area of the merely 'subjective', there to be examined by the hermeneutic disciplines.[30] In our opinion, however, we are not dealing with a polarization between rational objectivity and irrational subjectivity so much as with a distinction between different types of investigation; on the one hand 'established' philosophy (in the Kuhnian sense) and, on the other, less customary and less institutionalized areas of research. This might be seen as a distinction between concern for that which can more easily be heard and that which gravitates toward the area of the 'unheard-of'. 'The eyes are more exact witnesses than the ears',[31] we learn from the boundless wisdom of Heraclitus. That which lends itself to being heard is susceptible to so much interpretative labour that effectively, from the point of view of 'legal' evidence, so to speak, the eyes are more credible witnesses. The lesser 'reliability' of the 'ears' as objective witnesses is, however, an index of the vast cognitive and hermeneutic potential that can be explored only by listening.

As is well-known, in 'normal science' an agreement is generally reached which makes it easier for one person to agree on how to evaluate what another person says. 'Normal' scientific discourse is thus articulated basically upon a consolidated set of conventions; whatever counts as a relevant contribution or genuinely responds to an inquiry is judged according to this set.[32] We move on an epistemological level when there is not simply an understanding of the dynamics in action but also a desire to codify these dynamics in order to extend, demonstrate and seek a rational basis for the knowledge of the object under study. We reach a level of epistemological commensurability when sufficiently established investigative methods are made available to us.[33] And this does not occur only in the 'exact sciences'. It might also occur in the epochal cycles of philosophy, art and politics to the extent in which they become 'normalized'. Even though it is unwarranted to believe that thinkers in such fields have revealed the 'deep structure' or 'authentic nature' of knowledge, it is nevertheless appropriate to bear in mind that when a branch of research becomes sufficiently institutionalized it is relatively simple to isolate the basic assumptions which underlie its articulation and use.

In some limited aspects, hermeneutics might be conceived as

the study of an atypical discourse conducted from the viewpoint of a normal discourse; an attempt, that is, to gain some sense of what is unfolding during a phase in which we do not (yet) have the instruments we need to 'begin an epistemological account of it'.[34] From this viewpoint, therefore, the demarcation line between hermeneutic and epistemological research can not be drawn simply on the basis of a distinction between 'natural' and 'human' sciences, between facts and values, between explaining and understanding. A more fruitful differentiation, according to Rorty, might be based upon the criterion of a *greater or lesser familiarity*;[35] a distinction based upon our developing the habit of paying heed to formerly unheard-of messages, voices, clues. We assume a hermeneutic position when we do not completely understand the experience that we are faced by; and we can do this when we have the strength to admit our inadequacy, to abstain from negation and to opt for an interpretative procedure as a result.

We often get lost in the course of the complex labours of a listening process and, in spite of hobbling faithfully on, no kind of understanding or explanation of our lost state, or of the opaqueness of 'evil', can be construed: and even though we try to adhere to the 'better' aspects of our rationality no direct sense can be made of what we engage in. And yet, the implacable evidence of listening in fact evades any kind of 'logical' or 'moral' vision of the situation as it rather tends to reveal an unexpected ('unthinkable') insight into the *potential* of the relationship itself.

The notion that there is some permanent structure of knowledge which can be brought to light and articulated by philosophy (perhaps by making of it a kind of 'visible marionette'), with the risk of turning it into an idol, is equivalent to supposing that cognitive purposes, like the rules that govern research, are common to any discourse on a given subject of study. Thus epistemology works on the basic assumption that all contributions to a given discourse ought to be commensurable and translatable into one another.[36] Hermeneutics, on the other hand, might be understood as an attitude that distances itself from this basic assumption, as a reverent approach to all anomalies, aiming to revalue the work involved in a willingness to listen, a work that becomes evident in those interpretative efforts that involve and even transform the researcher. In Rorty's view, something is commensurable when it is 'able to be brought under a set of rules which will tell us how rational agreement can be reached on what would settle the issue on every point where statements seem to conflict.'[37] These rules tell us how to construct an 'ideal' situation, in which all traces of disagreement are revealed as non-cognitive, as a linguistic problem to be expunged or, in any case, a passing phenomenon that can be solved by means of further work of the same kind. From an epistemological view-point it is essential that agreement is reached on the methods to be adopted when one *must* agree. In the meantime, however, the interlocutors can also 'agree' to disagree since they are satisfied with the basic rationality that holds them together.[38] One of the characteristics of epistemology can be recognized in the basic assumption which makes it 'necessary' to find larger and larger areas of agreement with other thinkers. And the belief that one can construct an epistemology coincides with the conviction that such a rational area of agreement actually exists. Such an 'area' may ultimately ban other modes of expression, articulation and communication.

## LINKING HERMENEUTICS AND KNOWLEDGE

One of the first 'cognitive' effects of listening suggests that there is not much that can really be seen from *one* point of view, and that parallel perspectives on the same 'object' may actually reveal different worlds; in the listening approach there is no one direction of interpretative choice that can claim better results. Of course this multi-faceted view that comes up in the challenge of listening does not allow for an account based on a linear and consecutive causality, since each story could be re-described and re-written in several ways. Listening actually impoverishes us from a 'rational' point of view because if we seriously engage in paying heed we may even come to a state of helplessness and disorientation. And yet, even though in some respects the challenge pulls us away from the articulations of 'real knowl-edge', on the whole and in the long run it may contribute to a new (and not to an alternative) style of philosophical work; a sort of work which seeks neither to comply with standard ration-ality nor to shape the world according to its views; we no longer know what discourse we ought to reproduce mimetically in accordance with certain basic meta-rules and no longer wish to 'shape' culture according to certain principles of current rationality. 'Reality', 'nature', 'the world' thus escape any restrictive construction and almost elusively turn to renegotiate the relationship.

It is perhaps outmoded to recall the deeply engrained respect of certain maritime and agricultural cultures with regard to their environment as well as their quasi-religious dialogue with nature, constantly aware of the 'impossibility' or blasphemy of violating natural events. A similar outlook seems to reappear in some representatives of our changing contemporary science, an outlook which allies itself with a fuller logos of listening and discourse. Prigogine and Stengers, for instance, remind us that:

> At the very moment in which we learn the 'respect' for nature imposed upon us by theoretical physics we should also learn to respect all other cognitive approaches. We should learn to refrain from judging any form of knowledge, practice and culture emanating from different human doings, and should learn to promote instead modes of conjugating such cognitive ways and of creating new channels of communication. This is the only way to confront the unprecedented demands of our times.[39]

The stiffening of a distinction between facts and values may be conducive to obscuring the very possibility of there being alternative or complementary descriptions of something beyond those contributed by standard rationality and normal science; tacitly they imply the suggestion that once we have ascertained the facts there is nothing left to do but to operate a non-cognitive, unexplainable *choice* of value judgements, the choice of a perspective for evaluation which is in no way linked to knowledge and research. And yet what remains persistently occult is the question whether the kind of language whereby we try to describe the world and our cognitive relation to it, does actually coincide with an attitude that we stipulate regarding ourselves; an attitude which is a condensation of values, hierarchizations and instinctual derivatives. And the adoption, or prospective adoption, of a different language may be perceived as tantamount to a 'contrary' attitude. According to Rorty, only the hypothesis of a neutral translucid vocabulary with which to describe humans and their doings would make plausible the distinction between enquiries pertaining to facts and discourses pertaining to values.[40] And if it is an illusion that such a vocabulary exists we then force ourselves to feign to 'pretend' that we can split the same person into an individual who knows and an individual who lives. Epistemological debates are sustained by the trust that there is a common ground of rationality which may function to unite us even if speakers are not cognisant of it. And in order to be rational we must identify the terms in which every contribution to the discussion must be translated if an agreement is to become possible. In epistemology, 'conversation' is only useful as implicit research or as a precursor of research.

With the cognitive presumption of a vast underlying rationality and consequent logocentrism, we permeate the higher spheres of education and culture and thus induce a climate of latent arrogance at the exorbitant cost of a detachment from the interwoven complexity and unfathomable depth of 'reality'; we become increasingly remote from any chance of listening and prone to the 'conflagration' or 'raging fires' of 'pride'.[41] But then, the refusal to listen is resolved periodically in the shattering vibration whereby natural and social 'reality' breaks its way and makes itself heard even in the most élitist and exclusive of logocratic games. In a non-listening perspective, current rationality surreptitiously absorbs all knowledge claims with the ultimate result of silencing any 'illogical' voice that might be heard in the course of the debate and which might create links that we regard as unnecessary. The discipline of listening directed to both our 'inner' and 'outer' world would probably contribute to making the various ramifications of knowledge conversant with one another in as much as we become aware of the limits of our epistemic and 'professional' backgrounds. Research would thus outgrow the state of a technique based on the qualities of neutrality, anonymity, indifference; research would thus integrate probity and rigour into an evolutionary path which no longer avoids the challenge of *philo*sophy in its pristine and more extensive meaning. Paradoxically, the listening approach may represent a most drastic and rigorous way of knowledge in as much as it frees us from the adhesion to a dominant anthropology. Through listening we create a defence against any form of logocratic terrorism which may enslave the mind. And the enslavement of the mind does not take place because any cognitive outlook may be false or inadequate but because it tends to absorb major issues into minor models.

In an open organization of knowledge, even the experiences of pleasure and displeasure might become instruments of philosophical research as they no longer function as ends in themselves but are amenable to be used as intermediate passages towards a more complex equilibrium. An experience of pleasure may not be confined to the status of an occasion of enjoyment but may be transformed into the announcement or uncovering of unapparent features in the complexity of interactions. Similarly the notion of pain may no longer be relegated to the non-cognitive level of frustration but may enhance an awareness of features and factors which cause disturbance. The less pleasure and displeasure are regarded as mere fluctuations of one's inner life the more they can be introduced and used in the enrichment of our philosophical concerns. In general terms, indeed, it would be very perplexing if we were to talk about 'knowledge', especially in the social sciences, as if it were totally remote from the experiences of joy and pain; knowledge would thus come to be restricted to a minimal sphere of human functioning, with hardly any relevance to the live complexity of the knowing person. In fact, in philosophical enquiries, just as in other branches of knowledge, such 'emotions' as pleasure and pain are only apparently absent and no exceptions or immunities are to be seen, as can be demonstrated by the intricate history of scientific conflicts. 'We must not forget', Wittgenstein suggests, 'that even our more refined, more philosophical doubts, have a foundation in instinct'.[42] An oversimplified outlook on human relations, an outlook based on the assertive power of western logic, influences us so massively that we may actually become blind with regard to certain 'essential' aspects of our concerns for knowledge. Cognitive interactions, for instance, may be interwoven with early affective experiences whereby we construct the pattern of our basic interactions. In any of its varieties 'knowledge' may be far from neutral and void of emotions; on the contrary, it may be deeply engrained with instinctual derivatives connected with domination as a one-way form of relating – and thus a pseudo-interaction. It is these rational-emotive components that confer 'authentic reality' on our cognitive doings. At least in this respect even epistemology can be associated with hermeneutic concerns.

In spite of constant dialogic ostentations, the absence of a listening culture may still induce a basic system of 'yes' and 'no'. If this is still the latent structure, then we must be correct in every segment of our own pursuit as if we were unbreakably bound by some non-dialogic, deductive logic. When one is listening, however, it is not so important to be 'right' at every single step of the process. It is not essential that what we receive should be translatable in articulations which are legitimate, lucid, correct, coherent, unassailable. When concerned with listening one can repeatedly be wrong in a propensity to create a more enlightening relationship in which *even* the object can teach and instruct. We are confronted with a situation in which we have to take provisional, impossible steps in order to continue to listen and thus consent that something may come across.

## THE PROBLEM OF SEGMENTATION

By its very nature, a non-listening language sustains the tendency to institutionalize a mutual suspicion between areas of research, an attitude possibly conducive to an increasingly rigid and drastic subdivision of responsibilities. Furthermore, in accordance with such an 'urge' to subdivide into categories, all sense of responsibility with the life of (and on) the earth ends up by being banned. If this process of 'fragmentation' is continued, in fact, any sense of overall responsibility can not help but recede indefinitely until it loses all meaning. The insurmountable bulkheads between different areas of knowledge are perhaps one of the most obvious consequences of an underlying rationality that is able to induce cognitive advancements even when it is hardly capable of generating forms of mutual listening among different disciplines. A perspective of reciprocal listening would, in fact, allow for the cultivation of a knowledge in which techniques and types of discourse might fertilize one another to the point at which a philosophical space might emerge without hierachies based upon peaks of observation that encourage the breaking-up process. When we still do not sufficiently know our own personal and social 'weaknesses' we are incapable of understanding those specific instances that determine the development of different cultures. We may persistently continue to believe in a scientific or ideological fetish and, with satisfaction in our heroic sacrifice, remain enchanted by it to the bitter end. Nor are we disturbed by the latent search for power inherent in such attachments since the power that we seek when we climb on board any cultural vessel at all belongs to the symbolic cluster in which we have taken refuge, rather than to ourselves as individuals. We may feel strong and lucid precisely because we 'think' as emissaries of another thinker or train of thought in such a way that our own existential identity is protected and our own probity untested. It actually becomes possible to stop listening to oneself altogether if we insist upon staying on board a specific 'vessel'. Sometimes, as we plumb the depths of our experience, the recognition of the fragility of that which we are trying to propagate and of the possibly disproportionate effort bestowed upon the task becomes more visible.

Even though the linguistic games of philosophical texts – ever dignified and glittering with lucid arguments – seek to avoid a self-satisfied virtuosity, they do not only represent a condensation of the finest human qualities but also, possibly, reveal symptoms of their tendency to distance themselves (escape) from the complexity of life. They are elaborations whose power can often be admired, but in which, nevertheless, a certain danger can be glimpsed: the tendency to become an end unto themselves, to forget the extent to which they are interwoven with the development of the human condition, and to branch out into increasingly defined and watertight compartments. We sometimes raise our eyes towards philosophers with a feeling almost of reverence or inadequacy. They seem to be adepts of the most aseptic, neutral way of thinking, imperturbable in their analytical detachment, inaccessible to any form of disturbance. At other times, however, the superior neutrality of philosophy can almost seem to be a youthful game carried out in a dimension free of risk. 'Dangerous' thoughts may thus be entrusted to other disciplines.

And yet, a propensity to dwell by a disquieting thought rather than hurry to elucidate its possible linguistic expressions effectively transposes us onto a different level and perhaps creates a sense of discourse that can even testify to a mutation in the 'system'. Proximity to the listening approach may release a faculty for breaking-up with respect to 'closed' discourses and an ability to reorganize the most rigidly constituted symbolic circuits.

## THE PHILOSOPHICAL USE OF ANOMALIES

'What is important about depicting anomalies precisely? If you cannot do it, that shows you do not know your way around the concepts',[43] Wittgenstein warns us. And in order to 'know' our way around at any price, one is tempted to withdraw into a shell-like deafness that allows us not to pick up the manifestation of anomalies; ultimately this temptation prevents us from knowing our way around these powerful concepts with which we constantly deal. If we are not listening carefully for anomalies we may end up by ignoring them altogether and, as a result, also ignore the predicament that we do not know our way around the very concepts that we continue to expound and impose. In the development of the human sciences the conviction that one has an exact knowledge of certain aspects of the individual has often become entrenched, in spite of the fact that knowledge of greater scope may derive precisely from those 'anomalies' which would invalidate or refute our established cognitive claim. The philosophical apex of any discourse on the human sciences can be sought in the direction of inexplicable transformations, at the point at which a sudden leap, a riddle or surprise forces us to stop and 'think'. When we worry about incongruities that seem to resist all conceptualization we even become involved in the analysis of 'alien' contributions that stimulate respect, with the hope of drawing upon a concept or viewpoint which is capable of 'solving' the problem we confront. Our most stalwart efforts, however, often seem unrewarded and we are frequently bombarded by completely opaque and meaningless cultural events until, unexpectedly, we accept a hitherto unthought-of path or make ourselves available to something that has previously been ignored.

'There is no such thing', Gadamer points out, 'as a method of learning to ask questions, of learning to see what needs to be questioned.'[44] It would be even more justifiable to say that there is no such thing as a method of learning to listen to something.

How, then, can the admission of ignorance and questioning emerge? Let us say first of all that it can come about only in the way that we have any sudden idea . . . The real nature of the sudden idea is perhaps less the sudden realisation of the solution to a problem than the sudden realisation of the question that advances into openness and thus makes an answer possible. Every sudden idea has the structure of a question.[45]

And yet, unfortunately, this scenario already contains the established conviction that messages can only orbit around a specific 'question': messages, signals, symptoms or cries ('anomalies', in fact) that are not summoned up by our questioning can not be received and inevitably get lost. And thus, ultimately, even as masters of questioning, we may remain disorientated, unable to make our way around our own concepts.

Taylor suggests that the main reason why predictions are not possible in the field of history and philosophy is that humans are 'animals' that define themselves.[46] Changes in the way we define the human condition produce mutations in the condition itself; thus humans can only be understood in constantly different terms. Furthermore, changes in human history generate conceptual grids that are incommensurable with each other in the sense that no common matrix of expression exists to define them.

The psychoanalytic 'revolution', for instance, perhaps derives less from the systematic focusing on unconscious motivation than from the determination to establish a methodology of individual listening as the essential basis for all interpretative relationships. By means of serious listening, whatever is 'anomalous' simply ceases to be suspect for the sole reason that it is atypical.

Hermeneutic efforts often make it possible for us to respond to – or correspond with – cryptic messages deriving from different linguistic games; at the same time, also, we are not interested in searching for the equivalent expression in our own linguistic world. In fact, the capacity for elaborating commensurability – for finding, that is, equivalent expressions in different cultural areas – constitutes only *one* of the ways in which we can interact and cope with differing 'worlds'. And when this method fails to work we make use of any other method that might function, such as, for instance, when we stop translating and try to learn something from the *others'* games. 'When you read the work of an important thinker', Kuhn goes so far as to suggest:

look first of all for the most obvious absurdities and ask yourself how such a rational person could possibly have written them. When you find an answer . . . when these passages begin to have meaning, at that point you will realise that some of the most central passages, that you thought you had already understood, will have changed meaning.[47]

If hermeneutics points to an attempt to explore what can only be understood with difficulty, and epistemology represents the study of ways in which we actually know, one might consider the former as the discipline of humanistic research and the latter as the discipline of the 'natural' sciences. This distinction, however, may turn out to be extrinsic and superficial in as much as epistemology might refer to a method used in the *normal* sciences – whatever the object of study – and hermeneutics might refer to a method used in those fields in which 'normality' has not (yet) been attained or is unattainable. The dynamics of exclusion or excommunication, moreover, spring more easily from the normal sciences than from research into fields that are dense with 'anomalies'.

Learning to 'know our way around' anomalies and peculiarities might have a value that escapes any 'normal' system of evaluation. Canetti's disarming exhortation perhaps argues to similar effect: 'The least person has a claim to being found again and listened to. The happiest has to face the unhappiest. The time for such confrontations is viewed as more important than any vocational or familial demands.'[48]

Whatever form the 'negative' dimension of listening adopts, whether as insistent suspicion, constant renunciation, the emergence of contradiction or coexistence with the incomprehensible, it still is a vital aspect of a philosophical propensity for that which is opaque, open, perplexing. It is precisely at this point that the mild, surprising and strong nature of listening is revealed: it risks all, never retreating because it possesses no territory and, therefore, occupies no space. Listening draws upon those depths where 'truth' does not lend itself to representation by means of institutionalized languages.

# Chapter 4

# The power of discourse and the strength of listening

## NOTES ON THE POWER OF DISCOURSE

When responding to the philosophical need to recover the inherently problematic nature of language we should, furthermore, bear in mind the potentially defining aspect of every act of speech.[1] The secretly defining character of linguistic expression can bring about such a marked hypertrophy of our language that it almost becomes deformed until it appears to be no more than an élitist and potentially violent game. Logical-discursive interactions may be seen as élitist in the sense that they tend to represent the articulations of those members of a culture who are unable to live devotedly within language but who, on the contrary, possess it with extraordinary mastery, *hauteur* and, often, even with elegance and grace. Those who are incapable of speaking the incisive[2] language of the highest cultural games remain excluded from such despotic doings. Given the vagueness that arises from this lack of differentiation (between mastery of language and respectful dwelling with language) any attempt to establish an 'impossible' listening dialogue with those who survive at the extreme boundaries of the 'empire of logos' must ultimately be considered as a worthless pursuit.

This obviously does not imply that formalized ratiocination does not aim to include even the most 'marginal' aspects of the human condition: such aspects, indeed, become 'objects of study' through the customary application of the celebrated suffix that generates, for example, neonato*logies*, thanato*logies*, psychopatho*logies* and so on. Any particular segment of the cultural universe which still remains to be investigated is circumscribed and made an object of knowledge by attacking it with the most thorough and refined logical methods. The concomitant possibility of stopping to listen or of allowing oneself to be instructed by it (the 'object') appears so illogical as to be regarded as excessively obtuse or blasphemous.

It is paradigmatic that the actual founder of the 'revolutionary' therapeutic method truly based on listening is not always immune to that logocentric tendency that ignores the expressive potential of the object of psycho*logical* investigation. One might note, for example, the way in which Freud begins an essay written for a conference:

> Throughout history people have knocked their heads against the riddle of the nature of femininity . . . Nor will *you* have escaped worrying over this problem those of you who are men; to those of you who are women this will not apply – you are yourselves the problem.[3]

We are dealing therefore with the ability to speak of a particular object of study with other interlocutors, who must be 'scholars', just as Freud's 'people throughout history' must be men; and the object of study as such should not be concerned with expressing itself on the riddle that it represents for the scholars. The enigma represented by any human being is degraded in this way to the level of object (of study) by those holders of a non-listening logos that, in the final analysis, benumbs the researcher and makes the research itself banal.

Lying beneath western metaphysical tradition, according to Vattimo, there appears to be a way of thinking that reveals a basic insecurity and pathos, to which it reacts over-defensively. He thus suggests that *all* metaphysical categories are violent.[4] Canetti's note is not dissimilar: 'The sciences bite off pieces of life, and life shrouds itself in pain and grief.'[5] It would, however, be utopian to ask those who hold power to disarm themselves, giving up their privileges, and then listen to the 'good souls' who hope for a different kind of noetic coexistence for humans. It might be the case that the 'marginalized' will then demand their rights. And if they were ever capable of organizing themselves to the point of seizing power it is possible that they would lose their creative energy and the situation would simply become a power 'turn-taking'. But if the 'rising forces of the spirit', so to speak, tend to be excluded from power it seems inevitable that they be silent, losing, sterile. While the paradigm of this dilemma seems to resist tenaciously in the most varied of contexts, in the field of listening one tries to explore the possibility of following paths that permit one to release oneself from the latent 'vice' of this dilemma.

And yet, both the best accredited theories of knowledge as well as the enlightened distance that we try to create with the 'truths' that are the consequence of these theories seem to oppose any possibility of release from a dilemmatic condition. Authentic dialogue is undermined not only by modes of thought considered as forms of cognitive or ideological violence, but even by standpoints that appear to be absolutely non partisan, neutral, antithetical to any kind of intrusion. Canetti insists: 'Part of thinking is its cruelty, aside from its contents. It is the process itself that is cruel, the process of detachment from everything else, the ripping, the wrenching, the sharpness of cutting.'[6] The halved logos underlying the power of our culture can be expressed through both assertive and critical means. In both cases an essentially colonizing thought, and one that is rarely conducive to coexistence, seems to be the result. One could even say that the logos that knows how to speak but not how to listen represents the model of power in its primordial form. If technological and scientific development represents the goal vouched for by the logic of our culture, and if no other power capable of counterposing technological advancement exists, we are forced into believing that a technical civilization is the way in which the non-listening language dominates unopposed.

As an initial approximation, we could remark that this way of articulating our body of knowledge seems to be confirmed even by the development of 'innovative revolutions': these always occur within the same logical co-ordinates that determine the philosophical and ideological standpoints to which the 'revolutions' are opposed. As this coincidence can be easily revealed we might better explore the development of an orientation that is not simply an alternative (which would inevitably fall back into the same logic) but a possible complement, conjugation or coexistent interaction. Proper hearing, thus, might perhaps induce an evolutionary transformation in the coexistence of philosophical schools.

Even though historians may have asserted that people learnt from the mistakes of the past, now that the future seems so uncertain the past might even come to be regarded as irrelevant. And if the vision of a difficult future hovers above the judgements of the so-called élites in the world of thinking, this is frequently confirmed by the hypothetical man in the street, a ready witness to his own lack of personal prospects. This condition, which is endemic by now, can release a healthy scepticism in the face of any system of cognitive or political power which might be suspected of inadequacy or presumption. A lack of faith in the holders of logos can contribute to weakening an infantilizing dependence which may ultimately lead to the benumbing and devitalizing of initiative. Faced by the alarming and denied inadequacy of the solutions that are offered from above, the individual is then obliged to contrive solutions from the *humus* of the condition in which he lives. Listening is one of these solutions. Even the recrudescence of flight from political understanding can be a sign that reveals the growing reluctance of people to participate in a cultural system as long as they are confined in the role of consumers of prefabricated spectacles.

The producers of the body of knowledge (like its users) almost seem to be committed to discovering ever more ways of translating into languages that can be 'exported' everything that is invented by 'accredited' managers of rationality. A conviction transpires that the users will perpetuate their need to learn such ratiocination to avoid the danger of falling outside the dominant language. Lyotard points out that 'Along with the hegemony of computers comes a certain logic, and therefore a certain set of prescriptions determining which statements are accepted as knowledge statements.'[7] Bearing in mind this almost paradigmatic comment will help us to clarify our thesis: everything that is sufficiently and suitably enunciated is in practice accepted as an enunciation of knowledge. The prospect that this knowledge leads to an increase in the risks of extinction of philosophical pursuits does not even constitute a problem worthy of note since any knowledge that is sufficiently and suitably expressed (deployed) has a progressive tendency to establish itself as the only knowledge there is. And any discourse initiated outside the dominant body of knowledge turns out to be so very difficult to think and articulate that it almost seems unheard-of, simply because it is unhearable: something only suitable for lapsing into madness or irrelevance.

If we only consider the reduced-by-half notion of 'logos' that has prevailed in the itinerary of western thinking it should not surprise us to recognize that 'truth' is not located outside power, and that it is not without power itself. Truths based on multiple constrictions, themselves bearers of inevitable effects of power, are generated in our culture. Foucault,[8] for instance, claims that each discipline presents its own 'politics of truth' which rules the kinds of discourses that are to be accepted and the epistemic conditions that make it possible to distinguish between true and false enunciations, the way in which both are to be sanctioned: the politics of truth also establishes the procedures that are valued in order to arrive at truth as well as the status of those whose task it is to design what functions as true. The philosophical disquiet aroused by this probably complex state might be expressed like this: we wonder if it is necessary to confine the notion of 'truth' to the area of achievements derived from such a curtailed rationality. One ought to accept as a consequence the prospect that manifestations of truth be linked in a circular way to the systems of power that produce them as well as to the conditions of power induced by truth (and in which truth is reproduced).

The elegant argumentative compositions that are scrupulously distributed to 'disciples' might constitute the written draft, or statement, of the discursive imagination of a small number of conceivers and organizers of rationality: knowingly or not, they may thus succeed in bridling other minds' ability to think. Those modes of reflection that we consider to be indisputably sound, and impose as such, might be revealed as nothing more than dominant voices, voices that have achieved supremacy, or the greatest public diffusion, in the whirl of the higher epistemic castes. The power of logos is such that in the attention that we give to its most glittering emissaries, we almost become dazzled tributaries, thus spending a life of thinking as though it were a coin that one surrendered to others. What we call 'agreement' and 'consensus' remain major philosophical problems.

Productive power represents, effectively, the noetic apogee of the west. But this is not surprising if we only consider that 'productive forces' represent the conclusion and the culmination of the dominant ways of thinking in western tradition. Our language is in fact embodied in vast theoretical systems as well as in the scientific power of producing and eliminating with ever increasing ease. It is the sort of language that 'competes with the gods', that confronts the creative power of the 'divine word' and that, in any case, does not need to listen. Severino, for instance, insists that the technical ability to produce and destroy is basically the power to lead things 'from nothingness into being and from being into nothingness'. [9] It is indeed a language rooted in a delusion of omnipotence and such that it inevitably creates the risk of detonations or Babel-like conditions. And yet the philosophical disquiet that constantly revives us might be expressed in Canetti's words:

> Because for us the collective powers are urgently back again, it is inconceivable that an intellectual man does not think about his relationship to them. No matter how hard he may strain to elude their power, something in him acknowledges them. He feels 'guilty' about his resistance.[10]

A 'guilt' for ourselves to ponder on and from which a renewed philosophical force might emerge.

## NOTES ON THE STRENGTH OF LISTENING

If we were apprentices of listening rather than masters of discourse we might perhaps promote a different sort of coexistence among humans: not so much in the form of a utopian ideal but rather as an incipient philosophical solidarity capable of envisaging the common destiny of the species. That the philosophical strength of expressive language is limited (as compared to that of listening) can be seen when even the slightest 'wrong' is avidly used by a linguistic apparatus that is always ready to make an exhibition of itself in all its analytical power, however weak it is in its capacity of *coping*. Massive contingents of interpretative articulations round upon the 'negative event' when the strength of a simple word would be enough to dissipate it. The negative event thus thrives parasitically on our own arrogant culture, always ready to leap into action, as though resentful that it might remain unused. As a tribute to the splendour of our logos the event is 'magnified' until the 'banks' that might contain its cultural detonation are no longer capable of holding it. And then we once again invoke that same rationality and try to defend ourselves from the deflagration.

The articulation of a message at the rational level or, in any case, at a level encompassing that of the presumed uncouth ingenuousness of the person to whom it is directed, sometimes seems to reproduce an infantilizing and guilt-producing paradigm. 'Why have you remained in error so long? How could you have believed that . . . ?' is the sort of question that the 'normal' rationality of a dominant tradition seems to ask so frequently. A 'duty' to salvage 'philosophy', 'science' and 'culture' from the misleading beliefs attempting to undermine them insinuates itself into this deceptive prospect. The more incisive and appropriate the terms the more a compelling influence seems to come across through them. And if any strong and virtuous mind, however simple, uncouth or witty his 'traits' might be, refuses to be enchanted or remains irremediably outside the game, or, even worse, attempts to make himself heard, it will be made clear to him that his interests are *very* far away indeed from the questions being discussed, that certain problems do not concern him and that he would be better off restricting himself to achieving those merits and honours that his subrational condition holds in store for him.

The bewitchment of these authoritative voices appears to persist as long as they address us directly (as when we attend a lecture or read a book) and when the voice 'speaks' to someone else and we perceive the interaction, an inner awakening re-creates a critical distance, a philosophical *vis* or *virtus*, in the same way as glimpsing how a conjuror performs a trick. The nature of the virtue, or strength, released by this attitude may constitute an issue that is never sufficiently fathomed. Undeniably, there are even facets of one and the same mind, or moments of the same journey, that can be dominated by the most varied bewitchments and thus prevent the authenticity of the experience of listening; they are ensnared by an incessant whispering that instigates to reject any transforming dialogue.

When a thinker turns his attention to the humble, though exacting, labour of listening it is almost as though he were impeded or held back from this inappropriate operative level by some élitist power (possibly envious of its strength); it deviously insinuates to the thinker who tries to listen authentically that he could well be a member of a high and rational order, so to speak, capable of discerning essences and linguistic paradigms from the myriad of interactions; an élitist power which has become internalized seems to ask rhetorically why there should be any need to listen, when one has not only achieved a mastery of language but also of the metalanguages whereby one can soar to the level of the relations that exist between discourse and reality, or among different types of discourse.

It might also be possible to convince the interlocutor to take advantage of this mutual 'friendship' in order to bring to completion those tasks that are intended to solve the stubborn ignorance of mankind, if only the 'others' would agree to 'listen' and give their assent. The temptation above all suggests that major and minor holders of the logos should coalesce with each other and forget about certain 'sub-rational minds'. Let them simply 'listen' and then follow superior modes of reflection. In order to extend the scope of dominant rationality, its representatives may even be prepared to forget past conflicts and to consult together to consolidate their positions. When the caste barriers of the logos close once more there is nothing left to do but attribute tasks, diagnoses and constraints.

Certain orientations of thought, in fact, would not even be capable of aspiring to, or understanding, the germinality and strength of listening, not simply because the capacity to listen is virtually absent but also because there is no propensity to develop it in any way. In this sense, perhaps, much of our colonizing thought is waging a useless 'battle' in that it can not think of arriving at a level (or, rather, of creating a dimension) that it neither hopes for nor envisages. It is considered self-evident that each of us should aspire to a particular style of knowledge without worrying at all about the developments or dangers that might result from it. But in order to recognize the invasive presence of cultural tendencies that, even in their validity, are capable of making us obtuse, it seems essential that we make at least a few steps, even if only out of curiosity, along the path of listening. However slight these dawn-lit signs may be, they represent a strength that surpasses power strategies by drawing them into a different light.

Even the extraordinary lucidity of discourse or text could be construed as a bewitchment in itself. Those who are exposed to it are unable to relate the words that have been heard or read, and even when we manage to 'reproduce' the most authoritative sources of discourse we are surprised to discover that they seem to exhibit a notably diminished power to explain or enlighten. All that is left is the impression that it is an honour 'to listen to' and internalize a certain 'voice', and that everything the 'tradition' says is rationally superior. The desire to seem equally superior and rational by agreeing to the voice as rapidly as possible is an inevitable consequence. And when one is aware of voices that are even more melodious and enchanting, one pretends to be capable of a superior critical spirit and tries to outdo the voice with even more cogent and persistent enchantments. Should a lively mind join in the discussion in a different tone, he may come across as if speaking in a clumsy and uncouth way. If he then contradicts the enchanting and subjugating 'agreement', the only result is to make a cold anger flare up in those who are attuned to the luminous source of knowledge. A discerning act of listening, therefore, demands a strength and rigour that are difficult to subjugate and that deserve constant exercise. A listening atmosphere is not improvised. It is, on the contrary, the product of a strenuous process of conception, growth and devoted attention.

One could even say that an incomplete rationality (eloquent but deaf) may actually project its constraining tradition into the future, inducing a culture of imitative thought. Such thinking can only be imitative as it cannot transform itself by means of germinative listening and only hears what may perpetuate its basic structure. The development of this 'culture' tends to be a mechanical progression of reflected articulations, identical at every point and permanently oriented towards ever more *conquests* in the area of knowledge. Barely aware of its own limits, modern culture seems to lack the time and logical space it needs in order to cultivate a 'pristine', 'unspoilt', quality of thinking more suitable to sustain the innovative concreteness of experience. Some of the myths that constrain culture can only be disenchanted by a way of thinking that may draw upon the source of its own *strength*, not so much in the form of an introspective isolation as in a solidarity of reciprocities that will allow for authentic listening. On the other hand, one can continue to articulate ever new arguments amenable to various systematizations that lend themselves to repetition and to the reproduction of discourse-as-power. The source of strength that derives from inward listening appears less as an accountable thought and more as a spontaneous way of thinking, so to speak, allowing us to discern different, truer aspects in the very same features and myths of our culture. Only by re-assuming them in this way can we acknowledge their life. In the absence of a capacity to recognize this life we seem to be moving in a diversified but enforced theatricality which occupies the entire spectrum of our cultural expressions.

A person who simply listens is possibly not much, but he is not isolated in the sense that he is connected once again to a network of vivid, moving and complex dynamics. The attitude of listening can spring from even the most unfavourable situations and can be filled with strength whether it finds itself in the position of receiver, or referent, or in the 'favoured' position of sender. As each system is held together by its antithetical tension with the unavoidable threat of entropy, one might even suspect that a system of knowledge is interested in 'listening' responses; and each interactive novelty, such as a possible attitude of listening, 'can supply the system with that increased performativity it forever demands and consumes'.[11] In listening, however, a force is released that can not be transformed into power without itself vanishing. Listening, in fact, faces all difficulties unarmed and lets unfold what must happen. The only way of keeping a tradition of listening alive would be that of pursuing an aim that the traditions of power would not even be able to envisage or believe, an aim that does not participate in the acquisition of power and that looks simply foolish as a result. Since the work does not propose success, compensation or the overturning of antithetical positions, it is carried out in such a way that makes the germinal dynamics of listening unnoticed and secure.

Within the perspective of formalized rationality the deterioration of the celebrated object of knowledge appears to be *inversely* proportional to the capacity of articulation or expression of that object, and to the strength of listening exerted by whoever holds the greater contractual power. All this seems obvious on the manifest level. At a deeper level interactions can be revealed to be immensely complex and the destructive potential of the 'normal' system seems to unfold according to a space-time circularity that can be interpreted perhaps as a sort of *nemesis*. Protectionist devices of all kinds prove to be rather insignificant, therefore, when compared to the fundamental co-ordinates of a language-knowledge more suited to domination than cohabitation; in our basic logic it is only possible to advocate an ethical attitude with regard to something or someone who can *say something to us*, someone who can make himself heard. And yet the point at issue is whether we are capable of hearing a message and whether we select or predetermine what we can hear. And whatever 'says' nothing to us is unworthy of reciprocity and can be 'disregarded'.

On the other hand, however we pose the problems of human ethology and planetary ecology, what prevails is an archaic predatory code that integrates sadistic (and eventually self-damaging) relations which can only be diagnosed with enormous difficulty. An ever renewed and laborious insight into the basic articulations of the rationality we inhabit is not in the nature of a 'sermon' or of analytical affectation. On the contrary, if we all too simply attempt to computerize problems of ethological-ecological balance we could ultimately render them commonplace or 'sentimental'. Respect and listening, on the other hand are organized along rational lines that lead directly and increasingly away from banality. In the experience of metropolitan man, according to Vattimo, philosophy might speak once more in its 'weak' mode, which also demands a dismissal of the 'violent' characteristics that metaphysical tradition has vouched for. The emerging idea is that of a 'weakness' that distinguishes and distances itself from power, that neither disguises nor annuls itself, that neither attacks nor flees; such 'weak' mode, then, appears to be grounded upon an extraordinary strength.

## A DIFFERENTIATION BETWEEN THE CONCEPTS OF POWER AND STRENGTH

In our attempt to differentiate in some way between the conceptual areas of 'power' and 'strength', all we can do is stumble and grope. Any other proceeding – effectively a 'procedure' – would automatically draw our effort into an epistemic orbit that would probably show little interest in focusing upon such a basic distinction. Even though the two terms presuppose and underlie each other in a sense, some kind of differentiation seems to be essential if a notion of strength, too often unduly reabsorbed into a concept of power, is to emerge and to be sufficiently articulated. Unlike what is pursued in circumscribed and specialized investigations, the notions of power and strength are often used in the most varied philosophical areas of our culture as though they were interchangeable terms. A culture, for example, can show little interest in distinguishing between the power (or faculty) to annihilate and the strength (or capacity) to restore, reintegrate and let live.

In our theoretical frame of reference it is inevitably difficult to adhere to a sense of language connected with listening, or to focus on the sense (in terms of orientation and purpose) of our linguistic power. It is almost as though every cultural form resisted all efforts to identify its own basic interests.

Even those alternative cultures that rise up in opposition to the ruling body of knowledge possibly do not suspect that they are constrained within the coils of that same language, which knows how to speak but not how to listen. And how could a thinker change direction, contradict and correct himself? It would only be possible if he were not committed to works of subjugation and verbal bewitchment. It would amount to admitting some fragility in the relationship with the salient criterion he adheres to, a terrifying procedure that would have the effect of breaking the magic wand that confers prestige on the inhabitants of our logocratic culture. At the same time, though less audibly, we can glimpse a search for a virtue or philosophical strength sufficiently alive to allow us to try to neglect power. The practice of listening in fact does not in any sense imply assent; on the other hand, when dissent is raised to a 'philosophical' level by the inherent mechanics of a logocentric system it tends to endanger the quality of listening, and to confine itself in an epistemic fortress in which 'freedom' of thought proves to be illusory. If, however, we continue to explore the possibility of a more germinal and profound freedom we can aspire not only to the faculty of justifiable dissent but also to the strength (and virtue) of listening.

In some of his writings Severino represents the destiny of our culture in terms that might be more philosophically instructive if he *differentiated* explicitly between the notions of 'strength' and 'power'. Omitting this distinction he suggests that:

In the horizon of Western culture the supreme law remains that of the struggle for existence. It can be expressed in the following way: the *rational* (equalling true, beautiful, fair etc.) is whatever exists as a fact or, rather, whatever is strong enough to establish itself – the whole complex of existing political and social systems. The *irrational* is everything that lacks the strength to become or to remain a fact. There is no point in a culture trying to seek values other than strength; and it is inevitable that science and technical development, as the two supreme producers of strength, should lead the world. Does an alternative to Western culture exist? Is there any point in looking for one?[12]

Yes, on condition that we recover the primal vicissitudes of thinking and the capacity to notice that 'strength' and power must no longer be confused.

It almost seems as though our ways of thinking might become self-reflecting at the cost of their progressing loss of vitality in an uninterrupted flow of discourses. In this perspective we could notice the symptoms of degradation of our symbolic system; a danger otherwise impossible to even anticipate. In this way, thought might become 'wan', endowed with a dynamic that is no longer credible in spite of its warranted articulations and ready to dwindle into polemics at the slightest sign of difficulty. This lack of strength is in fact trying to regain its balance by a search, as secret as it is unrestrainable, for power or some link with power. The lack of strength of the more popular and accredited 'discourses' seems to follow a parallel course with an unrecognized pride in their liberty of movement and neutrality. It may be instructive to suspect that this neutral liberty is rather abstract, rhetorical and prone to conform to the precepts of the most primitive mechanisms determined by phylogenetic inheritance. Humans tend to proclaim their freedom on account of their powerful verbal and cultural constructions, possibly in an attempt to ignore the extent to which our theoretical developments are derivatives of underlying conditions and how easily they can be drawn back into the twists and turns of sterile argument. The most archaic interactions dominate in culture as a result of the insufficient *strength* of our powerful thinking, however admirable it might be in its expressive discourse and in the immense rationality of its western technology. From the *techne* of our origins to the techno-*logy* of the present and on towards the *logics* of the computer age, the enormous subjecting power of the logos can in turn be subject to the most archaic interactional cues. Western thought seems to have moved too far away from the strength of the listening word.

It has been suggested that the 'utopia of the living word' is not to be envisaged by overcoming the contradictions inherent in classical rationalism, but by attempting to overcome the reasoning language that speaks and produces them. Commenting upon the works of Benjamin and Freud, however, Rella, for instance, notices that both authors have proposed nothing other than 'rendering fit for cultivation those territories in which previously nothing but madness had grown',[13] penetrating them with the 'sharpened axe of reason' in order to 'fortify the Ego' and to perfect 'its organization', so that it can 'annex new areas of the Id'. It might be instructive to note that the recurring images in these fragments extrapolated from Benjamin and Freud refer specifically to a (mutilated and yet powerful) form of our logos that we have tried to show: a rationality that ought to function as a 'sharpened axe', that ought to confer even greater 'force' upon the Ego so that it can 'annex new areas' of the unconscious, according to a territorial logic which is both colonizing and predatory. The search for a listening dialogue, therefore, seems to be obliged to coexist with the distinctly 'territorial' features of our rationality.

In the famous work by Spengler,[14] in which no recognizable attempt seems to be made to transform the 'given' historical situation, the decline of western culture is presented as inevitable. No effort of thought or will could alter the course of our destiny, according to Spengler, as it appears to be impossible to flee from, or exorcize, the danger of decline. In such an oracular work we can see the binding power of the primordial myth of fate resurging once more. The domain of philosophical work seems to be struck by a paralysis that makes it assent to be crushed by an inexorable destiny. Once again we run the risk of falling into the void of a dilemma. Either we move conceptually according to western logical and dialectic methods, defending uncompromisingly the quality of our own philosophical procedures; or, as our only alternative, we lie down in Spengler's wake and compete in the compilation of 'contributions' based on a propensity to unmask, demythify, desacralize and deconstruct: either a procedure that exults in its own abilities or a pantoclastic, suicidal trend. This second approach also pretends to deploy a greater perspicacity or cognitive power; precisely because of its daring ability to anticipate catastrophic outcomes on the cultural level (and thus 'proving' the uselessness of thought), it arrogates to itself a higher degree of conceptual acumen. In a listening perspective this is not a binding dilemma, as it is necessary neither to move within the self-validating area of pre-established paths nor decree their indisputable extinction by a ponderous use of arguments. The dilemma itself forms part of a logical structure from which we are trying to establish a healthy, unnoticed distance.

There is a further dangerous temptation in the search for a cognitive reordering based on secure rational articulations. If these resources were workable there would be no need to try to risk anything else and one could ultimately 'clear up' most linguistic confusions and aberrations; drawing upon the power of ever new expressive modes of our rationality, one has the comfort that derives from a 'faith' in the validity of an end that legitimizes in terms of itself the path or means used to reach it. And only when the epistemic field has been reordered through the power of the dominant logos can one devote oneself to the 'pitiful' and inessential pursuits of listening.

One of the paradigms used to construct reasoning, classical causality seems to ever reproduce itself in cultural relations: texts and sources of a lay sacredness are instituted and knowledge descends from this 'sacredness' as with an underhand necessity that determines and shapes awareness while itself remaining unaltered. These text-sources can be replaced, upset and revolutionized without the authors ever entering into an authentic dialogue with those who read or 'listen'. A cognitive account that would make it possible to construe a listening subject who elicits articulation or a receiver who, by responding to the message, contributes in an unexpected way to the life of the discourse itself, is not favoured in our culture. The receiver of the (written or spoken) word is colonized above all by causal logic. Motives-for are frequently and wrongly used as if they were causes. It sometimes actually seems as though the listener has to be kept at a certain distance, and any creative intervention he might make eliminated at the very beginning, as if one were keeping at bay a vandalizing rabble, only capable of sublogical uproar and completely a-philosophical exhibitionism. Effectively this appears to be the situation, since listeners as such do not exist, except as human material susceptible to impregnation by a hegemonous self-referring rationality that establishes its developments by means of an admirably accurate articulation. It would therefore be madness to look, or listen, for anything else. And yet in a cultural situation involving blind alleys it is possible that the patient and rigorous 'madness' of listening might return from its concealment and contribute to enlighten our philosophical prospects.

It would seem, therefore, that there are no listening subjects but simply objects in a relation that is not founded upon dialogue, possibly a sadomasochistic (and therefore sterile) interaction deflected into the cultural dimension of language. Logocentrism therefore appears to be misleading to the point at which it perverts the creative function of listening. And anyone who dares resist the servile condition of pseudo-listening can only choose between the glosses of the dominant ratiocination produced within the chorus of adherents on the one hand; on the other, those who wish to avoid the silent imposition of muteness, may opt for the construction of a competing powerful doctrine. This 'new' set of theses and assumptions may initially be regarded as equivalent to the dominant rationality, then more cogent and finally hierachized as its opposite. Between these positions, in the last resort, an agreement is negotiated in such a way that it can be imposed upon other 'listeners' who are struck dumb and deprived of power.

The higher educational system also seems to be focused upon the development of those linguistic skills associated with greater contractual value in a logocentric-logocratic society, and thus intent upon discrediting the values of listening in the most drastic manner: by not even noticing their existence. One could even say that the nature of listening is thus presented in a perverted, misleading way. In the deficiency of a reduced-by-half logos (capable only of expression) there is a blindness whereby any attempt to listen is viewed as the sad and humble practice of those who could not possibly excel in cogent articulations. In a logocentric perspective the power of language determines a situation in which the incompetent are relegated to what is considered the desolate limbo of listening. The practice of genuine listening, on the other hand, is not associated with any institutional or hierachized structure and, in any case, can not propound itself as a competitive alternative to any 'religious' or lay doctrine. Any development entailing a claim to be its exclusive pursuit, so to speak, would ultimately represent a perversion of such a practice. No tradition of listening could be identified that draws upon or belongs within a specific institutionalized community.

As the culture which produces technology becomes increasingly capable of incisive and coercive assertion it finds in military devices – which actually define cultural areas of the earth – the paradigm of its inverted symbols; they, in fact, impede the logical space (which they are supposed to create) for communication and reciprocity.

As is well known, even the most elevated language of cultural treatises often serves to conceal and, at the same time, express some of the paradigms that are inherent in the most archaic territorial dynamics. And yet, even war-like practices, transferred on to the symbolic domain, do sometimes become clearly visible: 'He sweats peace out of every pore. But his mouth is teeming with war',[15] as Canetti has noted. The unfolding of our basic logic determines such an imbalance between power and strength that ultimately its expressions turn into lifeless, powerful positions defined in terms of themselves. Perhaps with the re-emergence of a propensity to listen – the other half of our rationality – we can glimpse a lasting source of philosophical strength.

## ON THE ACCEPTED MEANING OF 'STRONG' AND 'WEAK' IN WESTERN CULTURE

One train of thought in our culture is sometimes described as 'weak' in order to distinguish it from another mode of reflection to be considered 'strong', and from which 'unique, ultimate, and normative' assumptions can be derived.[16] It is not, however, plausible to claim that one trend of thinking is, in fact, 'strong' and that another type of philosophical research is 'weak'.

The body of knowledge that is differentiated from 'weak thought' can be shown to be anything but strong. It is in fact the sort of thinking that succumbs most easily when confronted with the slightest pressure from the vestiges of the reptilian brain that operates alongside cognitive structures in human beings.

The central theatre of western rationality (which is presumed to be 'strong') is periodically shaken by horribly destructive festivals which unfold with total indifference towards the 'strong' thinking that finds itself incapable of resisting the dullest mechanisms of human nature. A thought that, nevertheless, resumes its usual logomachies as soon as the period of terror has come to an end.

When faced by the incursions of the more archaic dynamics, our 'strong' thinking seems to be defenceless and, in any case, anything but strong. It is, therefore, characterizable more adequately by such words as 'powerful', 'exact', 'daring', 'efficient', 'cogent', possibly 'violent' and 'coercing', but not necessarily 'strong'.

The segment in the spectrum of our thinking which is generally considered scientific and rational might be more fragile than it appears to be: perhaps for this reason it is, conveniently, proposed in the most powerful and assertive ways. If classical or 'normal' rationality were strong they would be better able to resist the incursions of those territorial mechanisms that regularly produce extinction and fragmentation. 'I respect the weakness that is not an end in itself,' remarks Canetti, 'that makes everything transparent, that surrenders to no one, that encounters power tenaciously.'[17] There is a noteworthy strength in *this* weakness.

A clarification of terms might be useful in an attempt to get away from the hooks of ambiguity and thereby free oneself from unquestioned dominant assumptions with which, at the same time, one tries to construct an 'impossible' coexistence. In order to describe in a different way a listening type of philosophical contribution it might be more suitable to speak of *modes* of thinking that can be qualified as 'mild', 'moderate', 'modest', 'available', 'vulnerable', 'welcoming', 'patient', 'contained', 'tolerant', 'conciliating', 'receptive', 'pitiful' (with reference to *pietas*), 'humble' (with reference to *humus*), 'poor' (with reference to parsimony), 'disciplined' (with reference to *discere*), 'vital' (with reference to *life*): all those qualities that are not based on weakness but on a devoutly exercized strength.

It is not easy to free ourselves from the benumbing effects of a culture in which the characteristics of maturity and strength can be too easily qualified in terms of weakness. Nietzsche has already warned us of this ambiguity and misunderstanding:

The *ambiguous* character of our *modern world* – precisely the same symptoms might at the same time be indicative of either *decline* or *strength*. And the signs of strength and emancipation dearly bought, might in view of traditional (or *hereditary*) appreciations concerned with the feelings, be *misunderstood* as indications of weakness.[18]

Perhaps 'participation' in the dominant culture is more subtly coercive than we are prepared to admit since we even dare to use our standard language of power, or 'dominant plot', in order to describe (as 'weak') a way of thinking that tries to free itself from that language.

Furthermore, the counterposition 'strong-weak' seems to have a markedly classical derivation. In Book IX of his *Metaphysics*, Aristotle states:

> And since contrary attributes cannot be induced in the same subject, and *science is potency which depends upon the possession of a rational formula*, it follows that whereas the 'salutary' can only produce health, and the 'calefactory' only heat, and the 'frigorific' only cold, *the scientific man can produce both contrary results*.[19]

Such 'products' can be grossly misused. A linguistic expression such as 'weak thinking' seems to be derived tautologically from the standard vocabulary of 'thought-as-power' or 'thought-as-control' according to which everything that in its terms is considered defective is described as futile, inadequate, tenuous, inconsistent, subrational – in other words, 'weak'.

Linguistically it would appear that one must either fling oneself against thought-as-power in all its varied expressions or, alternatively, merge with and submit to it by adhering to the language that considers itself strong and that attributes connotations of weakness to anything that tends towards diversification.

The philosophies of deconstruction, dismantling and demystification can be traced back once more to an over-powerful and intrusive logos, endowed with analytical, demystifying and deconstructing acumen and yet closely associated with the logical power of the logocentric assumptions of western tradition. Deconstruction could be viewed as performing the role of an invective by means of analytical instruments.

These modes of reflection can be transformed into a deconstruction whose purpose is the perpetuation of itself in the sense that no deployment exists that is not bound by the underlying intention of subjecting everything to a destroying *lysis*. Listening, on the other hand, precludes no orientation – whether destructive or constructive; it is not susceptible to incompatibility and thus can not take the place of some of the procedures that characterize a considerable amount of philosophical activity: on the one hand the glossing of the most prestigious texts of the moment or, on the other, a destructive criticism intended to demonstrate its inadequacy, alter it substantially, or even overthrow it. Since it is not a substitute for any of these activities it does not posit itself in an oppositional or exclusivist dialectic. Listening is probably something quite different and demanding.

The sort of thinking that is carried on in listening cannot be regarded as weak since it can only derive from a sufficiently developed inner strength. And yet the thought that is practised in listening bears no power. A more suitable distinction, therefore, might be established between thought-as-strength and thought-as-power. Inasmuch as they can easily be eliminated both children and plants, for example, would be 'weak' (as are the Socrates and Gandhis who punctuate the path of human history) even though, effectively, however powerless, their strength is considerable. It is illuminating to have to recognize that all thought which is not consolidated in tangible forms of power is generally considered 'weak'. At the same time we can not ignore the fact that the qualities of attention, tenacity, patience, respect, resilience, rigour and farsightedness that contribute to the development of 'weak' thinking constitute a way of relating that is based upon strength.

With the prevalence of a misleading and illusory negation of a thought-as-strength that we are still unable to value, for everything which somehow is articulated outside the dominant logocratic paradigm the attribution of weakness is unavoidable.

We might be moving in a language so disproportionately arrogant and Babel-like that the enigma of listening can not even be entertained: a language that perverts itself in its incomplete expressive and coercive modes, which reduces itself by half, and which can only exist on condition that it is the most powerful, and that it gain ever more power. Among these Babel-like languages the most 'valid' and 'persuasive' is inevitably considered the 'strongest'. Human beings have by now acquired the ability to raise their cognitive voices, to render them ever 'stronger', up to the domination of the earth, the splitting of matter or to the unexploded equivalent of pseudo-symbolic expressions materialized in what are called 'deterrents'.

# Chapter 5

# Listening to philosophical tradition

## PHILOSOPHY AS ACCESS TO TRADITION

The avid assimilation of western philosophical tradition often seems to be aimed at a better articulation of how we have arrived at our current knowledge claims, that is, the sort of knowledge which now permits the technological control of both the animate and inanimate world. The smallest detail that might have contributed towards modern thinking is in fact sought out in the 'classics' and occasionally even the 'oversights' committed by the great thinkers of the past are accurately 'deplored'. If, however, we listen more carefully to our cultural history, if we try to auscultate it, these 'deplorable' errors may change their appearance and even help us escape from the narrow path of the dominant cognitive system. If we adopt the attitude of philosophical listening we do not seek support from classical sources so much as perhaps evidence of the complexity of interactions and concerns.

By listening patiently, humans in the process of becoming fuller persons are able to tell us how their specifically human physiognomy is established. Through a philosophy of listening whereby the most archaic images rise to a symbolic level in order to speak, we may gain some familiarity with the personal and group archetypes that, in the most imaginary ways, talk of fall, exile and loss, just as they do of restoration, mutation and awareness. In my opinion something can 'speak' if it is listened to, rather than there being something it might say, that one would subsequently attend to 'by means of' listening. What is revealed by the untiring effort of dwelling by, is not so much the logical completeness engraved in a phase of human history as its fertile emptiness, its evolutionary openness. As is well known mythological and exegetic disciplines agree in suggesting that myths actually celebrate the reinterpretation of an earlier story. Philosophically, however, we should perhaps remark that it is the capacity of paying heed to a story that allows the unfolding of its meaning; the narrative does 'exist' because it is listened to and thus its sense may come across and develop into further myths. A listening propensity thus appears as the condition for all accounts. An account of connected events in order of happening depends on the maturation of a dialogic disposition. The refusal of the history of something is tantamount to refusing it altogether.

In the often rigorously high-flown haste that goads us on to settle, for example, whether 'essences' are to be found in single objects or in some hyper-Uranian dimension, it becomes difficult for us to meet – or be met by – everything that lies, as it were, between here and the 'heart of things'. In our logical urgency to arrive at that point (apart from missing everything that lies between where we are and where we want to be) even the atmosphere of awakening thoughts, the springing to life of philosophy, may ultimately get lost.

As we draw upon our philosophical tradition, we might easily become disappointed if our 'knowledge' were to be restricted to a familiarity with sets of debatable opinions which are hierarchized into a conglomerate under the pretext of a universalizing 'scientific' value. As a result of this we might be tempted into presuming that we can free ourselves of the tradition, and thus run the risk of forgetting, losing our bearings and foundering. Alternatively, we might create an option for learning to discern and absorb ever more as our capacity for dialogue increases or, even, undergoes a mutation. We might let ourselves be 'overwhelmed' by the incipient gleam, the daybreak of philosophical thinking (instead of simply trying to capture it), in a procedure that is quite distinct from the classification, systematization and comparative evaluation of accounts. Referring to the desire to be conversant with western tradition Jaspers remarks that 'every assimilation springs from the depths of our own life. The more resolutely I live the premises of my epoch, the clearer is the language of the past, *to which I listen*.'[1]

It is not simply a question of 'hunting' for more cogent, imposing truths in the deep waters of our historic past. We should also attempt to create a communion that 'springs from the depths of our own life'. Sgalambro points out trenchantly that 'Kant can be quoted, not as a living spirit, but as a thing left lying somewhere to be used at will. These sacred relics no longer contain a soul but merely decorate our texts . . .'[2] Hunting out a thinker's exact doctrine eventually seems to end in a constrictive and predatory procedure that lies outside the fertile labours of a listening-based communication – a propensity that we might know little of.

When we prepare ourselves to learn from the 'utterances' of a thinker we often tend to pursue a policy of cultural, a-philosophical 'acquisition', placing our faith in a listening capacity that is either atrophied or insufficiently developed. Heidegger points out:

> that we imagine we are approaching . . . a saying in an objective manner and without presuppositions when we take cognizance of it . . . We take cognizance of it, we add it to the knowledge which we imagine we possess anyway of such matters. But this 'cognizance-taking' . . . seemingly not burdened with any prejudice, is in fact an interpretation as charged with presuppositions and prejudices as is possible . . . It rests on the stubborn and *widespread prior assumption that one can enter into dialogue with a thinker by addressing him out of thoughtlessness*. And here thoughtlessness is to be found not so much where someone untrained in philosophy asks his question, but rather where every seemingly pertinent and apposite citation from all of the world's philosophical literature is indiscriminately thrown in.[3]

In a dialogue in which 'we do not address' but, on the contrary, allow ourselves to be overwhelmed by the message, the evolutionary 'risk' cannot be compared to the grave danger of a benumbing sense of security. Heidegger, for example, also claims that:

> discerning minds understand that Heraclitus speaks in one way to Plato, in another to Aristotle, in another to a Church father, and in others to Hegel and to Nietzsche. If one remains embroiled in a historical grasp of these various interpretations, then one has to view each of them as only relatively correct. Such a multiplicity necessarily threatens us with the specter of

relativism. Why? Because *the historical ledger of interpretations has already expunged any questioning dialogue with the thinker – it probably never entered such dialogue in the first place*.[4]

The point at issue is why it is so difficult just to enter such a dialogue. And further on:

> The respective difference of each dialogical interpretation of thought is a sign of an unspoken fullness to which even Heraclitus himself could only speak by following the path of the insights afforded *him*. Wishing to pursue the 'objectively correct' teaching of Heraclitus means refusing to run the salutary risk of being confounded by the truth of a thinking.[5]

But if the risk, according to Heidegger, is salutary we might somehow deduce that 'the historical ledger of interpretations', to the extent to which it protects us from coming into contact with the 'truth of a thinking' that could overwhelm or sweep us away, represents a cultured 'normality' that is secretly diseased and pathogenic.

The 'salutary risk' in question is that of making the act of listening ever more rigorous in order to see whether some creative thought capable of overwhelming us might recognizably emerge from the heritage of the tradition. This type of 'investigation' can no longer simply be described or imagined according to a linear, causal notion of logical consequentiality. On the contrary, we should do all we can to discern the dynamics of a multidimensional field, a network of 'circular' causal relationships in which we find ourselves reciprocally forming part either of the problem or of its solution. Inhibiting a philosophical listening attitude can reduce these inexhaustible manifestations to a state of preventive extinction. When we adopt a connubial listening propensity we are no longer guaranteed – or bound – by a guiding thread of linear causality: the thread that *calms* us, according to Musil, is that of simple succession; inserting that famous thread of the story which passes through everything which has happened in time and space even though everything has already become no longer recountable and no longer follows a thread but has spread itself out across an endless surface.[6]

## THE CONJUNCTION OF PERSPECTIVES

A more promising path for contemporary thinking could be developed by forging together those inner means whereby we may become capable of 'hearing' new resonances from the past, thus promoting a conjunction of different cognitive horizons. As the opening remark of one of his last contributions, Jaspers states that philosophy grows stronger because of the way it resumes and profits from its history, and also suggests that the strength of contemporary thinking lies less in the creation of new basic concepts than in the new messages of past thoughts that it enables us to rediscover and 'hear'.[7] The philosophical seriousness of listening is revealed by the *way* in which it receives ideas that emerge from the tradition. The prevailing ways of approaching the past can, in fact, pervert both listening and ourselves whenever the concern is reduced to a game based on the reckoning and recomposition of philosophical findings. Nor can the philosophical 'way' of drawing upon tradition be restricted to a simple and possibly illusory observation of a 'theoretical' nature. The listening way is directed, rather, towards an involvement in proofs and experiments intended to test the potential of our own epistemophily.[8]

The listening horizon can reawaken in us something which is not easily reached through the exercises we perform within the domain of current, normal disciplines: proper hearing, in fact, reveals itself primarily in an endless confrontation with the secret fascination that benumbment holds for us. Something which seems unreachable if we take normal theoretical paths can emerge, with an almost unhoped-for spontaneity, from an intensified philosophical disposition to be taught by the depth of our philosophical past.

'It is true that we can compare a picture that is firmly rooted in us to a superstition;' says Wittgenstein:

> but it is equally true that we *always* eventually have to reach some firm ground, either a picture or something else, so that a picture which is the root of all our thinking is to be respected and not treated as a superstition

he concludes.[9] An interest based on listening is not sustained by a disjointing, or Manichaean, attitude, in which case one may tend to devalue a contribution because it is rooted in a 'picture' or 'superstition' from which we may want to take a distance for a number of reasons. In the modesty of the listener the idea of identifying the image and thus even of being able to 'uproot' it intellectually from a philosophical orientation in which it originates is not a central concern. Nor even is it relevant that the salient axiom should be placed under scrutiny for the plausible reason that it is comparable to a superstition. The choreographic paradigm, so to speak, of the advancements taken by western philosophy seems to avail itself precisely of the detection of the image 'which is at the root of all our thinking' in any preceding cycle, only to accuse it accurately of being a principle of unfounded knowledge (almost superstitious, even though partially 'justifiable') and replace it with more enlightened and cogent cognitive assumptions: a paradigm that can be perhaps illustrated in the saying *Amicus Plato sed magis amica veritas* (although Plato is my friend, truth is an even greater friend); a paradigm that appears to be reproposed in various forms throughout philosphical history. Listening, however, is not to be envisaged as yet another position so much as a path of a coexistential nature aimed at such an understanding of the message (theory, system, or other) that will allow it to live on and develop in the direction of further conjunctions and cross-fertilization.

In Jaspers' opinion what we are waiting for from past history and what may come forward to us is nothing less than the maturation of human nature as it is revealed in thinking.[10] If the enigma and peculiarity of human nature are rooted in an unutterable crossing of innumerable horizons, an intellectual approach that favours a predominantly 'spiritual' or 'biological' horizon – a segmentation[11] – may end up by usurping and disfiguring a depth that can barely make itself heard and which, ultimately, deprives us of its generative contribution. 'The understanding of the word of the tradition', insists Gadamer,

> always requires that the reconstructed question be set within the openness of its questionableness, i.e. that it merge with the question that tradition is for us. If the 'historical' question emerges by itself, this means that it no longer raises itself as a question. It results from the coming to an end of understanding – a wrong turning at which we get stuck. It is part of real understanding, however, that we regain the concepts of an

historical past in such a way that they also include our own
comprehension of them. I earlier called this 'the fusion of
horizons'.[12]

A further form of conjunction, or 'fusion of horizons', is recognizable in the compatability, or complementary nature, of a
listening approach when compared to certain logocratic ways of
speaking which ultimately go on 'decreeing' indefinitely. If we
link listening propensities to philological methods, Vico's claims
might perhaps come across more clearly:

> Philosophy contemplates reason, whence comes knowledge of
> the true; philology observes that of which human choice is
> author, whence comes consciousness of the certain. This
> axiom . . . includes among the philologians all the gram-
> marians, historians, critics, who have occupied themselves with
> the study of the languages and deeds of peoples . . . This
> same axiom shows how the philosophers failed by half in not
> giving certainty to their reasonings by appeal to the authority
> of the philologians, and likewise how the latter failed by half
> in not taking care to give their authority the sanction of truth
> by appeal to the reasoning of the philosophers . . . [13]

Cultivating a propensity for conjunctions, possibly similar to
Heidegger's concept of 'dwelling by something', we may become
exposed to the live story of mankind, with which we might
establish a kind of *consonance*. Perhaps to similar effect Canetti
suggests that as the earth becomes more densely populated and
our way of socializing more 'mechanical' we may have to resort
to music as a source of philosophical life:

> There will come a time when music alone will provide a way
> of slipping through the tight meshes of functions; leaving music
> as a powerful and uninfluenced reservoir of freedom must be
> accounted the most important task of intellectual life in the
> future. Music is the truly living history of humanity, of which
> otherwise we only have dead parts. One does not need to
> draw from music for it is always within us; all we have to do
> is listen simply, otherwise we would learn in vain.[14]

Still another example of the search for the conjunction of horizons is presented in Ricoeur's tireless hermeneutic research.
He argues, for instance, that although Hegel comes after Kant

chronologically we, as belated readers, go from one to the other; for us something in Hegel has surpassed something in Kant, but something in Kant has also surpassed something in Hegel, given that we are just as radically post-Hegelians as we are post-Kantians. In Ricoeur's opinion contemporary philosophical discourse is structured by this exchange and permutation.[15]

## LEARNING TO THINK FROM ENCOUNTERING THE PAST

Philosophical thinking is often directed at the past in the search of a theoretical starting point – *terminus a quo* – for every discourse on human nature and knowledge. As we know, historical notions are sought out and then exhibited as essential elements, guaranteeing the seriousness of the enterprise. In order to deal with any problem at all, a perspective is offered that retraces the path backwards to some initial aspect of the object of study in order to confer more credit to the pursuit in front of us. The past is explored, revisited and kept in safe keeping as a community memory that contains the treasures of those manifestations of the creative spirit which do not decline. And yet the past is also a museum both of 'horrors' and of endless 'errors' in the evolution of knowledge. Our community memory of such evolution often reveals itself only in a mythological form. Myths in most traditions refer to the dynamic core of 'human nature', which can be approached through the narration of events that display structures applicable to other similarly structured interactions. And the truth value placed upon certain myths does not derive from their antiquity. Their long history is probably due to their knowledge-enhancing quality. In our work the truth value of a myth may come across to us in the form of a listening 'instrument', a rough guide in the attempt to auscultate those enigmas and depths that might otherwise induce an over-hasty cognitive rejection and, therefore, the elaboration of thoughts that can be deduced from areas which are for us more easily practicable.

Vico, for example, wrote:

That the flood was world-wide is proved, not indeed by the philological evidence of Martin Schook, for it is far too slight, nor by the astrological evidence of Cardinal Pierre d'Ailly, followed by Giovanni Pico della Mirandola. For this latter evidence is too uncertain . . . But our demonstration will be drawn from physical histories discerned in the fables.[16]

Clearly, however, the use of fables demands a clear, radical listening that cannot be curtailed by the exclusive adoption of empirical techniques or means that banalize the story. In such a context, which may determine a restriction of perspective, an inability to listen seriously to the fable silences those 'physical histories' that would otherwise filter through it and be visible if we were capable of a relationship that was both more involving and more rigorous.

Opaque and unusable thoughts from the past assume *ipso facto* the cognitive status of errors, lacunae, mistakes or eccentricities that exempt us from laborious thinking and lead us to alleviate the burden of understanding by invoking a reassuring rationality that could ultimately benumb and deceive us as far as our potential for thought is concerned. According to Heidegger:

> Even if we have devoted many years to the intensive study of the treatises and writings of the great thinkers, that fact is still no guarantee that we ourselves are thinking, or even are ready to learn to think. On the contrary – preoccupation with philosophy more than anything else may give us the stubborn illusion that we are thinking just because we are incessantly philosophizing.[17]

The attempt to guarantee ourselves a secure fortress of certainty might lead to a degrading of our most evolved features, whereby we even attempt to move in enigmatic and provisional cognitive situations, to reach for our most profound resources and activate new forms of creativity. From Nietzsche's work, for example, we may learn that the courage of one's *own* opinions represents a common weakness[18] since the nodal point in a search for truth lies in the capacity, and courage, to detach oneself from one's own convictions.

But what is 'difficult' is less the content of what we try to listen to than the way in which we approach things; a method that cannot be reduced to the predatory or accumulative grasping of whatever is in question. According to Heidegger:

> Public opinion today cherishes the notion that the thinking of thinkers must be capable of being understood in the same way as daily newspapers. That all men cannot all follow the thought

processes of modern theoretical physics is considered quite in order. But to learn the thinking of thinkers is in essence much more difficult, not because this thinking is still more involved but because it is simple, too simple for the easy fluency of common notions.[19]

It may require a disposition to be detached from more than one variant of standard rationality. 'Thus tradition is not simply a process that we learn to know and to be in command of through experience', according to Gadamer, 'It is language, i.e. it expresses itself like a "thou". A "thou" is not an object, but stands in a relationship with us':[20] if we do not respond by proper hearing it can shrink away and be extinguished, depriving us of the life that the encounter might have generated.

# Chapter 6

# The philosophical problem of benumbment

## TOWARDS AN AWARENESS OF BENUMBMENT

In a culture that is almost saturated with the din of innumerable messages intent on formulating codes, priorities and orientations, the inhibition of our listening potential could be regarded – paradoxically – as a genuine philosophical option. In order to safeguard authentic philosophical resources one may develop 'non-listening' defences which in fact tend to protect one's inner self, perhaps naturally inclined to philosophy.

The person who has not been sufficiently listened to by means of a maieutics of thought (philosophical midwifery) does not seem capable of listening vigilantly to our resounding culture, but only of becoming its victim. Adhering to a pristine 'philosophical bent', therefore, this person ultimately refuses to listen at all.

Looking for a kind of free trade area in philosophical life can also lead to diverging results, possibly exemplified by the search for meditative experiences or artificially altered states of consciousness. Hypothesizing a natural philosophical tendency we might see in this search for different or altered states of mind the rejection of a hypertrophic culture that does not allow a more genuine sort of rational life.

It is almost as though the individual tacitly said to himself: 'I am trying to find a way of not thinking because I no longer want to think the thoughts of others'; or else: 'I wonder why I should carry on thinking if I find myself entertaining thoughts that do not allow my own philosophical development but only a culturally mimetic form of survival.'

In an attempt to break down this mimetic imposition the

individual strives to fold down the edges of the frame in any direction he can, in the sense that the only way to live, rather than merely survive, is to find an exit.

'Devastation', Heidegger remarks 'can haunt us everywhere . . . by keeping itself hidden':[1] thus we move forward under the burden of an obscurity that seems to weigh upon the world not as something extraneous but, rather, as something humans have engendered. As a way of monitoring such an unnoticeable advance of 'devastation', the listening approach can not possibly be viewed as a variant of passivity; it does not entail any silent sado-masochistic collusion. On the contrary, everything that is *not* listened to *correctly* is actually submitted to, accepted and absorbed. We can no more avoid thinking of coming to terms with the bio-physical atmosphere surrounding us than we can ignore the myriads of messages in which we are constantly immersed. That which we are *not* capable of listening to reaches us in any case, in ways that may induce passivity or unutterable torpid states whereby we are increasingly restricted to ever more mechanistically territorial contentions, whether in favour of or against something. And all of this may occur in the form of lucid rational articulations. Reducing the issue to its basic terms we might say: deciding not to listen does not mean that we become exempt from organizing or metabolizing the vast array of messages that are, nevertheless, addressed to us.

Listening, on the contrary, involves the utmost concentration and, as a consequence, the reawakening of our epistemic potential. By remaining vigilant we can attempt to hear without the fear of becoming the victim of what the others are saying. It is almost as if we become amenable to being linguistically overwhelmed in proportion to our lack of listening awareness and ability. It is often recommended, in fact, that the 'herd' should not listen to bad advisers or read unsuitable material and that they remain untouched by dominant ideologies of every kind simply because it is difficult to even hypothesize in these 'others' a capacity for vigilant listening. The interactive modes that are commonly envisaged, in fact, are either that of 'listening' and falling victim to a possessive and exclusivist discourse that binds the 'hearer', or alternatively, 'listening' in order to be able to rebut by a more powerful offensive logic that fragments the expression of the 'speaker' and thus produces assent to one's theoretical system; an ongoing search for 'rational' agreement, for 'producing' consensus.

By the same token, deriding the blandest forms of cognitive obtuseness is grafted on to the general system of philosophical benumbment: by conforming, in fact, to the taste for silent derision we ensure that contempt for the 'benumbment of the masses' remains superficial. As a result even our contempt becomes susceptible to further mockery in a benumbing spiral.

And when humans are encouraged to 'listen' we may be dealing with a violence perpetrated in an unrecognizable form in as much as persons are attacked by media intent upon inducing the acquisition of theories, emotional states and 'needs'.

Trying to abide again with the original *logos* of listening, we may realize that the 'passion' for benumbment can not simply be qualified as obscurity and error since it actually gravitates toward the lack of any distinction, where no differentiation between 'good' and 'evil' may be vouched for. The distinction between truth and error, clarity and obscurity, only holds as long as even the slightest choice can still be made between them. And the first elements to fall into the whirlpool of epistemic torpor are precisely the functions of choice, distinction and differentiation.

The inability to listen (and thus identify the threat of epistemic torpor) can only result in a surrender to the pull of benumbing trends. Jaspers eloquently suggests that in the 'rule of daytime' there is clear and open communication as process, whereas, in the 'rule of night', communication is based on a momentary unification in common annihilation where confusion is presented only to draw everything within itself;[2] *the calls of the 'night'* are not amenable to being introduced into the rule of day, or sufficiently explained, and thus propagate and re-sound everywhere. Instead of listening conceived as warranting growth, a form of habitual 'listening' inadvertently prevails; this then becomes a trend that finally acts as both a 'norm' and a benumbing limitation. In the light of a philosophy of listening, one could say that the *curriculum vitae*, or *cursus honorum*, could be revealed as a *curriculum morbi* characterizing the inhabitants of the most powerful doctrines.

One can not legitimately suppose that such a *curriculum* be transformed, since it appears to change by degenerating into something formless, silent and obtuse. If the richness of humans and nature 'says nothing' autonomously we can justifiably point to a ruinous dependence on obtuseness, in the same way that we consider 'obtuse', for example, someone who is unable to grasp an elementary theorem. And, moreover, whatever deviates from conformity to standard rationality and from its shadowing limitations is simplistically viewed as nothing more than a banal infraction of the norm. All this is part of a 'superstructure of considerations' since the most commonly accepted and habitual forms of 'listening' (that is, the dominant 'forms of life'),[3] are regarded as perfectly legitimate norms, even when they are 'forms of death'. We are incapable of understanding exactly the central notion of rational habit and thus perhaps unable to recognize its binding character. We are unable to recognize this binding function in as much as we are the inhabitants of a culture hierarchized by a logos that knows how to speak but not how to listen and thus constantly avoids genuine dialogue; it primarily tends to induce *competing monologues*. In order to escape an immobile and non-listening vision of reality we resort to an endless sequence of antithetical standpoints and, even, invent 'dialectical' schemes of position, disintegration and recomposition. And when we are bound by the enormous power of an immobilizing perspective we look for a way out in the simplistic, and reductive, overturning of positions, ideals and preferences.

If we summarize the situation, an alternation of 'praise' and 'crucify' seems to emerge, exempting us from those 'deeper' transformations that are unique in permitting renewal. If we are not sufficiently open to listen to what might be called enigmatic and deep, nothing is left us but the boredom of remaining in the same theoretical frame; and the desire for a mutation, or disruption of structures, might even induce the 'conviction' that the latest trend will surely resolve our state of cognitive boredom. The history of philosophy is often presented as one that bristles with denunciations, upsets, blows, denials and schisms – almost as if these dynamics could resolve the threat of cognitive blindness which is associated with the human condition; as though, finding ourselves inert in our *care* for knowledge, we resorted to 'philosophy'. It is a matter of constant concern: the continuous, irreducible desire for novelty might represent nothing more than an inadequate surrogate for our limited capacity for cognitive renewal.

In order to avoid lapsing into the lethal position of an immobile vision and, ultimately, in a sort of philosophic stillness, we make do with the illusion of apparently inexplicable disruptions even aimed to attack our own standpoints. Musil, for instance, even speaks about a widespread 'passion for belieing oneself'.[4] Moreover, our attempts to describe the endemic passion for benumbment seem to fail simply because every attempt to describe accurately belongs to an incompatible register. The 'impossible' attempt to articulate a passion for benumbment – something which originates and sustains itself – could only result in annulling the passion. And any one of the innumerable manifestations of this passion for benumbment would sound artificial and banal whenever we indulge in the presumption that it can be adequately defined in the rational terms at our disposal. This suspicion of artificiality and banality seems justified since any expression of benumbment which might be brought into the domain of rational argument would inevitably be denied and annulled. Perhaps the rationality of our culture is unable to recognize a passion for epistemic obscurity and torpor. It is, in fact, an 'illness' that rationality neither wants, nor is capable of conceiving, since it has no idea how to confront it. And, whereas our rationality does not want to know anything about it, humans are silently drawn to it – both individually and socially. In this predicament, however, we can invoke that aspect of our logos that has been largely ignored, that of listening. Proper hearing might be able to make us aware of the undertow dragging us towards benumbment and, in so doing, offer us a better position from which to avoid falling into one of the many forms of torpor. It is a question of grasping the rampant extent of a tendency that our 'logic' induces us to underestimate and manage in an inadequate way, with the provision that we can then reinterpret *ex post facto* its absurd, clamorous and devastating results. It is a passion to which only the most radical listening can react, since it is, precisely, the only approach capable of detecting – *hearing* – it.

## TOWARDS A DESCRIPTION OF BENUMBMENT

When the capacity for symbol formation tends to degrade, the recourse to presumed sources of knowledge and the search for some kind of trend in which one can believe become increasingly vehement. It is as though everything were contradictory and truths brushed against each other without coming into actual contact and without generating any reasonable trust. Everything can be interpreted in one way and then reinterpreted in the opposite way. One can even explain universal history as a process of constant evolution and, at the same time, see nothing more than biological decadence and artificial absurdity.

It seems that the more we reach for a valid 'philosophy' in which to go to work, the more our capacity for generating a genuine language that will allow us to evolve as individuals is muffled and atrophied. Scholasticity. In the collective elaboration of dominant propensities and central knowledge claims the 'listener' is usually completely passive, and often happy simply to recognize a certain familiarity with a few of the terms in the linguistic articulations more in fashion at the time. In this cultural quicksand the risk of gravitating towards a ruinous degradation of language, almost a linguistic regression, is increased. Heidegger eloquently remarks:

> The wasteland grows . . . It means, the devastation is growing wider. Devastation is more than destruction. Devastation is more unearthly than destruction. Destruction only sweeps aside all that has grown up or been built up so far; but devastation blocks all future growth and prevents all building. . . . Mere destruction sweeps aside all things including even nothingness, while devastation on the contrary establishes and spreads everything that blocks and prevents.[5]

Symbolic animals appear to be devoted with 'historic' regularity to prolonged rituals of collective destruction. Perhaps we can legitimately suspect that our linguistic games do not only represent intellectual pastimes or childish playthings but that they constitute, more than anything else, a way of keeping our 'minds' occupied and, possibly, of *not* seeing. Linguistic games might respond to an irresistible, paradoxical, need to close one's 'mind', to avoid unsolved problems and obscure forecasts and to hide, if possible, in an innocuous cultural torpor.[6] We devote ourselves with inexplicable tenacity to learning ever more complex games, even though we are defenceless against the most serious forms of threat and absurdity. Heidegger, for instance, insists that:

> Today we speak of 'loss of center'. People everywhere trace and record the decay, the destruction . . . We are surrounded

by a special breed of repertorial novels that do nothing but wallow in such deterioration and depression. On the one hand, that sort of literature is much easier to produce than to say something that is essential and truly thought out.[7]

Those who hear and read learn from innumerable written works and speeches what are to be regarded as the salient features of human coexistence. They also receive an enormous amount of material to be used for interpretative purposes on every subject. An inundation of impassioned communications of a historical, philosophical or psychological nature pours over current problems; such contributions, however, bear the mark of somewhat hasty and irresponsible thinking. There is, in fact, little sense of responsibility involved in the dispensing of communications which may be ultimately benumbing. The point at issue is that 'telling' or 'being told' may be more detrimental than we are prepared to believe. And even in order to demonstrate the inconsistency of whatever is 'futile' or 'benumbing' with a surprise ending (such as the unsuspected victory of truth over falsehood), not only symbolic but also pseudo-symbolic constructs,[8] engrams, are impressed upon the reader, listener or spectator. It is hard to see how two opposed but linked engrams, or the diffusion of pseudo-symbolic noise can be justified. On the biological-cultural level utterances of all kinds continue to function indefinitely, as a result of reverberation, or 'inertial force', even when they have apparently come to an end. This phenomenon might represent a warlike practice of an 'inferior' quality.

A Heraclitean fragment comes to mind: 'Not understanding, although they have heard, they are like the deaf. The proverb bears witness to them: "Present yet absent".'[9] 'Ghosts?' Philosophical benumbment might produce ghosts, both present and absent. If the capacity for inner listening is put into jeopardy or left to degenerate, our theoretical developments might turn out to be of no use; and this would not simply be a sort of philosophic vacuum, since even a vacuum 'contains', at least, space. The surrender of the inner world escapes all attempts at description. We can not even say how it presents itself or comes across to us since it does not do either at all. When we look in its direction it is as though we were blind. Human beings do not defend themselves in any way because being drawn back into blindness or deafness is completely painless. On the contrary, one might even hurry towards blindness whenever one feels too close to benumbment.

By an inexplicably powerful 'necessity' that neither tries to justify itself nor render itself plausible, the passion for benumbment is shown to be diffident or indifferent when confronted by a willingness to engage in dialogue. Moreover, there are neither purposes nor tasks to fulfil in the passion for benumbment: it is nothing but an enormous draw, or attraction, towards dispersal.

A listening attitude, on the other hand, does not refuse to recognize 'intellectual collapse' as a limit, even though it is assiduously devoted to the promotion of cognitive life. An honest propensity to engage in dialogue can lead to challenging or risking defeat, a sort of 'cognitive death', but it certainly does not seek it out, in the sense that it neither desires nor fears it. Benumbment, on the other hand, is closely linked to a relation of desire for, and fear of, annihilation. An attraction towards it is enforced, even in the fatuous illusion that it can be repulsed. In our passion for benumbment we fail, or refuse, to recognize anything or anyone that has mildly spoken to us and is still capable of doing so. This would imply response, gratitude, dialogue. The propensity to listen can even be degraded and extinguished as a result of exhaustion if, in the spreading of benumbment, we restrict ourselves to pursuing those events that it wants or, without distinction, does not want. And the benumbment that deflects us blindly from listening to our 'inner world' does not even permit us to see whether we are the initiators of anything.

In the works of Jaspers we find two juxtaposed expressions indicating the 'rule of daylight' and the 'passion for night'.[10] The latter is described as 'hurtling into the absurd'. There is no guarantee that philosophy is immune to it, that our rationality is above it. Jaspers remarks that nothing appears to equal the power exerted by this passion that remains invisible to others and that closes every absurdity within itself.

Unless one is capable of understanding and, therefore, discerning the hypnotic tonality of the attraction for benumbment one may lapse into the antiphilosophical error of confusing hearing with listening. Simple hearing can be tuned into a passion for benumbment, whereas philosophical listening reveals it to us in all its devastating absurdity. And when we have the presumption of 'freeing' ourselves of something that makes itself felt in an ineluctable manner although it can not be revealed because we can not properly listen all the way through, at that point we become debtors of an agent that exempts us from all the labours involved in a serious relationship with language. We seem to be moving in a culture in which we are all somewhat in debt to benumbment.

## LISTENING AS PHILOSOPHICAL EFFORT

The problem of listening, in its irreducibly dual form as a willingness to listen and to be listened to, might be reproposed in this way. If our listening 'capacity' seems to be too enfeebled, like a potential that has never been allowed to develop, the 'desire' to listen may point to an absence, or need. In that case our philosophical path leads us, paradoxically, to an affirmation of listening in the absence of it. A philosophical procedure might arise from this that consists in a re-definition of philosophical work as endeavour, labour, effort.

Those who attempt to re-possess language in this way no longer seem to be particularly interested in drawing from the teaching offered by the core of standard rationality. They feel a need to work rigorously, and not so much in the search for alternative sources as in reaching for a mutative effort. It would be misleading in fact to conceive of listening as a philosophical attitude that one could describe in terms of inertia or fragility. A listening dialogue demands, or, rather, presupposes, sufficient strength to sustain blows of any kind and still remain alert. In the absence of such strength, no suitable demarcation line capable of distinguishing between any two (or more) features can be perceived.

If the interactive endurance is not strong enough to avoid confusion and safeguard dia-logue then our philosophical horizons might become indefinitely obscured. Philosophical work is an 'effort' if listening is to be both accepting and critical, trusting and diffident, irrepressible and yet consoling. The coexistence of these irreducible 'contrasts' is the very strength it anchors to. Drastic in the clarity with which it presents itself and welcoming in its function as an aid, the effort of listening is seriously threatened by benumbment and only a listening 'self', therefore, 'trembles'[11] when faced by the 'demon' of being engulfed once more: and it is exclusively because of this terror that the whirl-pool can be avoided. If it is impossible to make a connection, or a convergence, between historical existence and theoretical thinking this does not mean that we should gratuitously expose ourselves to the passion for benumbment. The ability to listen, which allows us to hold firm and remain vigilant at the borders of obscurity, might be the condition that makes it possible for us to remain open to further linguistic and theoretical fields of concern. We are thus released from those causalistic 'expla-nations' for which we have developed a kind of addictive toler-ance: basically, unrecognized shifts in the meaning of 'because'; or, motives are not causes. In Wittgenstein, for instance, we read:

> The insidious thing about the causal point of view is that it leads us to say: 'Of course, it had to happen like that'. Whereas we ought to think: it may have happened *like that* – and also in many other ways.[12]

The ideological use of knowledge, as is well known, appears to be more like a 'lay-religion' which is somehow expected to supply guide lines in every field. On the level of affects, moreover, ideology is envisaged as a miraculous defence against anxiety, whereas dialogue, on the contrary, demands that we try and bear uncertainty. And yet the capacity for dialogical listening might never be developed or made use of: 'Yes, a key can lie for ever in the place where the locksmith left it, and never be used to open the lock the master forged it for.'[13] And the strength needed to listen to something unheard of might actually fail, precisely because things may be unhearable when listening has only been trained to pay, effortlessly, the minimum price established by dominant logics. Wittgenstein suggests: 'You could attach prices to thoughts. Some cost a lot, some a little. And how does one pay for thoughts? The answer, I think, is: with courage.'[14]

The pursuit of listening can not be associated with one or the other philosophical orientation. It is *a form* of rationality that can be thought of as underlying, going along with or reaching beyond, but not as being in opposition to anything. It is an effort that tends to free the movements of consciousness from those metaparadigms that predetermine it. Otherwise any cre-ative need for innovation might relapse into the aims intended for it by the assumptions of dominant ratiocination. We can 'think' about knowledge because we have been told authoritatively about its basic structure. It almost seems as though every irrepressible endeavour to 'transcend' standards had to flow back into the ways of our salient criteria. These refer to a consciousness that is imitative, reflecting, rather than 'false', inasmuch as we are dealing with limits imposed by culture itself and not only by a class or dominant group. Living under the influence of our mirroring and complacent consciousness is not the same as living with an openness to life. It involves constantly assuming and construing the 'format' of life, searching for it beyond our reflecting state, without knowing much about benumbment, the concealment of life, or how to overcome it. Even if we are enlightened by bearers of charisma or philosophers of genius, a resurgence of creative thought is more likely to be an event stemming from a listening space that people can *try* to install for one another, however inexpressible that expectation might be.

According to Gadamer, the inner listening tuned to such expectation is perhaps a more demanding process than merely knowing or grasping something since it is associated with a return to oneself and since 'it always involves an escape from something that had deceived us and held us captives'.[15]

The function of knowledge can, therefore, be perverted at the very moment in which it aims to provide security, and thus even permits the pseudo-philosophical attitude of 'excommunication' and derision. A life of knowledge can only be sustained by an awareness and effort that knows no respite, as though every attainment were also a 'thorn'. For every advance in knowledge one has to accept an oppressive interrogation that does not allow security, but imposes a state of constant vigilance. The 'price' of philosophical activity is revealed whenever a lucid and cogent articulation attracts the insurgence of problems even more irresistibly than they were previously elicited.

## THE ORIENTATION OF PHILOSOPHICAL WORK

Without presuming to grasp 'the source of our thinking', it is perhaps both possible and necessary to *try* and move closer in some way to it: only by approaching the 'source' does it become possible to try to deprive the 'facts' and myths that predetermine our culture of their enchanting power; facts and myths which might then appear to us as derivatives of the divided-by-half nature of our rationality and of fictional dialogic interactions. Some features would no longer be tied to the form in which they appear and one could thus approach forms of life with a changed perspective. The extension of an enchanted and somnolent torpor may become visible if only we look at the daily presence of madness existing by mutual consent (quite indifferent to the logical splendours of our culture), or the innumerable acts of collective destruction (even more indifferent to our superb structures of knowledge). And when our work is fruitless, in the sense that it seems to mean nothing or to be leading to nothing intelligible, we could redirect our research towards a more radical depth of intention. Wittgenstein suggests that 'One keeps forgetting to go right down to the foundations. One doesn't put the question marks *deep* enough down.'[16] As we listen we move in the direction of creative thinking without allowing ourselves to be submerged by culturally induced patterns whereby we decompose and recompose the most elegant articulations indefinitely: it is almost as though one had to learn to move about in our cultural galaxy, over-saturated with messages, with a capacity for abstaining from grasping and using them.

In this network of arguments and reflections we seem to be moving along a razor's edge – like tightrope walkers – almost as though we were on the point of falling, on the one side into triumphant, non-dialogical discourse, and on the other into a state of irremediable passivity. In both cases we would be victims of a kind of ideological hypnosis. A will to deny or damage ourselves intellectually could be seen also as a desperate manoeuvre to cope with our inability to listen in depth. When reality bores us we may decide collectively and unconsciously that something new is called for and, as long as it is remarkably different, we are indifferent to its implications.

And how could we begin to learn about genuine listening? First of all by eliminating all grossly misleading meanings of what listening is. Among the most deceiving of these is the idea that listening is something imposed by the holders of standard rationality upon those who can not or should not speak. A large part of the linguistic interaction that underlies human coexistence is certainly not listening so much as endurance or forced feeding, hypnotic induction or epistemic violence; a linguistic game that one would prefer to stop playing as it is ultimately futile and fatuous.

When 'life' and 'reason' are isolated in too artificial a manner from 'death' and 'madness' by the excessive power of dominant rationality (beyond which nothing can be legitimately envisaged) the complexity of living and thinking becomes relegated to epistemological illegitimacy; as a result they become unheard and unseen, even though they are interwoven with culture itself.

'If in life we are surrounded by death, so too in the health of our intellect we are surrounded by madness',[17] says Wittgenstein. If, therefore, we are prepared to make contact with whatever lies at the borders of a healthy intellect we find ourselves intent upon listening to whatever may be disclosed beyond the border, or limit, that surrounds our rational life.

But when a codified 'inner' life and the normative science of our epoch no longer have much to say to us we can finally try to transform the setting and include a life-enhancing awareness of death. When philosophy seems to be silent and without purpose it becomes possible to resort to an exploration of limits. When the burden of the dominant culture is a hindrance to 'philosophical courage' we can begin to demand courage from everything that has been banned, and make our departure. If we wonder where the philosopher should go and whether he should hurry we might reply in the words of Canetti:

> But what is urgent? What he feels and recognises in others and what they cannot say. He must first have recognised it and then found it again in others. The congruence creates the urgency. He has to be capable of two things: to feel strongly and to think; and to *hear* the others and take them seriously in a never-ending passion. The impression of congruence must be sincere, undimmed by any vanity . . . It is the most precious but also the most terrifying thing that a man can experience. He must be able to keep it upright when it threatens to crumble, he has to nourish it incessantly through new experience and effort.[18]

# Chapter 7

# Silence and listening

## THE FUNCTIONS OF SILENCE

If we consider silence dialogically, we might frame the hypothesis that an orientation towards discourse, rather than towards listening, provokes far more a sense of cognitive security and far fewer demands. It is almost as though a non-listening speech tends to favour 'simple' mechanisms that divide and extinguish, whereas listening requires a laborious attitude more consistent with problems of integration and living. And the *gathering* that allows these qualities to unfold is not so much concentrated on a single point to the exclusion of others: it is a silent acceptance that tends to unite through the attitude of integrating and letting live. The silence stemming from this gathering perhaps simplifies without reducing and overcomes without winning: it re-creates time and space as a depth that may become inhabitable by every language.

If we are still capable of considering silence at all and of escaping for even a single philosophical moment from the relentless concert of the logos-in-progress, we might be able to exercise our listening potential and reveal features emerging in the *modes* of western language – before they hide. In other words, we should be able to listen in spite of the din.

It is by means of a listening silence that we can, for instance, hypothesize the practicable re-connection of the divergent poles of manifest meaning on the one hand, and a sequence of further possible meanings on the other. To recognize only the first pole might be equivalent to preventing the development of the inexhaustible metaphorical complexity that constitutes the life of language itself; it might be the exact contrary of Socratic midwifery. The vector that moves away (in the opposite direction) from the word as mere sign discloses levels of inner life whose existence, or survival, is dependent upon listening to those numerous levels. Any connection created in the space between these two diverging poles owes its birth and, above all, its survival to some form of silent gathering. As a result of this silent attention, threads of mental life are granted that coexistential resonance, or recognition, which allows an incipient structure to be inserted into the life of thinking, rather than being rejected or else reduced to the most elementary semiotic mechanisms. Heidegger suggests that we may consider language as a set of binding signs that anyone can use or else as something unfathomable and inexhaustibly rich. 'These two ways of thinking about language are so distant from each other that their diversity would not be sufficiently appreciated even if we tried to describe it as the ultimate opposition.'[1] Probably only an accepting silence is capable of re-uniting or making practicable the array between these two extreme possibilities. In the absence of a vivid awareness of this distinction, as essential as it is elusive, we run the risk of disregarding the value of these poles which, nevertheless, underlie and imply one another. It is not simply an abstract relationship which can be enunciated, but one that is *functional* in so far as it is philosophically inhabitable and practicable.

From an evolutionary viewpoint we might envisage the emergence of the ability to listen authentically (as something distinct from simply receiving a signal) not so much in terms of perfecting linguistic capacities that have been attained, but rather as a kind of unutterable rupture, as a silence that indicates a crisis beyond healing. The evolution of the higher primates probably can not be accurately conceptualized as a process in which existing semiotic faculties are pushed to their absolute limit, but as a 'hole of memory', a fissure in earlier gestural habits; a new reality is equivalent to something that does not exist because what is discovered is only what is already there. It is almost like a failure in memory, a sudden silence in the routine of survival, a cognitive support that disappears and leaves one dumbfounded.

If language represents a specifically human way of 'transcending' biology in order to arrive at the level of culture, we can nevertheless see that the patterns and archetypes of that transcendence call for a 'dialectical' procedure which contrasts these archetypes with their own 'opposites'. If, however, authentic

dialogue needs to have *time* for the silence of listening, a system
of dialectical opposites does not seem to have any *room* for a
listening silence. As suggested by Durand, 'ascension' is imagined
as something opposing a fall and light as something in contrast
to shadow. And yet light tends to transform itself into lightning
just as an ascent tends to look down to the 'herd'. Thus transcendence, according to Durand, is in all cases an armed occurrence – as can be seen in that transcendent arm *par excellence*
represented by the arrow, and in the 'sword of justice'.[2] These
are the cutting arms that are found united, before all others, to
the *daytime rule* of the imagination. It is significant, for instance,
that even a 'humanistic' approach to culture is ready to diagnose
in the normality of the 'healthy' the same kind of pathology that
official culture 'cures' and fights against in the 'abnormal'; *as if
oppositions and alternatives were a necessity*. Cultures also seem
to have a tendency to invoke alternative discourses and, thus,
come to represent the extreme form of an oppositional way of
thinking that infiltrates contemporary efforts. We are weighed
down by the humiliating realization that whichever logic we use
to prevent ourselves from being overwhelmed is itself ultimately
a bearer of violence. A more authentic kind of philosophical
aspiration, however, even appears to be prepared to become
dumb for a second in order to create, or allow, a breath of
silence, a philosophical fast that purifies the noetic atmosphere
as a moment of transmutation that is not simply a repetition of
ebbs and flows. Whether it is enchanting or intolerable, accepted
or rejected, according to Sciacca, the force of silence is as deep
as the 'infinite' of our inner world.[3]

As long as we remain firmly attached to our capacity for
creating silence the 'external world' will not be able to completely
reabsorb us by aggravating the danger of an illusory monism
that excludes the serious problem of relationships: either everything within us, without the world, or everything outside us, in
the world. And every undeserved (arbitrary) exclusion of a voice
entails the paradoxical effect of producing more noise. For as
long as the function of silence is somehow respected we do not
run the risk of getting lost in the meanders of our own verbalization or, conversely, of losing ourselves 'centrifugally'. If the
'spiritual domain', so to speak, has laws we must assume that
they may provide counsel, before us and inside us, without
leaving any trace or provoking any resonance, as long as a

cognitive stance prevails which is not truly philosophical and thus involves the usual rustle and noise that make humans obtuse. The search for a listening silence continues nevertheless to attract us in the most unusual ways: 'The sounding and, we might say, eloquent silence of truth insinuates itself noiselessly into our minds', writes Augustine.[4] And yet, at the apex of the trajectory traced by western thought, a remark like this might seem to be nothing more than a poetic fragment of dubious value or a simple archaeological piece. Even a few segments of our coexistence may give an idea of the unlimited number of floating and menacing messages that saturate the cultural milieu in which we function. The question of environmental degradation in terms of the excess of something and the extinction of something else, is hardly ever addressed with regard to the world of language; even the linguistic domain could be irremediably damaged by an unmonitored saturation of written or spoken words and by a concomitant lack of silence. A sufficient 'degree' of silence could be regarded as a medium suited to enhance the linguistic life of the symbolic animal and to avert irreversible deteriorations.

When we try to conceive of a listening silence as an effort to give space to the inexpressible, the celebrated comment of the 'first' Wittgenstein – 'Whereof one cannot speak, thereof one must be silent'[5] – is revealed as a somewhat circumscribed philosophical statement. It might sound censorious and quite at variance with the maieutic silence of the person who listens in order to allow something apparently inexpressible to emerge. In a maieutic logic, considerable dialogical patience is sometimes necessary so that the inner experience which is less suited to being 'spoken' can be expressed (and therefore elaborated) in some way, rather than continuing to be concretized in the most regressively reductive forms. The enormous evolutionary impetus that is gained by the experience of being listened to and, therefore, of being able to express oneself, constitutes a phenomenon that cannot legitimately be undervalued in a dialogic context. A hypothetical individual who is suffering, or confused, might respond to Wittgenstein's comment by saying: 'But if that of which I am incapable of speaking is what invalidates my cognitive life, why should it be precisely that which cannot be said?' We can, however, glimpse a further meaning in Wittgenstein's statement if we distance ourselves even more from the manifest tradition of western rationality. We might even understand it to mean that only when we know how to be silent will that of which we cannot speak begin to tell us something.

That which must be discovered 'urges' from inside, so to speak, and this urgency might represent the authentic form of our philosophical propensity; and since it is still 'nothing' that is urgent, this nothing-at-all, celebrated in silence as the dawning moment of listening, ought to be respected. If anyone had a claim to know the philosphy of listening one would begin to assemble it by continuing to follow the normal cognitive structures even though they would be transposed to what is regarded as a more fertile concern. We can find ourselves sliding into an even more insidious epistemic area whenever language is misunderstood to the point at which it is coerced into the sole function of expression and excluded from the fertile horizons of proper hearing. Listening and speaking ought to be carried out mutually since the ability to create a silence, and thus determine a new perspective, belongs to those who can speak in so far as speech represents a decision or a choice; silence is radically different, in this case, from an expressive inability or stuporous state of imposed muteness, just as the rituals of fasting would be difficult to envisage in a community that was always on the verge of starvation. The philosophical attention devoted to the concern for listening now coexists with a deafening cultural scene. And in the increasingly tight interaction of language games even our coexistential ability to deliberate pauses of regenerating silence might be put in jeopardy.

## SILENCE AND DIALOGUE

The highest function of silence is revealed in the creation of a coexistential space which permits dialogue to come along. Heidegger suggests that:

> *In talking with one another, the person who keeps silent can 'make one understood' (that is, he can develop an understanding), and he can do so more authentically than the person who is never short of words.* Speaking at length about something does not offer the slightest guarantee that thereby understanding is advanced. On the contrary, talking extensively about something covers it up and brings what is understood to sham

clarity – the unintelligibility of the trivial. But to keep silent does not mean to be dumb. On the contrary, if a man is dumb, he still has a tendency to 'speak'. Such a person has not proved that he can keep silence, indeed he entirely lacks the possibility of proving anything of the sort. And the person who is accustomed by nature to speak little is no better able to show that he is keeping silent or that he is the sort of person who can do so. He who never says anything cannot keep silent at any given moment. Keeping silent authentically is possible only in genuine discoursing . . . In that sense one's reticence makes something manifest, and does away with 'idle talk'. As a mode of discoursing, reticence articulates the intelligibility of *Dasein* in so primordial a manner that it gives rise to a potentiality-for-hearing which is genuine, and to a Being-with-one-another which is transparent.[6]

When an individual is in a condition of instinctual satisfaction (such as when there is a state of satiation at the beginning of our developmental history) he may not be sufficiently motivated to try and increase his dialogical ability. We are probably quite aware of how necessary patience and firmness become when we are faced by fervent requests for more 'humane' and closer interpersonal relationship. 'There ought to be more authentic, and "warmer" relationships between people' is a heartfelt and often repeated longing. Incensed affective links as well as the alluring ideological use of philosophy (geared to minister to emotional problems) can indeed constitute the equivalent (however much the reverse might seem to be the case) of an attack aimed at destroying the listening space;[7] an approach contrary to Socratic midwifery. Even demands for intense mutual friendships can represent an unconscious attempt to merge with the interlocutor and, in so doing, compromise any chance of dialogic evolution. One would thus sacrifice dialogical *distance* and the isolation needed for communication. Sciacca eloquently remarks that:

nothing isolates more than silence: it offers protection against lightning . . . Silence is an isolator but, simultaneously, the most efficient conductor; it does not rebuff lightning, but simply makes it slide into its bottomless pit. And inside, the serenity of cremated storms . . . inside, the calm of its consummate knowledge of every storm. The flood is a drop of water in the desert of silence. Vigorous with the potential for every word, silence is the efficient conductor of fertile communication . . . [8]

The strength of silence, however, can also be perverted and abused in the most outrageous way when it arrogates to itself a position beyond language and prevents any possibility of a relationship: the 'interlocutor' can not exist as the receiver of a message and, therefore, can not possibly be heard. 'Silence' on something in fact prevents that something from gaining access to any categorization. At a first approximation, it appears that silence can be used in at least two ways, both as an instrument of listening and as a non-verbal form of communication that can carry a variety of meanings – from acceptance to total refusal.

In its creative function, silence basically represents a way of being *with* the interlocutor; it indicates, that is, a proposed interaction, an invitation to the development of a time-space in which to meet, or clash, in order to share in the challenge of growth. In Sciacca's vivid language:

> With silence we express the most varied and conflicting states, sentiments, thoughts and desires. Silence is meaningful. There is the silence of fear and terror, of wonder and stupor, of pain and of joy . . . Silence is anything but an 'absence'. In our philosophical life it is the opposite of absence: it is the fullness of the present instant. 'Dumb silence' is a contradictory expression. Instead of describing the same thing the two terms exclude each other: silence is not dumb and whatever is dumb is not silent. Silence is a form of communication . . . dumbness, on the other hand, isolates and excludes us from all communication . . .

And later:

> The silent person is not taciturn. People are taciturn because of sadness, temperament, illness; they are silent in order to pay attention or concentrate . . . ; silence always reveals a level of profundity . . . One can say nothing without being silent, without listening in silence. Silence is always in a state of listening or of waiting for something.[9]

It is indeed significant that silence is usually regarded as being something opposed to dialogue or as the expression of a desire to keep one's thoughts inside a well-defended fortress; from this circumscribed (and misleading) point of view Socratic midwifery would be reduced to the task of understanding the 'silence' of the other in order to help him overcome it and express himself. Silence, on the contrary, can be a very fertile way of relating, aimed at the inner integration and deepening of dialogue. From this point of view, silence rarely becomes an object of philosophical attention. In my opinion the creation of an empty space, or distance, within a dialogic relation might be the only way of letting the deeper meanings and implications of that relationship emerge. The nature of silence, as a gap or distance in which germinal meanings can be developed, may be 'described' in the following lines by Lao Tze:

> We put thirty spokes together and call it a wheel;
> But it is on the space where there is nothing that
> the utility of the wheel depends.
> We turn clay to make a vessel;
> But it is on the space where there is nothing that
> the utility of the vessel depends.
> Therefore just as we take advantage of what is,
> we should recognise the utility of what is not.[10]

This 'nothing', this emptiness, can be compared to silence and is probably called 'nothing' because it is not manifest or immediately perceptible: it is not a question of thoughts or emotionally tangible events but, possibly, only of that which organizes them from within and allows their springing to life. Resorting again to Sciacca's words:

> Silence is an essential part of sonority and sounds in fact 'sound' because silences are in function; a discourse without pauses – incomprehensible. Silence is not an interval . . . but the bridge that unites sounds; the 'vacuums' of sound, the 'fullness' of sounds; the shadows of a painting, the 'emphasis' of the colours; the pauses of music, the 'beat' of the notes.[11]

We could say that, for fear of functioning in our constant 'imbalance', with its implication of vacuums and silences, we adapt ourselves to living in a comfortable common sense overflowing with words. In general, we might say that human beings are constantly doing something – speaking, thinking or dreaming. This continuous involvement with language might be considered an automatic, repetitive defence against the separation anxieties that silence can represent. The discourses we make can not always be justified in terms of the relationships in which they occur. Silence, therefore, when regarded as an 'opposite' situation to speech, must not be considered necessarily as a defensive or offensive stance. It might instead indicate a healthy desire to set aside certain automatic defences that are only intended to fill emotional vacuums. Silence can also represent a desire to abandon quasi-symbolic or pseudo-symbolic expressions that are only fictitiously oriented towards the stipulation of truth conditions. The abandonment of these verbal fillers can, furthermore, indicate a renewed chance of testing further processes of inner cognitive organization.

Often used to describe negative, melancholic and narcissistic states, the same term 'silence' is also needed, paradoxically, if we want to indicate a desire to abandon automatic verbal sequences that fill our games; this same willingness is also, in my opinion, the origin of a more mature capacity for recognizing and tolerating the gap (distance, or hiatus) between the self and the others, between language and reality. We must recognize that this hiatus is what makes necessary and possible the development of our more authentic dialogical interactions, even in those critical dialogic situations involving the expression of instinctual derivatives. One way of escaping from difficult dialogic situations is to try and involve the interlocutor in a 'friendly' relationship; another method is to frighten him so much that he is forced out of the dialogue completely. In some cases, however, whenever it is impossible to trap the interlocutor in a 'friendly' relationship, or when one is unable to shatter the dialogue by subtly destructive messages, there is yet another way of annulling a listening distance: that is, by filling the silence with a profusion of appropriate utterances. By completely saturating the reciprocity space one can ultimately annul it. And, as a subsidiary avoidance measure, one can fling oneself into extremely rapid passages and ephemeral connections between the various thoughts as they emerge. In this way the links between them are constantly broken even though one has the illusion that new and improved discussions are being created. The speaker can linger over a thought, only to flee from it precipitously as soon as the risk of having to absorb the impact of the connection between two or more thoughts becomes imminent. Perhaps, the adaptive transformations that are required for (coping with) life can only be attained if we become capable of *abandoning* something, such as for example an explicatory *Gestalt* or a basic assumption for which one has developed a cognitive 'addiction'. Thus, what we really need is *a silence* or the detachment from an hypothesis that is constantly and unconsciously introduced into the way in which we confront a problem and which, itself, makes the solution of that problem impossible.

## TOWARDS A 'DESCRIPTION' OF SILENCE

If we conform to the accepted belief that silence is neither seen, heard, nor 'pondered upon', and that it is therefore essentially something that is not given, it might be a dangerous concern to attempt to 'discuss' it and thus force the limits of language. Silence, furthermore, is clearly not a condition in which one finds oneself for situational or psychopathological reasons since, as is well known, such 'silences' can be filled with the din created by archaic and regressive derivatives. Silence is more like an inner virtual condition to which we can aspire as well as a precondition for further development.

However unsuitable to being explored or described, silence nevertheless appears to be irreplaceable for affective or cognitive renewals of any structural relevance: movements forwards, that is, destined to transform the inner condition rather than simply extend a coping paradigm that already exists.

When we say that, *as a matter of fact*, we deal with articulations and not with silence and that, consequently, we have nothing to do with it, the case might be that our *matters of fact* are only used to indicate the most banal form of hearing: a receptive capacity that is both limited and limiting, a reception that does not listen at all and renders everything trite. In less banal and more meaningful exchanges silence seems to actually mediate communication; so much so that even an appropriate word may disrupt a previously unexplored communicative level. In certain crucial dialogic confrontations we do communicate with silence and are sometimes tempted to shatter it with any futile or 'innocuous' articulation; this temptation derives from a need to look for a way out from an overabundant communication; expressions are then used not in order to say something but to attenuate the scope of what is being said.

In a logocratic, centrifugal state there might be a continuous loss of the inner strength that can make use of silence in the sense that one almost automatically competes for exhaustive, expressive articulations, becoming perhaps increasingly 'exhausted'. 'Anything your reader can do for himself leave to him',[12] insists Wittgenstein, almost exhorting us to the cultivation of a silent linguistic parsimony. The powerful mechanisms of expression draw insatiably from an inner strength in that they tend to become ends in themselves.

Attempts to open ourselves up to the experience of inner silence are neither casual, nor spontaneous, nor gratuitous. Sciacca suggests that:

> Silence has a weight . . . that we do not find in any word: it is heavy with everything that we have lived, are living now and everything that we shall experience . . . A whole life is gathered into a moment of silence. We hold it in our hand and it seems we founder into it. Not for nothing do we flee from silence, the only thing that confronts us with our own life. It recapitulates it for us there, in that instant, entirely present. It is a review that involves us without concessions . . . [13]

In the widespread benumbment produced by an excess of words, on the other hand, we give up the right to be taken seriously, at the same time withdrawing from the responsibilities that this would involve. When we agree to go along with the discourse of an interlocutor who implicitly admits that he is obliged to say just about anything, we give up the right to consider the other responsible for what he is saying. Dialogical relationships can thus degenerate into exercises of impossible logical seductions in which we do not even hope to be convincing. All we can hope for is to elicit attention with pseudo-revelations intended, in any case, to attract the other person's interest. When the 'exploration' of inner life is undertaken without silence it is deformed into an involuntary parody of the 'life of the mind'. This is why, as we progress, we say to ourselves that inner life is hardly worth taking seriously, as though the journey towards interiority were only capable of revealing emptiness and noise.

## SILENCE AND THEORY

Increasing emphasis in contemporary thinking is placed upon the need to clarify issues. And while the immediate sense of this need refers to a philosophical activity intended as an exercise of the utmost linguistic rigour and openness, in a more profound sense we also see the recognition of just how difficult, even *impossible*, it is to live without clarity. This could perhaps enlighten the enormous attraction of the numerous explicatory 'mythologies' Wittgenstein refers to in his conversation with Rhees. In the domain of human sciences, in fact, a stance that insists upon investigating until an 'explanation' is found often prevails: what appears to be a healthy scepticism and a refusal to accept accident or a lack of clarity in human affairs can thus all too hastily decline into a blind prejudice in favour of a particular type of explanation.[14]

McGuinness points out a common human tendency: when we name a phenomenon or become capable of operating in a given context, we acquire mastery over it and thus overcome our *inability* to grasp it as something simple or incapable of being contextualized. We feel that we have attained a higher level of awareness and congratulate ourselves: 'But of course we *ought not* to do that'.[15] We might derive some questions from this annotation, such as: 'Why do we like doing it even though we ought not to do it?'; 'What else could we do?'; 'Why do the alternatives seem to be unavailable to us?'. A predictive explanation, like an interpretative understanding, only tells us that in any discussion the explanation is *one* of many ways of thinking about certain things; we have no authority to assume that it is the *only* or the *best* way. The irresistible pleasure produced by an interpretative or explicatory approach might then partly derive from the abandonment of the labour, the 'waste' of time and the silence demanded by listening: we leap into the saddle of an explicatory discourse in order to seize the object and say to it: 'Shut up, I've caught you, now it's my turn to talk'. In the human sciences the enormous attraction of explicatory theories might be seen in the following way: at the very moment in which we 'arm' ourselves with a cognitive model we are, paradoxically, justified in losing interest in the object. We no longer consider it as enigmatic since it is our turn to speak to it – the object no longer has very much to say to us. This attitude can ultimately contribute to impeding our ability to think with clarity about vital issues.

Obviously these considerations subtract nothing from the enormous value of scientific research and theories since we are not so much interested in theories as in the 'relational' spaces between theories and the object of our knowledge. These spaces might be said to consist of periods of silence that can be used to restore the expressive potential of objects and persons. It is almost as though a dense cloud of theory, interpretation and explanation formed around the object, blunting *its* prospective eloquence. In a culture which is moulded by the advancement of the human sciences, we seem to be immersed in a kind of multifaceted understanding that exempts us from stopping to listen, since even a minimum amount of observation allows us to 'contextualize' the situation, that is, to arrogate the word to ourselves by depriving the other of it – erroneously believing that we have understood it. Not only does this attitude 'guarantee' the identity of the person who controls understanding, but it also establishes a one-directional, pseudo-dialogical circulation in which the only 'virtue' that is revealed is that possessed by the researcher, the adult, the analyst, the teacher and so on. *There is only as much movement towards the object as is necessary for distancing it even more.* And even therapeutic stances intended to contain, empathize and interpret can hide the risk of seeing the interactive field dominated by the 'perspicacity' and 'rigour' of only one of the two persons involved.

Aware of the partiality and provisional nature of cognitive models, we could moderate our assumptions and consider all explicatory ventures merely as a set of instruments to be used for reference; this, in my opinion, could lead to a more authentic orientation towards the object. Attempting to understand the *multiplicity* of models and the difficulties involved in their *integration* could also have the effect of a salutary demythification that would provide us with enough silence to live with, and let the other speak.

## SILENCE AND DISPUTE

The intense cultural activity of the west might seem to be intent upon perfecting its own languages, in order to refine them in such a way as to be able to 'break into', and conquer, the arena of knowledge, thus attaining *the last word* in a variety of cognitive areas. And in the concern for this pursuit the idea of making use of defeat, *as such*, is both inconceivable and unworthy of attention or of any kind of preparatory commitment: in fact every laborious act of preparation is primarily aimed at winning in any one of our cognitive games. Defeat is thus received with a sense of trauma that is void of meaning and, as a result, becomes even more traumatic, since the 'logic' in which we move is entirely concerned with winning, or at least with winning back. Not knowing what to do with 'humiliating' defeats that leave us speechless – in 'silence' – we can not even hypothesize our need for an adequate preparation capable of transforming the apparently unusable and destructive experience of a defeat into something altogether different. At the most, the directions that emanate from our rationality suggest that we learn how to lose 'with dignity' and that we resume as quickly as possible those preparations that can make the experience of loss valuable in terms of a *more* significant subsequent victory. It is unfortunate that even in philosophy, or perhaps primarily in it, the metaphor of 'battle' is considered of greater value than, for instance, those of gardening or choreography.

In the linguistic skirmish that lies beneath every field of cultural life, ever new attempts are made to falsify inconfutably or demonstrate conclusively a variety of issues and above all else to reveal the 'absurdities' of others. The most enlightening word is supposed to be the one which imposes 'silence' for a certain period, establishing itself as *the last word* as it marks in fact the various cycles – waves, fluctuations, fashions – of our modes of reflection. Lakoff and Johnson point out that:

> We don't just *talk* about arguments in terms of war. We can actually win or lose arguments. We see the person we are arguing with as an opponent. We attack his positions and we defend our own. We gain and lose ground. We plan and use strategies. If we find a position indefensible, we can abandon it and take a new line of attack . . . It is in this sense that the 'argument is war' metaphor is one that we live by in this culture; it structures the actions we perform in arguing.[16]

Looking at the situation with the inconclusive modesty of the listener, we might, however, recognize that each word has a consequence which might be able to live within us better than it can in the (battle) *field* in which the last word has been said. And whatever the last word is unable to exhaust involves a consequence, just as any subsequent word does. It is possible that every word is followed by another and it would be more enlightening to experience it from the very beginning as the last word but one. Whereas, in the powerful languages forged by dispute, we try to have the last word for ourselves, in the philosophical parsimony of listening the 'last word is the foundering of the silence of the one into the silence of the other: faced by the revealer of the unspeakable, we must abstain from speech'.[17]

Even the superior 'nobility' of the communicative, articulative, stance can be secretly bound by an unlistening language. In the exasperating event of not being heard even when we are trying to stop and hearken in view of dialogue, our frail propensity for Socratic midwifery may ultimately disintegrate and be altogether denied. In a serious confrontation there may be an abrupt degrading of '*philo*sophy' into indignation.

In the enlightened developments of rational knowledge it is possible that the original loving aspect of research – the first part of *philo*sophy – has been lost. It almost seems that knowledge forms part of an epistemic horizon that is saturated with a sort of tacit fury that only rarely and with difficulty can be scanned according to authentic dialogic methods. If 'dialectic', conceived as a critical discussion intended to promote the manifestation of truth, is envisaged as the superb tradition of our western ratiocination, we should ask ourselves whether the dialectical splendours of knowledge are not also, in part, a cover for simple hostility, or belligerent practices, conducted in the domain of articulation.[18] By unconsciously cultivating these warlike styles in a cultural context and, even, elevating them to the rank of ultimate dialectical principles, *a rationality that has more and more power and less and less strength is consolidated* – increasingly incapable of the farsightedness of listening. A rationality which does not consider listening moves away from agricultural models and gravitates toward hunting images condensed into the basic metaphors of our culture. And the function of a metaphor is to enhance the understanding and experience of one kind of thing in terms of another. Thus, according to Lakoff and Johnson, our conventional ways of talking about arguments presuppose a metaphor – 'Argument is war' – we are hardly ever conscious of.

> The metaphor is not merely in the words we use – it is in our very concept of an argument. The language of argument is not poetic, fanciful, or rhetorical: it is literal. We talk about arguments that way because we conceive of them that way – and we act according to the way we conceive of things.[19]

Wittgenstein remarks that:

> This language grew up as it did because human beings had – and have – the tendency to think in this way. So you can only succeed in extricating people who live in an instinctive rebellion against language; you cannot help those whose entire instinct is to live in the herd which has created this language as its own proper mode of expression.[20]

We can consider a stance based on silence and listening only when there is an instinctive rebellion against the constrictions of a language that tends naturally towards controversy, more able to 'battlespeak' than to listen; a language that seems to be primarily suited to being used *against philosophers* – both outside and inside us.[21] Such a language knows nothing of – (ignores) – the challenge of silence: 'It can be as hard to refrain from using an expression as it is to hold back tears or to hold in anger', remarks Wittgenstein.[22]

The most expert, complex and surprising arguments must necessarily be elaborated because, if they were not, we would not know how to manage when confronted by anyone who tried to accost us with comparable contentions. Since it is not even conceivable that a relationship of listening might exist or that silence might be practicable, the most suitable position would therefore seem to be that of training ourselves tirelessly to produce valid arguments whose primary function is that of confronting those of other thinkers. Ryle forcefully asks: 'What is the use of philosophy if it is only useful against other philosophers?'[23] In Wittgenstein we could perhaps find a sort of reply: 'Philosophy is a tool which is useful only against philosophers *and against the philosopher in us*';[24] strange philosophical tradition that seems to work primarily *against* someone (either inside or outside us) rather than *for* someone or something. 'My ideal is a certain coolness, a temple providing a setting for the passions without meddling with them', Wittgenstein also says.[25] The 'temple' of a listening silence – which provides a background and does not interrupt – thus seems to be an ideal for him. This ideal might represent a non-polemic cultural style to which it is possible to aspire.

'The real discovery is the one that makes me capable of stopping doing philosophy when I want to – the one that gives philosophy peace, so that it is no longer tormented by questions that bring *itself* in question . . .'[26] In this perspective we do not bind ourselves to a philosophical system in its exclusivist entirety, as we might do to a party or a person; paradoxically, the freedom to stop philosophizing is the same freedom that allows us to continue listening – to ourselves and to others. Arguments, discussions, wars, sadly end by exhaustion as if we had not yet developed a right, or freedom, to stop. If however, we adhere to an exclusively foundational concept of philosophy without being conscious of it we can certainly not stop philosophizing whenever we choose; not until the roots have been identified and the foundations laid can we try to engage in any other philosophical concern, and so it would be irresponsible to interrupt the work.[27] The 'discovery', therefore, is that one can suspend, or interrupt, without causing any damage. In our logocratic (and possibly entrepreneurial) haste to compete in establishing the winning principles of knowledge, or in counter-attacking those foundational orientations that appear misleading, it often becomes difficult for us to 'stop doing philosophy' and pause for a moment of silence. And so listening, obviously, is postponed indefinitely, or until we have finally completed the understanding of what exactly knowledge is. According to this grandiose philosophical stance it appears that the experience of letting ourselves be spoken to by someone or something capable of 'interrupting' our philosophizing is constantly procrastinated.

In the absence of a sufficient listening propensity, what we call the human Eros and our life forces come to suffer from the devaluing outlook of a rationality whereby communication substantially coincides with the power of speech and expression. If we adopt this perspective even our noble affections and the most enlightened philosophical pursuits might be closely reconsidered. Jaspers does not exclude the hypothesis that even such incensed interactions may rest upon elements of blind barbarism,

contrary to communication and underlain by a violence 'that
does not want to *hear* anything but itself'.[28]

In the words of Sciacca:

> To communicate is to enter the other, while watching ourselves
> carefully, to enter without usurping . . . To usurp the other is
> to annul him, to prevent him from returning the gift; it is the
> refusal to accept his discrete word; it is to violate his inner
> home without allowing him to enter ours, it is the arrogance
> of someone who believes himself to be an entirely fecundating
> force and refuses to receive. The univocal gift, without
> reciprocity . . . is not communication, but violation.[29]

And also: 'It is the delusion of destructive selfishness, the stifling
game of the one who soliloquises, making use of the other as a
passive listener who is ultimately excluded from communication.'[30]

And the triumph of a halved rationality (capable of speech
but incapable of listening) is almost automatically translated into
indifference: a common sentiment that may readily degenerate
into animosity. A knowledge, and therefore a culture, sustained
by the indifference of a non-listening rationality is being massively produced. Hostility, in contrast, appears to be an intense,
acute, and tiring emotion that is only experienced with difficulty.
The indifference of non-listening is incomparably more extensive
and less demanding. It extends in time and space without losing
anything; it abandons itself to its inertial course, drawn by the
mechanisms of a conventional, noisy language that impedes the
inner silence of the individual. And so we find ourselves unable
to go ahead autonomously. Perhaps, from a remote perspective,
humans might be seen as a species that moves in waves formed
of masses, as though the vestiges of the reptilian brain operating
in each of us (however disciplined it might be by more evolved
structures) did not function so much in the individual as in
extended groups; the mass to which we risk returning with the
powerful excuse of our great pseudo-philosophical ideals.

# Chapter 8

# Dialogic interaction and listening

## THE UNITY OF THE DIALOGIC FIELD

The output of knowledge tends to be expressed in an endless series of sophisticated ramifications, so specialized that they induce an incapacity for mutual exchange between discourses which then become increasingly fragmented and specific, or even seem to purport opposing theses. The problem of listening may then appear as an issue that should not even be touched upon; as something totally inappropriate or futile. Listening will, in fact, seem a worthless concern until we are capable of considering *as a whole* the myriad of subtly opposing accounts that culture constantly produces, and consequently tries to impose with western 'rigour' and 'elegance'. While we are presented daily with the possibility of choice (as with products) or of casting a vote, we do not have the 'opportunity' (or 'freedom') to envisage and theorize the grid-like nature of the vast cultural output that constantly shrouds us. Superficially our search for this greater awareness might seem to be a generic exhortation to tolerance (almost as though listening could be reduced to an instrument intended for the purpose of simple survival). When we examine the problem of listening more closely, however, we also come to confront the crisis of a culture tormented by splitting mechanisms and perhaps so lacking in methods of reconnecting that the most disquieting of questions – such as linking branches of knowledge – are forced into silence since they can not even be adequately articulated.

If the world community persists in its current pattern of development, perhaps the planet we shall be inhabiting at the beginning of the next millennium will be more crowded, ecologically unbalanced and 'spiritually' vulnerable than it is today. Acknowledgements of such possible crises, however, are not so much 'forecasts' of what may happen, as the expression of an attempt to delineate the conditions of human coexistence as it might develop in the absence of adequate transformations. All too easily, in fact, we tend to use or eliminate any 'object' – whether animate or inanimate – that does not *tell us* anything: and everything which is other than us can tell us nothing until we are *prepared* and ready to listen. The danger of environmental deterioration can probably be connected both to our benumbment and to cultural saturation with competitive expressions. We wonder once again what the profound lack can be in the rationality that underlies a scientific culture with which planetary trends are inextricably interwoven. We are, in fact, the repositories of a 'logic' from which the most powerful languages have been generated but which, nevertheless, tends to atrophy the ability to pay heed to problems concerning coexistential equilibrium as a whole. We are systematically struck by the difficulty of being understood and, at the same time, doubtful about easy conciliations: when an agreement deriving from reciprocal consent is produced there is always the risk that it is based upon an episodic opportunity for alliance rather than rooted in mutual recognition, susceptible to regenerative growth.

When faced with the inexhaustible labours of a philosophy of listening the very myth of truth as power may begin to vacillate: somehow its foundation, the idea of a centre or geometric *locus* in which its postulates and genetic mechanisms are decreed, is withdrawn. Through listening a development unfolds that seems both open and enigmatic (clearly perceptible but equally clearly unfathomable): a development of relationships that become knitted together into an ever increasing involvement. Ultimately, logical conceptualization as such no longer appears as a guarantee of the inevitable improvement of situations: 'Concepts *may* alleviate mischief or they may make it worse; foster it or check it', remarks Wittgenstein.[1] The presumed innocence of knowledge tends to provoke more doubts than ever before. Listening, in as much as it is a container of open discursive practices, is proposed to us as an attitude in the face of which there is nothing simple, natural, innocent, detachable from the great machine of relationships and relativities that composes our world.[2]

There exists a way of 'listening' geared to detect the typical traits that characterize an interlocutor's expression, with a view to attaining a predictability of his moves. The accuracy and perspicacity of this way of 'listening' allows for the attainment of a contractual power of a predictive nature. Such a strategy can be instrumental in achieving an end in the same way as any other form of knowledge. This way of paying attention, therefore, can not be regarded as an authentic listening experience. It is a kind of self-interested and manipulative 'eavesdropping'. It is my belief that *not even* by overturning this type of 'listening' can the core of the problem be represented. The opposite of a self-interested monitoring would be implemented in the form of a 'neutral' objective method that ensured the 'truthfulness' of the message received. In such an attempt one would understand a subject's speech act by treating it almost as though it were a natural object and by placing oneself in an ideally disinterested position; the assumption being that it is possible to set aside all subjective dynamics as a 'suitable' expedient for ensuring the methodological neutrality of research.

## DEPTH AND VISTAS OF THE DIALOGIC FIELD

As is well known, a good part of dialogic communication is based on the possibility of at least one of the two interlocutors being able to understand. And yet in this way one would reproduce the paradigm of a rational power emanating from one mind that encompasses, grasps and contains another subject who is not equally skilled at understanding: an individual is envisaged upon whom is conferred the status of being able to be understood by a rational force, but not the status of being able to understand in turn, nor of being able to express an alternative mode of ratiocination.

Listening is not simply an activity of applied thinking in which, with a minimal amount of personal involvement, one occupies oneself with an object of study; it is, on the contrary, a procedure whose authentic advancement depends upon one's ability to re-enter one's own self. But it would be illusory and misleading to claim that the 'ability' to be oneself represented the result of a linear introspection – as though it were a kind of introflection of the perceptive gaze. According to Jaspers, if someone makes himself the immediate object of his attention he follows a final and dangerous path that leads to losing his sense of reciprocity and ultimately of his own identity. The man who only wanted to grasp himself – Jaspers concludes – no longer understands himself.[3]

All one would produce is a narcissistic reflection, a narcosis, or loss of self; in order to continue to function, our thinking would have to be 'doubtful' in some way: that is, it would literally have to be a thought that concerned at least *two* thinkers. The *dubium* (the 'double') implies a relationship between different, distinct and detached figures who, thinking in some way, listen to each other and, in order to really listen to each other, make *further* attempts to think; a way of reasoning, therefore, that is aimed at overcoming the equally terrible conditions of fusion and isolation. The resolution of narcissistic conditions derives from producing a dialogic field in which we can delineate a variety of conceptual levels, and in which we can connect them without confusion, and distinguish between them without splitting. An unlistening rationality is incapable of promoting an evolutionary path of this nature.

What we call 'objective knowledge' (the result of strict argument undeflected by 'irrelevant' considerations) provides us with defence mechanisms which can not be underestimated in as much as we become inclined to an idea of cognition rooted in the illusive belief that it is neutral and that it will protect us from any involvement with the repercussions of the cognitive event. Such knowledge may entail the presumption and the illusion that it does not share in the event it produces and in the problems that it generates; as a consequence knowledge-makers would be exempted from participation in such problems. 'Real knowledge' may claim to be neutral in the sense of being 'intellectually healthy', aseptic, uncontaminated by subjective or traditional obscurities. And yet, like any other human endeavour it may carry its share of insufficiently explored pathology. If we reach for a vaster horizon of events (and not simply for a deliberately 'small' synchronic and diachronic cross-section), we might then allow for a 'senseless' attitude, disposed to heeding our remote biological past, the future that we attract upon ourselves and the community of the living in an open, planetary sense; we might thus be able to recognize more easily in our condition of 'rational animals' a challenge for survival and an opportunity not to be missed. It is not a question of adhering to one of the antiscientific fluctuations punctuating cultural fashions (and 'opposing' the triumphs of rationality) just as one may follow with enchantment the advances of scientific knowledge. The point at issue is the capacity to create enough distance from a Cartesian, rationalistic stance – all too lonely and secluded – which presumes itself capable of summoning and repelling deceiving demons.

In my opinion the language of knowledge can degenerate to the point at which it arrogantly excludes all proper hearing: it might be a question of holding back such an attitude that increasingly involves not simply individuals but the entire species. And even though it is doubtful whether there are 'missions' characterizing the human condition, Kant's planetary vision should still be considered significant: he insists in fact that the human community can only hope to fulfil its 'destiny' in its *entirety*.[4] The degradation of language and, as an alternative, the cultivation of listening, respectively represent, in my opinion, the greatest danger and a preliminary task for the survival and 'destiny' of the human species. 'Man's role is thus a highly artificial one', argues Kant.

> We do not know how it is with the inhabitants of other planets and with their nature, but if we ourselves execute this commission of nature well, we may surely flatter ourselves that we occupy no mean status among our neighbours in the cosmos. Perhaps their position is such that each individual can fulfil his destiny completely within his own lifetime. With us it is otherwise; *only the species as a whole can hope for this*.[5]

The myth of Narcissus, who sees nothing but himself, might indicate the extreme opposite of an open dialogic field that unites the human race. Whether construed in individual or group terms a narcissistic inclination casts humans down into a tragic narcosis. Narcissus perpetrates his own destruction (drowning) through the total absence of dialogue – the response of Echo being a fake; he aspires to isolated autarchy.

## CIRCULAR CAUSALITY IN THE DIALOGIC FIELD

In an attempt to construe the unity of every genuine dialogic field we can rely on a more specific orientation that characterizes certain areas of empirical research: an orientation that we might roughly describe as a transformed conception of causality. Simplifying the question as far as possible we believe that it is legitimate to extend our notion of causality whereby we commonly say, for instance, that the adult listens *because* the child begins to speak. By transforming and broadening our conception of causality we could then justifiably affirm that the child begins to speak *because* the adult listens. As Heidegger suggests:

> It is the custom to put speaking and listening in opposition: one man speaks, the other listens . . . Speaking is itself a listening. Speaking is listening to the language we speak. Thus, it is listening not *while* but *before* we are speaking . . . [6]

The value attributed to a 'restricted' principle of causality may derive from a temptation to over-extend the application of cognitive instruments in use; in this case the tendency to persist in the style of an initial cognitive approach. The causality of classical physics might perhaps be regarded historically as a first stage, or childhood, of scientific thought; not so much in the sense that it is something to be abandoned or corrected, but rather as an understanding that may be inserted into a more complex context. And whereas causality, just like the method of verification through experiment, is being attenuated and made more flexible by contemporary science, it is becoming increasingly recognized that the deterministic principle of cause and effect is unsuited to accounting for the growing complexity of science and human life.

In the outlook of the epistemological school of Geneva one can show, for instance, that simple causality represents the initial form taken by our attempt to achieve explanation.[7] At this stage, cause and effect are as radically and hierarchically distinguished as the subject and the world; this is why its explicative power is promptly recognized as of the inception of the primary phases in operative thought. Circular causality, on the other hand, in so far as it stipulates an indissoluble link between two reciprocally causal relationships, and thus regards them as a whole, is presented as a somewhat tardy and laboriously attained concept. It represents an explicative scheme that is far more elaborate, even though its explicative character is less directly evident; it appears that circular causality is endowed with a less obvious significance. In order to create such a cognitive model and be satisfied with it, the mind seems to need to spend a considerable span of time at the stage of simple causality: in other words, humans need first to learn how to consider separately (one at a time) the two unilateral components of the causal schema, and then to learn how to associate these two relations of elementary causation into a more complex circular causality.[8]

There is a general tendency to remain within the framework of linear causality, that is, within an explicative description of reality which implies a string of simple causal relations between events. According to Halbwachs, just as a relationship of simple causation is the result of an abstraction that consists in isolating a certain correspondence between the events belonging to the class of causes and those belonging to the class of effects, similarly a 'linear' relationship is also, generally, an abstraction that neglects a vast array of factors.[9] Obviously we are dealing with a legitimate abstraction, at least as a stage in the analysis of relationships, since the schema of simple causal connections is the most striking among elementary explicative forms. Isolating a relationship of simple causality from the apparent chaos of innumerable connections sometimes offers us a partial explanation of reality and, thus, a criterion for creating some degree of order. And yet we find it seriously perplexing when we are confronted with causal relationships that are not linked to one another. 'At a certain point in the development of a science', Halbwachs contends, 'it is no longer simply causal relationships that provide the key to the explanation, but the connections that we can gather between them.'[10] In the epistemology of the human sciences, according to Halbwachs, we come up so frequently against links of *reciprocity in causal relationships* that we begin to wonder if they are not a general rule. As is well known, simple causality establishes a subordinate relationship, whereby each event in class A produces and determines an event in class A'. But as research continues we find with increasing frequency that, even though we have discovered the causal relationship A-A' at a certain time and under certain conditions, there are circumstances in which we discover phenomena that correspond to the relationship A'-A. The simplest case, according to Halbwachs, is that of reversible causality, A-A'-A, with the result that linear causality is broken and cyclic paths introduced.[11] This type of relationship is generally known as circular causality.

> With the connection of reciprocity in relationships between
> natural phenomena, a richer and more complex structure
> emerges than that of a simple linear connection. This structure
> has, however, a specific character. It does not destroy the
> explicative method that was linked to simple causality, but
> raises it to a higher plane by introducing the principle of
> reversibility . . . This is why pointing it out generally permits
> decisive progress in our understanding of processes.[12]

Furthermore, in the epistemology of the physical sciences no
research has yet presented a *credible* prospect of offering an
overall rationalization of the enormous stratification of its laws.
According to Wheeler the belief that if we were only capable
of penetrating ever more deeply into the structure of physics we
would see a final exit leading to an *nth* level, is increasingly
weak: and it is also feared that we are mistaken to think that
the structure can advance, *ad infinitum*.[13] We are thus faced by
the ultimate question of whether the structure of the physical
world, instead of ending as an infinitesimal element or as the
most basic structural field, or, alternatively, continuing indefinitely, does not finally lead us back to the capacities of the
observer himself, in a kind of circle of listening *interdependencies*.
Wittgenstein's comment is enlightening in this context: 'There is
nothing more stupid than the chatter about cause and effect in
history books; nothing is more wrong-headed, more half-baked.
– But what hope could anyone have of putting a stop to it just
by *saying* that? . . .'[14] Not much, clearly, since he would hardly
be listened to – in the sense that saying something which moves
outside the coordinates of a narrowly causalistic discourse might
– paradoxically – even seem 'stupid'.

And even in the epistemological vicissitudes concerning what
we call 'mental illnesses' we also find a gradual and tormented
transition from the notion of a pathology that is 'inherent' in
the patient to the elaboration of a theory of transference, and
then of counter-transference: an effort to link our labours with
principles of reciprocity and circularity.

## THE LISTENING EXPERIENCE AS EVENT

Largely rooted in the productive power of its languages, our
culture can ultimately constitute a constraining and limiting

matrix; whereas on the one hand it seems to be able (or, at least, to want) to respond to an ever greater number of questions, on the other hand it increasingly binds us to the position of questioning, thus distancing itself from listening and corresponding to events. And the prevalence of a reduced-by-half notion of rationality (able to speak, but not to listen) can actually create an overexpansion, a hypostasis of the question, as a result of which one can not even *doubt* that we possess a logical space in which questions are to be formulated. It is only when events assume a lacerating or seismic form (such as, for instance, episodes of irreversible environmental degradation) that we are obliged to recognize that there are no available spaces for the formulation of questions. It is only *then* that we become aware of the incompleteness of a culture founded upon discourse rather than upon a capacity for heeding and corresponding. 'To undergo an experience with something – be it a thing, or a person . . . – means that this something befalls us, strikes us, comes over us, overwhelms and transforms us', Heidegger insists.

> When we talk of 'undergoing' an experience, we mean specifically that the experience is not of our own making; to undergo here means that we endure it, suffer it, receive it as it strikes us and submit to it. It is this something itself that comes about, comes to pass, happens.[15]

And when the event tells us, beyond any shadow of doubt, that we do not know how to listen, some kind of homeostatic tendency inevitably comes into play which repairs the event, annuls its consequences and prevents it from 'existing' any longer. Catastrophic events, of whatever nature, may be construed as 'unforseeable' explosions that burst into our individual and cultural lives in order to tell us that reality does not correspond at all to our 'well-founded' accounts and that it is, on the contrary, something quite different. In its simplest meaning the event could be seen as the moment in which something 'happens' to us, as a result of which, however reasonably secure we are with our beliefs and habits (and thus with our 'reality'), we find ourselves suddenly exiled from everything; we say that the 'world has collapsed around us'. And, above all, the event tells us unequivocally that the only reality that functions at the moment is the reality of the event in which we are involved. 'The authentic attitude of thinking', Heidegger tells us, 'is not a putting of questions – rather, it is listening to the grant, the promise of what is to be put in question.'[16]

In a historical perspective, we might say that Heidegger sums up his thought in the following way:

> Once, however, in the beginning of Western thinking, the essence of language flashed in . . . But the lightning abruptly vanished. No one held on to its streak of light and the nearness of what it illuminated. We see this lightning only when we station ourselves in the storm of Being.[17]

A listening experience could actually come across like a storm and overwhelm us – silently – distancing us from the constant din of the discourses that saturate our culture, ready at all times to convey on the market the most sophisticated 'philosophical' devices *against* the storm. At a remarkable distance from such cultural orientation, Cannetti suggest that:

> Most important of all is talking to unknown people. But it has to be done in such a way that *they* do the talking, and the only thing one does oneself is to get *them* to talk. When that is no longer possible for a man, then death has begun.[18]

Conversely, we could then justifiably say that until we become capable of getting something unknown to talk to us we have not yet begun to live and interact.

The accepted event impinges vividly upon our cognitive organization in such an abrupt manner that any kind of discursive reasoning is deflected. In this sense it takes us back to our innerness, leading us back to silence; sometimes it can predispose us to hear properly and, even more, it tells us that we have not been able to listen inasmuch as the occurrence is presented as an 'accident', rather than as an event. The event perhaps might be seen to function as a sort of 'nemesis' of a reality that has been shrouded by our brilliant conceptualizations, stubbornly unheard and silenced. Every now and again this reality sends us signals, warnings to which we are practically deaf since we have been moulded by, and for, a culture in which listening does not pay. In our culture, for instance, maternity and paternity, like the experience of being born and dying, are understood as 'events' that pose problems and impose their presence to the extent that they are consciously experienced. Whether the event is terminal or initial it is always presented as a 'traumatic' reality that proposes or, sometimes, imposes upon us the need for greater transformations than those permitted by the logocentric choreography of our culture. The event is linked with something profound within us such as, above all, a resistance to the event itself. In our cognitive insatiability and our constant search for novelty, we do not, however, have any desire at all that innovative events be produced. However afflicted we are by boredom, we want nothing to be announced to us even though the deepest philosophical aspiration is rooted in the desire to be one to whom something happens – the protagonist of the event.

In its philosophical scope, listening involves the renunciation of a predominantly moulding and ordering activity; a giving up sustained by the expectation of a new and different quality of relationship. 'But, as we have seen, the renunciation is not loss', Heidegger reminds us.[19] Nor does 'sad' refer to the substance of the renunciation, but rather to the fact that it has been learned. 'That sadness, however, is neither mere dejection nor despondency. True sadness is in harmony with what is most joyful – but in this way, that the greatest joy withdraws, halts in its withdrawal and holds itself in reserve.'[20] Heeding an event from which we learn renunciation, paradoxically, does not demand extensive reflection in order to demonstrate its cognitive significance: it comes across as a thought that can be experienced without too much discursive mediation. The experience of listening, in this respect, is eminently suited to being regarded as a positive experience (even if it is 'sad'), since it is one of the most 'direct' that humans can have. And when the event is 'unthinkable' – something absurd or incomprehensible – we can not summon the words we need to talk about it. 'But when does language speak itself as language? Curiously enough', replies Heidegger:

> when we cannot find the right word for something that concerns us, carries us away, oppresses and encourages us. Then we leave unspoken what we have in mind and, without rightly giving it thought, undergo moments in which language itself has distantly and fleetingly touched us with its essential being.[21]

## THE LISTENING EXPERIENCE AS TRANSFORMATION

We can hypothesize a stereotype which brings together many thinkers and which seems to be *deeply* rooted in us in spite of the fact that we are ready to recant it promptly at levels of greater awareness: the stereotype that there is little, or nothing, that needs to be developed in the area of our listening capacity. If this cliché is made explicit we realize that it represents a defensive barrier against disturbing underlying problems. Researching into the philosophy of listening, in fact, represents a path that is unattractive and troubled in the sense that we risk fragmenting our protective devices in our reappropriation of inner layers which are ill-adapted to levels of awareness. Furthermore we might begin to doubt our own capacity for understanding and even that of our great 'masters' in every area of learning. We are so poorly prepared for the incipient awareness of the need to listen that an exhausting effort seems to be required. It is easier, for instance, to try to recognize people who are no longer with us (and thus no longer demand listening) and, at the same time, continue to ignore the people around us. And even the flourishing state of the anthropological sciences, as yet another instance, can end up in the production of 'studies of anthropology' primarily meant for the academic market. The idea that we may take seriously a different *genius loci*, be instructed and transformed by it, is in fact rather remote.

Listening philosophically to the lines of Stefan George:

So I renounced and sadly see:
Where word breaks off no thing may be[22]

Heidegger comments:

What the poet learned to renounce is his formerly cherished view regarding the relation of thing and word. This renunciation concerns the poetic relation to the word that he had cultivated until then . . . It is equivalent to 'abdication' . . . In his renunciation, the poet abdicates his former relation to the word. Nothing more? No. There is in the abdication itself already an avowal, a command to which he denies himself no longer.[23]

In the face of a 'command to which he denies himself no longer' a transforming relation is set alight, a germinal contact with the word, giddily different from dependence upon the sterile din of words in whose transmission we are ensured immobility and isolation. This cognitive dedication to the word of the other demands a philosophical methodology that involves the person entirely, since it demands a kind of inner abnegation. Without this inner renunciation the individual can only hold a dialogue with himself.

It is possible that only the more serious levels of this dedication confer the capacity – in a literal sense – to take in the profound truths characterizing human doings. Our undervaluation of this methodology is probably linked to our ignorance of its fecundity. We are not in fact dealing with epistemological concepts unrelated with the knowing person: he is an instrument of knowledge that must transform himself in order to know, rather than deform objects in order to recognize himself in *his own* illusory immobility.

An authentically symbolic language often elicits a singular feeling of scandal and repulsion: even though such a language is esteemed from a distance and demanded in times of need, it is never seen as an object of preference; it is, on the contrary, shunned. And even in cases of suffering or loss we may accept more willingly a pseudo-symbolic language based on stereotypes (whether traditional or brand-new) than the challenge of a transformational language. Humans seem to prefer discomforts and indescribable labours rather than transform, or even re-examine, their own symbolic organization; they seem to prefer placing their faith in formulas rather than in their own experience. Ricoeur suggests that:

> When a word says something, when it discloses something not only of entities, but of Being, . . . we are faced by something that we might define a 'word-event' . . . In a word-event I dispose of nothing, I do not impose myself. I am no longer the master . . . Obedience and liberty have their origin in this situation of non-possession . . . [24]

As is well known, we commonly speak of 'discoveries' or innovations in relation to the answers that are given to riddles in human knowledge. *Discoveries*, in fact, 'presuppose a pointer in the direction of an area of openness from which the idea can come, i.e. they presuppose questions', suggests Gadamer. 'Hence we say that a question too "comes" to us, that it "arises" or "presents itself" more than that we raise it or present it . . . Thus questioning too is more a "passion" than an action.'[25] At this point the observation that the raising of the question (even before it receives the answer) depends upon our capacity for listening to our inner world as it questions itself, comes across *a fortiori*. This first phase in awareness is presented to us as the more appealing and least tormented in so far as it is firmly anchored in the expressive ability of a self that is capable of questioning. A genuinely philosophical activity, however, begins at the point in which we are exposed to being disconcerted and disorientated by the unthought-of, and unthinkable, nature of the answer.

# Chapter 9

# On inner listening

## INNER LISTENING AND THE SOCRATIC *DAIMON*

At the outset of philosophical tradition the figure of Socrates marks a starting point in the development of western rationality: he represents so significantly the transition towards an age of cognitive advancements that the preceding philosophical period is usually referred to as the epoch of the pre-Socratic philosophers. And at least *one* of the salient features of Socrates the philosopher can be identified in his relationship with the inner *daimon*[1] to whom he constantly listens. And if this type of relationship tends to disappear during subsequent flights in our philosophical history, perhaps we do not ask with sufficient curiosity why it is that, after Socrates, messages *from within* which inspire, advise and direct us are no longer 'audible'.

Centuries later, an ever more serious split in our inner world seems to impede us from listening to ourselves; it even prevents us from distinguishing between those options that aggravate our condition and those that might alleviate it. I use the simple expression 'inner world' as a tentative safeguard from an over-specific terminology that can induce a commitment to doctrinal orientations in which one may remain inextricably bound.

As a first approximation, we might remark that the benumbment of our capacity for heeding ourselves induces a radical philosophical distortion perpetrated in terms of damage to the human potential; in the absence of inner listening we might erroneously claim to have reached a cognitive, or even (in certain *Weltanschauungen*), a social liberation, thus precluding the mutations that are needed if we want to maintain ourselves at the level of – or, rather, above – the technical and logical achievements that humans have created. Blunted in his capacity for inner listening, the individual gets lost in the manifold advances of a rationality that slips ever more out of his control. And the more he pursues it the more his 'philosophical strength', however inextinguishable, grows weak. At every level in our culture the experience of an inner vacuum, the sensation of a fragile identity and the terror that in the depths of the self there is nothing – no one – insinuate themselves. Similarly, if we consider our scarce interest in a past that no longer tells us much, however defiantly it re-presents itself in the form of revivals, we might think of a human community that can hardly confront the future.

Any focusing on the problem of listening might be regarded as the emanation of an educational policy that preaches linguistic 'altruism', or the surrender of one's 'philosophical' living space; whereas in fact it is a question of the preliminary *development* of a capacity for listening to one's own self (thus distancing ourselves from the futile tendency to claim that there is no point in learning to hear, as there is nothing like an 'inner voice' to which we should pay heed). On the contrary, we might legitimately hypothesize that no message is received precisely because we ignore the philosophical, Socratic, art of listening – to ourselves and to others.

In our cultural frame of reference we find that we soon master the capacity for picking up external social codes and also tend to censure our limited capacity for tuning into the dominant wavelengths. This state, which encourages us to pay attention to that which comes from the outside and at the same time tends to attenuate the possibility of a self-awareness capable of listening to itself, is reinforced by a developmental history that teaches us from the very beginning how to grasp the powerful and incisive messages that must at all costs be taken into consideration. At the outset of every ontogenetic story the voice of the 'others' (the speakers, versus the *infants*) is far more consequential than one's own: it is thus easier to tune into the speech of the other and follow in the wake of what we hear from outside, of what emanates from those who are in control of established rationality. It is up to the individual, as he develops into a fuller person, to know how to comprehend and recompose (wisely) these messages. And furthermore, in both a phylogenetic and ontogenetic perspective, practical advantages for survival depend specifically upon being able to manage relations with 'parental figures' in the broadest sense. In as much as we are capable of understanding the rules of the game we are guaranteed greater chances of social survival. One wonders therefore what the world of inner listening might offer that could compete with such a clear and ineluctable demand that we understand the messages emanating from those who possess any type of power at all. And yet, we might begin to recognize through inner listening that we are dealing with 'positions' that are phylogenetically archaic and ontogenetically precocious and which, nevertheless, determine our deep vicissitudes. It is not therefore 'necessary' that such subservient attitudes continue indefinitely if they are not for the purpose of ministering to our needs for continuity; to cope with such needs even the most antiphilosophical and limiting conditions sometimes tend to be perpetuated.

Analysing the fundamental terms in the issue, that is, comparing the ability to understand messages that come from outside with the capacity for understanding those that derive from the inner world, might lead to a preliminary clarification whereby a capacity for tuning into the outer pole, so to speak, is no longer to be deceptively overvalued when compared to the capacity for inner listening.

The more we are involved with a culture that seemingly exalts the individual while possibly rendering him ever more dependent upon external ruling and incapable of sustaining a by now fearsome contact with his own inner 'void', the more we become compulsively dependent on external messages and incapable of letting any inner message spring to life.

In order to examine more closely the initial question of the Socratic *daimon*, we could draw a preliminary remark from Goethe's work:

> He who would explain to us when men like Plato spoke in earnest, when in jest or half-jest, what they wrote from conviction and what merely for the sake of the argument, would certainly render us an extraordinary service and contribute greatly to our education.[2]

If we concede, however, that what is said in 'half-jest' or merely 'for the sake of the argument' has deep, strong roots, and if we also consider the possibility that what is said 'in earnest' or 'from conviction' rests upon disavowed features in our cognitive organization that protect us from intolerable anxieties, then it would no longer be so important to debate on the logical or psychological status of Socrates' inner 'voice'. It would be more enlightening, philosophically, if we used the opportunity to acknowledge that at this point in our path nobody hears daimons' voices any more and that everything we no longer have the 'time' or ability to construe is often palmed off as non-existent: probably there is no longer any logical space for unjustifiable wastes of time such as listening to something with which we may never be conversant.

Once again invoking Friedlaender's investigation we see that:

> The Platonists of antiquity assign to demonology a definite place in the structure of the master's thought. Modern interpreters are too enlightened to take Plato's statements on this subject very seriously. But how are we justified in regarding as mere play what is said about the demons if we consider the physical and physiological 'doctrines' of the *Timaeus*, or the 'philosophy of language' of the *Cratylus*, as integral parts of Plato's system? By the mere fact that we have a contemporary science of nature and language, but none of demons? . . . And while what the characters in his drama say about the world of demons is certainly 'play', it is – like all play in Plato's works – of a *deeply serious* nature;[3]

the seriousness and trepidation that are required when it is a question of guiding the fulfilment of a person's destiny or an educational process understood as an authentic birth and growth of the mind. Possibly the apex in the trajectory of western thought, our culture does in fact tend to ignore this voice, whose only concern is for the 'health of the soul'. And thus the most credible voice is ultimately represented as the most negligible. A Jungian scholar, Hillman, reminds us that 'Platonic and neo-Platonic writings confirm the assertion that the voice which spoke to Socrates through his personal *daimon* was that of Eros: the prototype of the psychologist, *whose only concern was for the health of the soul . . .*'.[4] We also read in Friedlaender:

> On yet another level, there is the 'divine'. Plato, in the speech of defense, even makes Socrates connect the two and call the phenomenon 'a divine and demonic element' . . . and even 'the sign of the God'. In Xenophon's presentation, Socrates

states that this power counseled or instructed him beforehand what to do or not to do.⁵

In Plato, therefore, it is a *daimon* that guides Socrates in the vicissitudes of his educational vocation; according to Friedlaender it is not merely a remarkable peculiarity of a single individual, but an essential part of the nature of the great teacher in that it safeguards the quality of education, prevents it from degrading into a purely argumentative pursuit and secures a connection with that element of mystery that is lacking in the instruction of the Sophists. 'Thus Plato must have regarded it as part of the *normal*, not as something abnormal.'⁶ And later:

> As human speech affects the ear, so the *Logoi* (to retain the equivocal term) of the demons directly affect the human soul. What ordinary people experience only in the relaxation of sleep is given to human beings with a pure, serene soul . . . in their waking lives.⁷

From this viewpoint, which in fact characterizes the prelude to western thinking, the search for personal identity actually seems to coincide with heeding one's own inner expression; a message whose origin is so deep (or so elevated) that, evidently, one opts from a contact anchored to listening rather than to the logical interrogation advocated by the Sophists. Rather than proceeding toward it, therefore, one should simply let oneself be approached by it. Heraclitus could be invoked in this connection: 'You could not in your going find the ends of the soul, though you travelled the whole way: so deep its Law (logos).'⁸
And Friedlaender insists:

> It is easy to see how this demon of the community can be reconciled with the demon of the individual, especially when we think of the correspondence between *Nous* and demon in the *Timaeus*. But we are not concerned here with combining the elements found in different contexts into conceptual unity. We merely wish to recognize what is common to these mythical symbols.⁹

Such symbols had a vital sense in the ancient world, and were probably derived from a listening attitude that had not yet been overwhelmed by the uncontested triumph of a rationality that concedes 'civil rights' to the weak Eros which exudes everywhere, but has no space for the strong Eros[10] that is linked too intimately to Socratic inner listening. To say that such 'symbols' do not exist and never have existed, that they do not speak or that they speak no longer because their time is over (serial, calendar time) testifies to a sort of schizo-paranoid approach whereby responsibility for the absence of dialogue would fall back on something other than us – and not so much as a 'conclusion' of the discussion, but rather in the very enunciation of the initial terms in which the question is presented. 'If I see nothing it is because there is nothing to be seen' – in the language of the prevailing visual metaphor.

Perhaps the *genius loci* of a community or the *daimon* of the individual may fare better in a silence that allows for listening than in the centrifugal dynamic of discourses that face outwards in order to achieve territorial control of their physical or cultural spaces. The point at issue is that of a philosophical attention that can only function as a 'gaze' rather than as a 'hearing' and is thus bound to be externally deflected. As Vico reminds us: 'Tradition says that Homer was blind and that from his blindness he took his name, which in the Ionic dialect means blind.'[11] And also: 'Homer himself describes as blind the poets who sing at the banquets of the great.'[12] According to Friedlaender the subtle and rigid distinctions of later interpreters of Plato:

> remind us of Goethe's remark that 'the original teachers are still conscious of the insoluble core of their project, and attempt to approach it in a naive and flexible manner. The successors are inclined to become didactic, and their dogmatism gradually reaches the level of intolerance.' Plato, on the contrary, still shows how the same things may be seen and named differently.[13]

Paying attention to inner inspiration, therefore, can be articulated in different ways and can be seen from different angles, thus avoiding the risk that such a vital aspect of the Socratic figure be ultimately banalized or simply indexed as a historic item in the mass of doctrinal treatises.

In the 'scientific' urgency of establishing whether one is dealing with a myth, a symbol, a concept or a figure of speech we might lose sight of the relevant fact that at the dawn of our rational tradition inner listening had a creative and salient function. 'Without the *metaxý* of the soul, without the realm of the demonic, heaven and earth would break asunder.'[14] In the *Phaedo* Socrates continues to communicate with his friends until the very last moment and insists that: 'No worse thing can happen to a man' than to become a 'misologist' or 'hater of argument'.[15] Quite: the dialogic, maieutic argument that listens, gathers and allows for life.

## INNER LISTENING AND THE CREATION OF TIME

In order to understand more clearly the function of temporality as a fundamental coordinate of inner listening we resort to a work in which Heidegger develops his own interpretation of Kant's first critique. The salient lines of argument of *Kant and the Problem of Metaphysics*[16] lead toward the interpretation of time as 'auto-solicitation'. From our point of view, however, we are less interested in the correctness of Heidegger's reading of Kant than in a link with the relevance that Heidegger attributes to the 'pure intuition' of time as the first *a priori* coefficient for all knowledge of the inner and outer world.

As a first approximation, it seems that civilized humans are no longer capable of a cognitive propensity for inner time as they are constantly suffering either from boredom or else from haste. The very same culture that devitalizes time also seems to be intent upon the massive production of prosthetic devices meant to safeguard humans from boredom and haste. Possibly much of the total yield of 'cultural' messages seems to be an antidote to the ever more serious problem of boredom in the sense that in a civilisation by now inextricably interwoven with media of all kinds, *everything* becomes a performance intended for a show. It even becomes 'necessary' to change things into a show so that humans can have some di-version and thus de-flect attention from themselves, turning centrifugally toward external stimuli of any sort: from the remains of a 'weak Eros'[17] that bobs on the surface of our culture to the banality of *thanatos* in its monotonous variants.

With regard to haste – our irremediable lack of time – the situation is not very different since technological advances are geared to develop instruments designed to make *everything* faster – growth, exchange, elimination – and thus to 'save' time or delusionally even 'produce' it. We are in the presence of a triumphal advance upon time, of an inconsiderate race against something that we no longer acknowledge and therefore do not even think of respecting.

With the technology of informatics and the achievement of 'real time', which constitutes precisely the annulment of the time spent in waiting, we move ever further away from biological time, undeniably contained within the limits of birth and death and scanned by such rhythms as sleeping and waking, diastole and systole. Structured by a sequence of rhythms that are in evidence as early as in pre-natal life, biological time is conspicuously different from the concept of time created by western rationality: a time, that is, which has lost all rhythmical flow and only speeds up in a planar, uniform and unhalting way. It is a notion of time that can be integrated more easily with a technology of treatment than with the prevention of pathological states; two different views of time, linked to horizons that seem to diverge ever more and that render one another both alien and alienated.

We are perhaps faced with an 'impossible' partnership: a paradoxical dialogue between outlooks that must seek each other in order not to dissolve; outlooks that can not understand one another, and yet must cope and compromise in reciprocity with an aim to survive.

A practice that is incapable of abbreviating, economizing or annulling time, the listening approach comes across with even greater relevance in the context of temporality. A listening dialogue is fertile inasmuch as it is willing to ignore time measures; the maieutic word, in fact, can only be expressed at just the right moment and with a philosophical patience that makes for a renunciation to bargain on matters of precedence.

Although there is a considerable theoretical distance between the two (and yet, some enlightening convergence) both Wittgenstein and Heidegger might be interpreted as exhorting us not to be constrained by problems of time when we are trying to comprehend messages. Wittgenstein: 'Sometimes a sentence can be understood only if it is read at the *right tempo*. My sentences are all supposed to be read *slowly*';[18] and, later: 'I really want my copious punctuation marks to *slow down* the speed of reading. Because I should like to be read *slowly* (as I myself read).'[19] Heidegger: '*We renounce thinking too hastily* if we palm off nothing . . . as simply nothing . . .'.[20] And he continues with a clear warning: 'Instead of entrusting ourselves to the haste of such an empty acumen . . .'.[21]

In this outlook, therefore, it is not a question of evaluating the correctness, or legitimacy, of Heidegger's reading of Kant, as we are confronting a task which may be qualified in quite a different way. In an age in which there is an incipient awareness that inner time is lost, or ailing, Heidegger does in fact attempt to investigate a dimension pointing to a way out from the deterioration of time. In Kantian terms the *a priori* category of time represents a transcendental coefficient of knowledge, a constitutive principle of all experience. And yet, even with regard to its cognitive function, 'time' seems reluctant to be explored, measured, controlled. Heidegger writes that time 'as pure self-affection originally forms finite self-hood in such a way that the self can become self-consciousness.'[22]

Perhaps the unusual (obsolete, unthinkable) act of listening to one's inner world could make us conversant with the cognitive and revealing potential of temporality as an *a priori* category for experiencing both our consciousness and the external world. Again, I am using the expression 'inner world' in an attempt to minimize the risks of linkage with theoretical terms that might prove to be too binding.

In *Kant and the Problem of Metaphysics* Heidegger seems in fact to be inscribing Kant's work in a contextual circle of his own making. Heidegger's attitude might be summed up in this way: 'You should not so much pay attention to what I am doing or to the way I do it, but rather to the circumstance that Kant's text allows me to try to show something vital for philosophy.' In his interpretation of Kant's work, Heidegger declares that his intention is to tell us something about the problem of metaphysics and to allow Kant to speak about it, so that in fact two elements are being presented: we have the word *uttered* by the text and we also have the word *heard* by Heidegger. The latter, however, since it has not yet been spoken, places itself in a particular position suitable for overcoming the manifest attributes of the Kantian word as utterance and thus for gathering whatever else it might bear. And so we can see that, in Heidegger's 'contextual circle' of attention, a *new* word is being uttered and is susceptible to being heard, permitting us to discover what the circle might have concealed. Philosophically, one might learn to live in a *virtual* space that separates the uttered word from that which is heard (and thus still absent as a spoken word) and that might, somehow, become a real space if it were inhabited and devotedly cultivated. The consistence and fertility of this space is based upon a listening attitude that brings the two 'words' into relation and makes their encounter possible. In the relation that is created by a 'virtuous' circle we thus have a word that is 'absent' but listened to, and a word that is present and uttered but which, nevertheless, is limited to its most manifest levels and thus needs to be heard properly if it is to develop and attain its full potential. A purely academic, or limiting, investigation may ultimately induce circles that spin emptily or which become vicious circles in which the great voices come into and go out of fashion; and even more 'vicious' circles may be produced in which debate simply delineates territorial areas of cognitive control.

'This connection and this separation of words', suggests Riedel:

> does not only play an active role in *speaking*, but also in *listening*. What is in question is the same event, simply unfolding at different levels . . . It is not therefore a question of something purely *logical*, in the sense of the assertion, but of something *acroamatic*, of something to be heard.[23]

'This something to be heard', he insists:

> is not the philosophical discourse as it manifests itself to the outside in the voice and messages of philosophers . . . In these cases, obviously, hearing *would follow* the discourse, it would be a merely acoustic phenomenon that would have nothing to do with the problem of the acroamatic . . . [24]

Returning to Kant's works, we read in his first *Critique* that 'It is not consonant with the nature of philosophy . . . to employ the dogmatical method, and to adorn itself with the titles and insignia of mathematical science.'[25] The validity of mathematical deductions is in fact ensured by a procedure 'whereby all errors are rendered manifest to the senses'.[26] Kant suggests therefore that philosophical arguments should 'be termed acroamatic proofs rather than demonstrations, as only words are employed in them . . .'.[27] In this important passage of Kant's work the connotation of *acroamatic* as something that qualifies the nature of philosophical 'proofs' comes forth clearly. In this type of discourse the function of listening is thus decisive in that it is a question of basing proofs upon the capacity of listening to something rather than upon the cogency of rational discourse.

Influenced by their growing awareness of time and of their being finite, humans do not so much fear the extinction of life as that of personal significance. And if the 'meaning of life' is considered of primary importance, humans want to know that their lives have value in the sense that they do create a significant mark. Presumably saying something, in whatever fashion, somehow acquires the meaning of leaving a mark through which one can surpass the domain of purely biological reality in order to gain access to the level of cultural duration. Uttering poetry, or science, or gossip are all possibly disavowed but comparable techniques whereby we try to imprint our own story in others and ultimately try to insert it into the cultural circuit of symbolic exchanges. Speaking is thus presented to us above all as an instrument for living and surviving, as of the phylogenetic 'moment' in which we have become symbolic animals. In this outlook listening could be perceived as an overabundant offer (sometimes even as a sacrifice) in which the meaning of the word received is allowed to be born, even if we have to postpone or forsake our share of expression. In this same perspective, writing possibly represents one of the most incisive ways of speaking – the specific way which is supposed to leave a lasting mark. The philosopher Socrates is the one who does not write. In this sense Socratic midwifery might constitute the 'emblem' of an attitude most suitable for promoting the birth and cognitive life of the interlocutor.

Heidegger's remarks in his preface to the second edition of *Kant and the Problem of Metaphysics* are perhaps enlightening:

My critics have constantly reproached me for the violence of my interpretations, and the grounds for this reproach can be found in this work. From the point of view of an inquiry which is both historical and philosophical, this reproach is always justified when directed against attempts to set in motion a thoughtful dialogue between thinkers. In contrast to the methods of historical philosophy, which has its own problems, a dialogue between thinkers is bound by other laws. These laws are more easily violated; the possibility of going astray is more threatening; the shortcomings more frequent . . .

Through their shortcomings, thinkers learn to be more persevering.[28]

The 'weakness' of Heidegger's reading of Kant might be summa-
rized by a comment of Pareyson's: 'One can talk about anything
in either a *simply technical* manner or in a *genuinely philosophical*
way, according to whether one holds on to a "classically" defined
object or confronts it with a sense of its ulterior and deeper
purpose.'[29] In the search for a philosophical method allowing for
a 'waste' of time and ready to open itself to listening, it is quite
true that even with regard to the slightest thing one is faced by
an alternative between an approach that is revelatory even when
it speaks of the least datum of experience and a discourse that
is restrictive even when it refers to the 'highest' truths; the
alternative between a philosophical discourse that always reaches
for ulterior features and a technical discourse that only talks
about what it is discussing. And of course there may be something else that can be understood on condition that 'time' is not
made an issue and that we are prepared to spend, and even
'waste' ourselves in the effort to stay on and listen.

## THE VICISSITUDES OF DISCOVERY

As it is commonly understood, the argument developed by Heidegger in *Kant and the Problem of Metaphysics* is centred upon
the interpretation of time as 'affection of itself';[30] in his view
Kant focuses upon the nature of temporality, as the one *a priori*
condition which sustains and engenders our consciousness. 'It is
specifically the concept of time as auto-solicitation', suggests
Verra:

> that determines for Heidegger the failure of the attempt to
> found logically Kant's critique: it consents to the need for
> finding a unifying principle of critical thinking, but seeks it in
> a direction that casts doubt upon the very model of rationality
> and logic of which Kant was a follower and whose disinte-
> gration he had glimpsed as the ultimate outcome of his chosen
> path.[31]

If we now turn to Heidegger's text we read, for example,
that:

> Time is by nature, pure affection of itself. But more than this,

it is that in general which forms something of the order of a line of orientation which going from the self is directed toward . . . in such a way that the objective thus constituted springs forth and surges back along this line.[32]

This 'springing forth and surging back', possibly equivalent to Verra's 'possibility of bending oneself in different directions'[33] and thus also 'backwards', seems to refer to an inner world that can exist on condition that we move toward it: this 'going from the self' is neither an automatic mechanism nor a necessity, so to speak, but a propensity that might also be lacking – or deteriorate – and is thus worthy of close consideration since it represents, according to Heidegger, the germination of all cognitive life and of metaphysics itself. But how is it possible to 'surge back'? How are we to understand such a disturbing metaphor when temporality as such has nothing that can be seen or explored? Presumably, surging back might represent a first step in the innovative direction of listening – an orientation dizzily different from the customary cognitive extroversions.

Heidegger suggests that oblivion is neither casual nor temporary, but is produced constantly and out of necessity. The principal philosophical disposition is therefore a 'recollection'.[34] But an authentic recollecting must always internalize that which is recollected; it must, that is, act in such a way that what is recollected progressively re-turns toward the self. In order to let the recollected progressively return it seems that we must go towards it or, at least, not flee in every direction, as if constrained by the appeal of external stimuli.

> As pure self-affection, time is not an active affection concerned with the concrete self; as pure, it forms the essence of all auto-solicitation. Therefore if the power of being solicited as a self belongs to the essence of the finite subject, time as pure self-affection forms the essential structure of subjectivity. Only on the basis of this selfhood can a finite being be what it must be: a being dependent on receptivity.[35]

The issue of the essential structure of receptivity thus comes to the fore in a cultural 'moment' in which we 'have less and less time' to look inside ourselves, an inner world into which we can probably fare better with the ear than with the eye.

Verra also suggests that Kant had already covered a considerable distance towards the elaboration of temporality, even though he had not 'taken up dwelling'[36] with it (in Heidegger's language): on the contrary, as Heidegger points out, Kant 'retreated', and 'stepped back', 'because, on the one hand, he had not completely freed himself from the traditional conception of time and, on the other, he had remained imprisoned by a "dogmatic" notion of the knowing subject that stemmed from Descartes'.[37] He 'must have had an intuition of this collapse of the primacy of logic in metaphysics'.[38]

Perhaps it not so much a question of 'collapse' as of withdrawing from the unconditioned control of a rationality (western thinking) that is perfectly able to speak but far less able to listen. Faced by such a prospect, retreat seems inevitable: renunciation, in fact, represents in a classical outlook an undesirable 'destruction' or the loss of all foundation.

And Heidegger insists:

> The internal sense does not receive 'from without' but from the self . . . Pure self-affection provides the transcendental ground-structure of the finite self as such. Therefore, it is absolutely untrue that the mind exists in such a way that, among other beings, it relates certain things to itself and in so doing posits itself. Rather, this line of orientation from the self toward . . . and back to (the self) first constitutes the mental character of the mind as a finite self. It is at once obvious, therefore, that time as pure self-affection is not found in the mind 'beside' pure apperception. On the contrary, as the basis of the possibility of selfhood, *time* is already included in pure apperception and first *enables the mind to be what it is.*[39]

A number of queries thus emerge: first and foremost whether selfhood represents an indisputable fact or a simple possibility of realization. And if it is really the function of time to make the mind what it is how can we know whether time fulfils its role and whether the mind exists as such; we must ask, therefore, if time is 'alive', if it works. Time, which can not be seen, touched or controlled by following it as we choose, is nevertheless capable of paralysing humans with boredom or disintegrating them with haste. If we actually believe that time 'enables the mind to be what it is', it is only fair to ask ourselves how we can have experience of it. And if, in our haste, our boredom or other forms of deterioration, time fails us, the mind might cease to be what it is. And what might a mind be when it is no longer what it is?

Faced by questions such as these we can at least outline a preliminary approach: in order to maintain contact with time we can adopt the rigorous exercise of whatever propensity for listening we may have – a concern as apparently banal as it is arduous to pursue. So arduous that it would seem 'logical' to retreat for fear of a 'collapse of the primacy of logic'. A listening propensity in fact involves some separation from the binding paths of classicity.

As an alternative to these paths we can aim at the restoration of authentic temporality and, more specifically, at an awareness of our own end as an attitude linked to the problem of our creative potential. The intellectual need to keep all interactive forms closely bound within a network of those cognitive categories that are 'normal' and practicable, just as the constant desire to 'know' what happens – even at the risk of falsifying knowledge – opposes not only the painful experience of loss but also impedes any endeavour of genuine creativity. Whenever, in fact, a climate of cultural constraint or cognitive cramp opposed to the creative life of thinking begins to prevail, the human being can no longer really live his own awareness of time; the experience of death inevitably assumes the stereotypical appearance of an absurd, prospective accident that must not, at any price, be spoken about. The mental mutism that forces us into a series of concealments does not only overshadow the striving for an awareness of our own finiteness, but also opposes genuine human creativity. The knowing subject, in fact, will become ever more reluctant to let himself 'die' even when cognitive 'death' is equivalent to relinquishing familiar models in order to be able to seek out models elsewhere, in a creative knowledge rather than in the mirroring of standard rationality. Frequently, however, our efforts to master creative processes are revealed as vain attempts at the control, or theft, of something from which thinking is supposed to arise. We palm off 'having' for 'being'.

And creative endeavours obviously do not pass through circuits of articulation traced by standard use but only through a heeding language able to accept a temporality that reconnects the inner events of birth and death. As we are presumably the only living beings capable of awareness of time and of our own end, in the absence of inner listening we must pretend not to know, then feign not to pretend, and so on. Humans would thus produce a mind that can not be 'what it is'. In this falsifying spiral in which the reality of one's own finiteness is denied (and that denial also disavowed) there is the risk of depriving oneself of the possibility of any kind of creative activity, almost as though by denying death – illusively – the fullness of creative life were also denied. The creative process in fact appears to be dependent upon the capacity for mobilizing attitudes that are simultaneously contrasting and reciprocal. Activity and passivity, orientation and confusion, 'springing forth and surging back'. We might say that creativity can be linked to that paradoxical capacity for knowing how to use our cognitive coordinates and, at the same time, knowing how to abandon our rational ground by not using it. The guide-line of inner listening can allow us to drop, or arrive, beyond the circumscribed spaces of that which is knowable in order to let something new come forth.

# Chapter 10

# Midwifery and philosophy

## MAIEUTICS: SOCRATIC LISTENING

SOCRATES: Come then, you are on the right road just now . . .

THEAETETUS: I can assure you, Socrates, that I have tried very often, but I can neither persuade myself that I have a satisfactory answer to give, nor hear of anyone who answers as you would have him; and yet I cannot help being troubled by the problem.

SOCRATES: These are the pangs of labour, my dear Theaetetus; you have something within you which you are bringing to birth.

THEAETETUS: I do not know, Socrates, I only say what I feel.

SOCRATES: And have you never heard, simpleton, that I am the son of a brave and burly midwife, whose name was Phaenarete?

THEAETETUS: Yes, I have heard . . .

SOCRATES: And that I myself practise midwifery?

THEAETETUS: No, that never.

SOCRATES: Let me tell you that I do, though, my friend: but you must not reveal the secret as the world in general has not found me out, and therefore they only say of me that I am the strangest of mortals and drive men to their wits' end . . . [1]

One of the most important aspects of listening is in fact discernible when cognitive frontiers are opened up without any 'frontal' attack, but only in relation to our availability to listen rigorously; as if our determination to go forward tentatively without knowing exactly our direction, but sustained by the readiness to listen – almost auscultate something muffled – were exactly what opens the way for the birth of thought. In the readiness to understand there is precisely an effort to follow up the inner consequentiality of someone's expressions: the disposition which gives life to a 'listening event'. The thing experienced itself becomes capable of utterance insofar as the interlocutor adheres to a rationality which is capable not only of saying, but above all of listening, and insofar as the interlocutor opens himself to the strength of thought springing to life in the other, free from the cognitive claims provided by his own interpretative parameters.

If we reach the point of discerning a consequential thread in the utterances of 'the other' over and beyond apparent fragmentation, listening is then converted into a maieutic process; this emergent consequentiality in which the fragments of one's own interior world organize themselves, perhaps represents thinking in the process of its formation. It is an activity which begins to distinguish itself from a flow of affects and which at the same time expresses itself as genuine thinking, because it is not passively introjected from external sources of utterance. On the other hand, if listening is not sustained by an authentic maieutic approach, all that can be derived from it is a more or less satisfying interactive impact. The most difficult among listening situations resolve themselves into being experienced as a collision, or insult, which can dissipate an inadequately developed maieutic capacity in the listener. The Socratic thinker can only learn his art from competent and authoritative midwives, such as Phaenarete – that is, those who are capable of facing even the most intensely difficult situations. Listening experiences do in fact extend from the 'easy' to the 'impossible'.

The message from the other will not attain its expressive potential except in the context of a relationship through which the listening interlocutor actually becomes a participant in the nascent thought of the person who is talking. But a listener can only 'enter' in a way which is at once paradoxical and committing: 'by taking leave', by standing aside and making room. The type of listening which can be transmuted into a process of birth and growth may perhaps find expression in the language of Rilke: 'If you want to make a tree grow, surround it with the interior space which you have in yourself . . . Only in your own renunciation can it take form and become truly a tree.'[2] And to find the strength to stand aside and make way for the incipient thought of the other, we need an 'attention' which only very skilled and authoritative midwives can teach us. 'This attention', Heidegger maintains, is that 'imperturbability, which will not allow itself to be disturbed in its hidden preparation for that leave-taking which is the essence of a sacrifice.'[3] Listening can in fact be assimilated to a highly demanding mode of 'thinking' which 'pays attention to the slow signs of what escapes from every calculation, and recognises in it the unpredictable declaration of what does not allow itself to be deterred'.[4]

The listening attitude may moreover be regarded as a genuinely interactive propensity, in the sense that it determines what the speaker will say as much as the speaker himself determines it, with the innumerable tensions that are created in a bipersonal field. The verbal interventions of the person who 'knows' how to listen as well as his silence impinge on the person who is speaking and thus ultimately reshape the physiognomy of the context underlying the dialogue. While we must undoubtedly acknowledge that the utterances of the speaker in reality represent his own contribution, we cannot set aside the influence of the person 'who intends to listen', with regard to the one 'who intends to speak'. The habitual use of the power of eloquence – that precious capacity to use language incisively and productively – perhaps might indicate a proportionate difficulty in listening. This power of eloquence may enter into collusion with the most deep-rooted defensive structures of the person who is trying to express himself, and by activating these it may provoke a halt in his nascent thinking. Constant attention appears to be necessary, in fact, to the struggles of those who are not 'capable of giving an answer', or cannot 'find a satisfactory one', or 'can't stop thinking about it', and admit their sense of bewilderment: 'I do not know, Socrates, I only say what I *feel*.' These difficulties reveal to us that at times we are not in a condition to take in some aspects of our own life of thought: thoughts never listened to, which we then come sadly to believe can not or should not ever be expressed. Perhaps it is a question of aspects of an interior world which has not been, and still is not, permitted to rise to the level of adequate symbolic expression, because it has been and still is an object of definition, devaluation, correction or invisible rejection by not listening.

The power of language becomes paradoxically involved in a

negative collusion, by which the rigidity of the most deep-rooted patterns is reinforced in the other person: patterns in which the suppression of what is most unacceptable has been carried out because it requires too much effort to listen to; 'inaudible' thus equals 'unheard-of'. The possessor of a language which is powerful, articulate, persuasive – who is unable to give it up in order to make way for the strength of an act of midwifery capable of allowing to be born and live what neither of the two may be aware of (unless each of them listens and makes himself listened to) – is transformed into an 'artificer' who intervenes in his work, making and de-making, or into a 'demiurge' who seeks to assemble something according to his own preestablished scheme.

In the context of western culture, there are frequent references to the celebrated maieutic method understood as the art of obstetrics transported into the context of philosophy. And yet in philosophical literature not a single reference is made to a 'second' art which is considered even more important and which is closely connected to the first: the art of prearranging the best unions. Thus we read in the Platonic dialogue:

SOCRATES: Did you ever remark that midwives are also most cunning matchmakers, and have a thorough knowledge of what unions are likely to produce a brave brood?

THEAETETUS: No, I cannot say that I knew it.

SOCRATES: Then let me tell you that this is their greatest pride, more than cutting the umbilical cord. And if you reflect, you will see that the same art which cultivates and gathers in the fruits of the earth, will be most likely to know in what soils the several plants or seeds should be deposited.

THEAETETUS: Yes, the same art.

SOCRATES: And do you suppose that with women the arts of planting and of harvesting are so different?

THEAETETUS: I should think not.

SOCRATES: Certainly not; but midwives are respectable women, who have a character to lose, and they avoid this department of their profession because they are afraid of being called procuresses, which is a name given to those who join together man

> and woman in an unlawful and unscientific way;
> and yet *the true midwife is also the true and only
> matchmaker*.
>
> THEAETETUS: Clearly . . . [5]

An elementary reading of the text tells us that just as the function of the midwife, transferred to the epistemic level, is that of bringing thought to birth, so also the function of the matchmaker is the infinitely more relevant one (in any philosophical perspective) of instituting 'unions' such as will favour the development of the best combinations (articulations, linkages) of thoughts. The capacity for wedding differing orientations, or fostering well-matched connections is therefore one of which matchmaking midwives are even more 'proud' than they are of their obstetric art. However, the 'proud' capacity for arranging good marriages is an exclusive prerogative of the matchmakers, in that they are *above all else* midwives: persons capable of fostering the birth and life of thought. In the absence of this basic and indispensible art, they could not carry out the function of matchmakers, a function which they rightly consider to be more important than their midwifery abilities. But since – Socratic Plato insists – the disorderly and stupid way of marrying off men and women is the work of a procurer, the wise and orderly way truly only belongs to those who are in a condition to foster the processes of birth. And thus all 'wedding' of thoughts which are not the work of midwife-matchmakers, like the 'brave and burly' Phaenarete, for instance, is classed as the work of procurers who, for over-circumscribed motives (and hence with no reference to the complexities of life), link, weld and combine without knowing anything of the art of bringing to birth. In the absence of a real maieutics of listening and thought, the very amalgamations of thoughts among themselves become the works of mere panders. If the weddings of thoughts are considered to be more important than the actual birth of thinking, it is a fact that Plato insists on the *indivisibility* of the two philosophical attitudes, and stresses this conviction with a very precise double articulation.

The first time, he tells us:

> SOCRATES:   . . . you will see that the same art which culti-
> vates and gathers in the fruits of the earth will

THEAETETUS: Yes, the same art.

be the most likely to know in what soils the several plants or seeds should be deposited.

SOCRATES: And do you suppose that with women the arts of planting and of harvesting are different?

THEAETETUS: I should think not.

In other words, either we learn maieutic philosophy, the art of bringing to life the best way of thinking, or else there is nothing but panderism, stupidity and disorder in seeking to put thoughts together.

## THE BIRTH OF THINKING

If we now try, on a philosophical level, to come closer to the unrenounceable method of the midwife and matchmaker, we can begin to articulate some basic considerations.

One is often tempted to maintain that the 'richness' of our inner world possesses a guarantee of existence in itself, and that the 'problem' merely consists in knowing how to select the words which are best suited to expressing and representing it in a context of consensus. In this way, we may be tempted to believe that words are 'like a grasp that fastens upon the things already in being and held to be in being'[6] – a grasp which seizes and compresses. In fact, however, the situation is far more complex, demanding and enigmatic than that. The organization of our innerness seems to exist on condition that it is heard, brought out – in effect brought to be born. It is not just a matter of entities lying there waiting to be linguistically seized and organized in the most diversified expressions. If a symbiotic or possessive link is established with the 'object' (whether person or thing), in the end this will tell us nothing, because right from the start there was no propensity for a maieutic form of listening, but rather a tendency to a fusive or confusive relationship – a form of exploitation. Even the most intense form of 'affection' experienced by human beings, for instance towards their offspring, may paradoxically resolve itself into an insult to the creative potential of the developing person. In the last resort, every approach to persons or things can be resolved into an interaction suited only to satisfying an obscure desire for dulling, by which the quality of the dialogue itself is robbed of its genuine nature and degraded to its opposite function.

If we envisage the practice of listening as a process aiming at the birth of thinking and interaction, we may then recognize that maieutics is an indispensable preliminary for any authentic form of *ethos*. Maieutic listening increasingly appears to be an essential condition in both a phylogenetic and ontogenetic perspective. 'An ethic of the desire to be or the striving to exist', in the words of Ricoeur.[7] In his view, this process is not regulated by a formal principle of obligation, and even less by an intuition of aims and values, but rather by the effort, or 'attempt', to self-expression which characterizes each one of us. 'Effort', but really also 'desire', because at the heart of this ethic there lies the identity between 'effort', in the Spinozistic sense of the word and 'desire' in the sense of the Platonic 'Eros'. The task of ethics ultimately coincides with the reappropriation of the striving to exist.

In the words of Heidegger, for instance, 'Being-with others develops in listening to one another'.[8] Again, Ricoeur helps us understand the maieutic quality of listening as a primary attitude which can provide the basis for the birth of thinking. 'We should start out from a point of view in which the autonomy of our will is rooted in a dependency . . . which is not contaminated by accusation, prohibition or sanction. Listening itself creates such a pre-ethical situation; it is a way of being which is not yet a way of doing, and because of this it escapes from the alternative of submission or revolt.'[9]

If we consider the challenge and process of listening, it can be seen prima facie as distinct from that other journey towards the construction of reality by means of a language which organizes and shapes. From a closer perspective, however, the opposition between speaking and listening does not exclude a meaningful resemblance. What warrants this affinity is always the creative function of symbolization. And, while this function attains open expression in language, in listening it is pursued in 'secret': a reversed image of creative language is described, as listening provides its negative pole, so to speak, and thus contributes to the construction of a more complete and integrated rationality. Listening as an innovative and renewing force begins precisely at the point where the action of the linguistic 'demiurge' is temporarily put to silence and where a different sort of creativity, that of the 'midwife', unexpectedly comes into effect. And any 'suspicious attitude' devoid of well-directed foundation can lead us astray, since it acts as a repelling force, which prevents us from welcoming thoughts which could prove fertile. The person who recognizes a maieutical listener in his interlocutor in fact is posing this tacit request: 'I don't ask you to believe what I say, but I ask you to think it, to make it the object of your interior world of thought; then my thoughts will enable you to recognize their own message of truth.' Responding to this request could constitute the basis of a properly maieutic attitude. In this way there seems to emerge the indication of a preliminary methodological feature which may be summed up in the need for an attention 'without' reserve and 'without' preconceptions to the revelations of life interactions in general. And the nascent strength of the maieutic dialogue seems to enhance a level of 'higher' order which makes certain new notions seem old, and vice versa. It is a 'method' which keeps us straight and holds us upright in ever more complex articulations and interactions even though it seems to deprive us of some of our familiar liberties: 'The greatest freedom may coincide with complete unfreedom.'[10]

If this propensity tends to make us resemble Plato's 'strangest of mortals', we should nevertheless remember that what is involved is not a question of the legitimacy of certain doubts, or of the features of current 'normality'; the point at issue is the occasional awareness of the non-listening culture in which we operate, and which makes for 'strangeness'. In the presence of doubts too uncomfortable to hear and acknowledge (what is 'unhearable' becomes 'unheard-of'), we automatically distance ourselves and describe such doubts as linguistically meaningless or incorrect – when even the minimum suggestion of them comes to our ears. Wittgenstein suggests that a mathematician would be horrified by his comments in the sense that the mathematical mentality is trained in such a way as to avoid completely any kind of opinion about the type of thoughts and doubts which he develops. Mathematicians have learned to consider such doubts as something contemptible, and embarrassingly infantile. 'I trot out all the problems which a child who learns arithmetic, etc., finds difficult,' says Wittgenstein, 'those problems which education represses without resolving. I say to those repressed doubts: "You are quite correct; go on asking; demand clarification".'[11]

When one asks, for instance, if someone is 'mad' or 'sane', we see that only the most rigorous listening can tell us something illuminating. In our view, the most varied linguistic dimensions coexist in everyday speech, from the most pathological and destructive to the most illuminating and formative. And the 'forgotten poetry'[12] of everyday language is not only poetic, but truly *poietic*, a constructive instrument, in that it is the indispensable condition which determines the development of every human subject. As is known, the 'poietic' force of early dialogic experiences and of modest everyday speech represents the guarantee of every individual process of human development.

'Attention to what words tell us', Heidegger insists, 'is supposedly the decisive step and directive on that way of thinking which is known by the name of philosophy.'[13] If the attention devoted to what words say is listening, then it justifiably follows that the quality of listening determines the features of that decisive 'step', which confers norm and direction on the course of philosophy. Further on he writes: 'Every science rests on presuppositions which can never be scientifically established though they can be philosophically demonstrated. All sciences are grounded in philosophy, but not vice-versa.'[14] Perhaps one could even concede that a 'different' or 'new' science might be based on a mutant philosophy capable of listening. McClintock, for instance, 'serenely' claims that good research requires, above all, a disposition 'to listen to what the material has to say'.[15]

## THE RISKS OF LISTENING

'Dire are the pangs which my art is able to arouse and to allay in those who consort with me', says Socrates, '. . . just like the pangs of women in childbirth.' Later he says:

I suspect . . . that you are in labour – great with some conception. Come then, to me, who am a midwife's son, and myself a midwife, and do your best to answer the questions which I will ask you. And if I abstract and expose your firstborn, because I discover upon inspection that the conception that you have formed is a vain shadow, do not quarrel with me on that account . . . For I have actually known some who

were ready to bite me when I deprived them of a darling
folly . . . [16]

In these passages from the celebrated Platonic dialogue we find
a suggestion of a process of birth closely linked to the readiness
to sustain a loss or an interior laceration. According to the
maieutic metaphor in fact, one who is born irremediably 'loses'
a vital secure haven, in order to set out on the dangerous path
of individuation, and one who gives birth equally 'loses' a vital
and symbiotic entity with which she must institute a complex
and possibly also dramatic sequence of interactions. In both
cases the risk element is essential and unavoidable. If we consider
that a transformation takes place as a result of the abandonment
of a 'propensity' comparable to a currency which is not yet out
of use, any new attitude must take on the semblance of a loss
of the previous mode of seeing things and of evaluating them.
'A benighted vital instinct hates philosophy,' remarks Jaspers;
'it is dangerous. If I understood it, I should have to . . . see
everything in a different light, have to judge anew. Better not
to think philosophically.'[17] And the activity of listening also
involves an unavoidable process of mourning, which is the prelude to incipient processes of knowledge. The point at issue is
whether it is possible to suspend or surpass the most surreptitious
or deep-seated automatic responses of approval or recrimination.
With a nascent capacity to renounce recrimination, the processes
of 'judgement' may appear in clearer form. And a scrutiny of
subtle accusatory articulations may bring out the lifeless dross
of the judging conscience encompassing our culture.

In Heidegger we read:

For at one time . . . the poet . . . reaches the place of the
ancient goddess of fate, and demands the name of the rich
and frail prize that lies there plain in his hand . . . The goddess
searches long, but in vain. She gives him the tidings, 'No like
of this these depths unfold'. There is nothing in these depths
that is like the prize so rich and frail which is plainly there in
his hand. Such a word, which would let the prize lying there
plainly be what it is – such a word would have to well up out
of the secure depths . . . The frail, rich prize, already plainly
in hand, does not reach being a thing; it does not come to
be a treasure, that is, a poetically secured possession of the
land. The poet remains silent about the prize which could not

become a treasure of the land, but which yet granted to him an experience with language, *the opportunity to learn the renunciation in whose self-denial the relation of word to thing promises itself to him.*[18]

When we cannot find the names or the words to describe the treasures which we have in hand, these are not transformed into the cultural values of our cultural 'land', or era. And we too have no clear idea of the nature of the jewel which cannot become a treasure of our land even though it is 'rich' and 'frail'. And if we take willing risks at this moment of extreme importance, in which we are brought face to face with the tremendous negativity of not being able to express the value of what we have in hand, or 'inside' like Theaetetus, if we are able to avoid running away from it, a more genuine experience of language will be disclosed to us, in the sense that we make a 'renunciation' which coincides with our assent to an act of learning. What sort of learning? This experience teaches us that there are not always words for what we have in hand (in mind, in the 'soul') and that it is precisely where we have to forego expression that we may nevertheless find an opportunity to realize, as if dawning upon us, that there may be something which is not yet translatable into the 'repertory' of our epoch, but which even so may subsist if only we know how to resist in borderline areas. And remaining in search of that treasure – undescribed and undescribable – is indeed assent to a revelation of something 'rich and frail', which cannot yet become a 'treasure of our land' or a 'negotiable currency' of our culture. We have learned that we are not the masters of a language that will produce on demand the precious constructs to which we presume we are entitled. Nor should we allow our rationality to drift on to the plane of an illusory sense of the practical, and opt for a general pessimism, for optimism or for any variant of indifference; we would thus accomplish no more than a naive protection and would only stay away from labour and risk.[19]

Perhaps we can recognize that at times we are tempted to ignore the inner depths of humans. We can give in to this temptation when we believe that we are dealing with 'foolish' or 'conventional' people, whom we perhaps tend to objectivize too unhesitatingly. It seems that we are almost inclined to treat them as natural objects. And yet the depth of persons, so to speak, may prove to be so unfathomable that we begin to ask ourselves whether our language is sufficient, whether it really has the terms to express what we are trying to approach. In exploring natural phenomena we justifiably believe that it is sufficient to change some specific terms or concepts, whereas in the challenge of maieutic listening we can be confronted with so much difficulty in reaching for language that we may even foresee the risk of having to 'transform' the whole of our vocabulary. Two different possibilities could be envisaged here: in one case we do not see beyond the boundaries of a logocratic culture which does not easily accept the prospect that it can be further integrated; and in this case, we are confined to sharpening the logico-symbolic apparatus which allows the greatest cognitive gains. In maieutics, on the other hand, the laborious events of the listening dialogue lead to transformations in our 'normal' rationality, and thus make possible an unforeseen quality of philosophical learning. We are confronted with two modes of reflection attempted on different planes, and yet both a long way away from 'success'. In both cases the pursuit involves risks and travail. Even in the case of the adept possessors of lucid linguistic instruments it appears that much disappointment results. And in the case of those who opt for the way of listening, the process cannot be devoid of difficulty, detachment and exhaustion. Operating in a culture which hinges on the power of expression and which is largely programmed for not listening, there is no doubt that conflicts and disappointments should continually arise if one engages in proper hearing: it seems almost as if we are to relinquish those logico-cultural paradigms beyond which there would be nothing but dross and folly. But if we recognize the persistence and plausibility of the *two* differing orientations, we may yet explore the fertility of their coexistence and the ways of healing the breach.

Even in the context of a deliberate process of listening, a close examination of one's own maieutic capacities may prove to be as instructive as it is laborious. The resurgence of doubt may override the validity of one's own standpoint and even the reassuring competence of the 'masters'. It seems almost that we have no resources to cope with the laceration of certain basic protective assumptions or no resources to redefine the state of affairs in a more responsible way. 'It is so convenient to be immature!' exclaims Kant. 'If I have a book to have understanding in place of me, a spiritual adviser to have conscience for me, a doctor to judge my diet for me and so on, I need not make any efforts at all.'[20] In this way, one does not even have the problem of having to try and listen to oneself. And again: 'I need not think, so long as I can pay; others will soon enough take the tiresome job over for me.'[21] The payment may be construed as an exchange attempted by means of 'normal' criteria and accredited utterances, which constitute the symbolic currency ruling the interactions within a culture. 'Thus it is difficult', the philosopher continues:

> for each separate individual to work his way out of the immaturity which has become almost second nature to him. He has even grown fond of it . . . dogmas and formulas, those mechanical instruments for rational use (or rather misuse) of his natural endowments, are the ball and chain of his permanent immaturity. And if anyone did throw them off, he would still be uncertain about jumping over even the narrowest of trenches, for he would be unaccustomed to free judgment of this kind. Thus only a few, by cultivating their own mind, have succeeded in freeing themselves from immaturity and in continuing boldly on their way.[22]

By the unnoticed provision of 'dogmas' and 'formulas' a predetermined way of thinking may be established in the form of a language which is aimed at expression and which cannot incline toward listening to oneself and to others. Such reduced-by-half-rationality tends to prevent listening genetically, or in its nascent state: knowledge claims are formalized in advance which do not allow a logical space for listening to oneself and to others in as much as the only plausible form of listening is reduced to absorbing the most successful rules and paradigms, or even counter-rules and counter-paradigms, provided by competing varieties of expressive rationality.

In the wake of pseudosymbolic linguistic degradation, 'nonexistent things' can be represented by words more easily and elegantly than unavoidable realities. In genuine symbolic life, on the other hand, a contrary propensity is developed. In fact, nothing escapes so easily from representation by the use of proper words than what is pretended or simulated. And yet, the greatest necessity of symbolic life is just that of bringing out into cultural life – letting unfold – certain 'things' whose existence is initially neither demonstrable nor necessary, but which, just because conscientious midwives acknowledge them as though they did exist, come closer to reality and to the possibility of articulation. ' "A whole world of pain is contained in these words!" How *can* it be contained in them?' asks Wittgenstein, 'It is bound up with them. The words are like an acorn from which an oak tree can grow.'[23] But nothing guarantees for us that the strong oak will grow; it is rather a project or a risky challenge in which we engage in order to avoid spreading sterile or abortive linguistic relations. Even more harmful in the development of one's thinking is being constantly misunderstood with regard to the essential feature of what we say even though expressed in ways that are still defensive, cryptic or timorous.[24] And even when one experiences a rewarding dialogue, one can still suffer latent damage inasmuch as the understanding derives from the 'goodness' or the 'superior' rationality of the other, and not from a response to the specific quality of our pristine message. In a non-listening culture, one may be rewarded without being understood, satisfied without being heard, and well-cared for without maturing.

## A METHODOLOGY OF LISTENING

According to Heidegger, reflecting upon language demands of us that we approach and adhere to the saying of language in order to 'dwell' in language: 'in its diction, that is, rather than in our own'.[25] Once again one is struck by an enormous difference in philosophical perspective. It is not a matter of using our conceptual accounts in order to impose them on something, but rather of abiding-by in order to listen, and to do so genuinely: which means to be in an indefinite state of hearing, freeing ourselves from any 'standard' limitations of time. Heidegger's thinking seems unambiguous when he suggests that we should 'take up residence in language'.[26] This 'taking up residence' can in fact be referred to a form of cognitive interaction which has no trace of 'predatory' or 'hunting' paradigms and no sign either of a tendency to colonize; it attempts to be 'agricultural' and 'pastoral', in the sense that it implies a coexistence and cohabitation, in which the risks, the produce and the destiny can be shared. We are a long way away here from the prospect of a rationality which is expected to triumph *over* nature, which can speak but not listen in the same way and thus loses genuine interest in what it deals with. The attempt is not yet one of the simple 'overturnings', which we encounter so frequently in philosophical thought, but rather a process heading towards an ulterior way of relating to language, a link which involves us in a committing way because it implies attaining 'its saying', and no longer just the monotony of our own. According to Heidegger, humans speak inasmuch as they listen;[27] this speaking through listening and receiving is correspondence proper. But once again, we may ask how it may be possible to respond if one is not disposed, or trained, to receive the speech of another. If this crucial point is not developed in its full breadth, linguistic investigation may be deflected to ever more restricted contexts, beyond which language may induce conditions of noisy expressions and dumbness.

On the question of knowing how to listen, we could argue at length about whether we are in fact capable or not. A salient criterion to invoke, however, is the distinction between not being able to do something and not wanting to do something even though one has the 'power' to do it. 'He refuses to', we read in Wittgenstein, 'means:

> it is in his power. And *who* wants to say that?! Well, what kind of thing we say 'is in my power? – We may say this when we want to draw a distinction. I can lift *this* weight, but I am not going to do it; I *cannot* lift that one.[28]

Abandoning this distinction is equivalent to falling into a preventive confusion in which it becomes increasingly difficult to differentiate what we can and cannot seek to do. Heidegger suggests that:

> To pay heed to what the words say is particularly difficult for us moderns, because we find it hard to detach ourselves from the 'at first' of what is common; and if we succeed for once, we relapse all too easily.[29]

In a philosophy of listening it is a question of 'finding' – or rather of beginning to experience by practising it – a way of thinking which is a commitment to what is problematic and 'worthy of being asked'. A philosophy of listening cannot go seeking (or 'hunting for') philosophical theses to be rendered 'normal' as an alternative to other perspectives; it should be conceived rather as a theoretical development which we are allowed to try out, like a still-uninterrupted path which we can follow.

In an over-restricted view of language, for instance, we could believe that we listen to someone because he is speaking, when originally he only spoke because someone had consented to listen: maieutics. According to scientific methods underlying cogent and predictive knowledge, we may remain confined within a context which is not suitable for the openness and self-gathering required by listening. The maieutic method appears to be aimed at welcoming nascent thought before it is irremediably 'shaped' by culture; adhering to this method the philosopher is intent upon 'gathering himself' in order to welcome with respect a thought or a significance before it lapses into imitative conformity with standard rationality. By only listening to what is more obvious and easy to decode, we cannot really say that we listen or know: perhaps we do not engage in the process of knowing, but gain bits of knowledge, perhaps feeling deprived of that single inner moment in which the maieutic dialogue can take place as a birth event. Often the thought of our interlocutor must first be integrated into the cultural repertory in order to become recognized by the person who is 'listening'. But a thought known in this way perhaps no longer bears much resemblance to its pristine physiognomy. Thus the snuffing out of philosophical midwifery is the precondition for the spreading of our thinking in unrelated, repetitive forms, contrasting only in appearance. If we were for one moment to entertain the fantasy that nothing less than the 'secret of being' were revealed to us, we should also have to suspect that it would be useless to man as he would not know how to listen to it; in fact he could only conceive of it on condition that he could reduce it in such a way that it be amenable to normal discourse, to standards of articulation, where it no longer could 'manifest' itself.

In our commitment to listening and in the effort to distinguish it from the productivity of thinking-as-power, there can hardly be any deceptive longing for, or risk of, relapsing into a sort of pre-logic golden age. The discipline and lucidity required by maieutic philosophy are a long way from any form of nostalgic idyll. In order to be such at all, listening must be rigorous: assenting to it demands that we 'work our way out of immaturity', 'cultivate our own minds' and even be prepared to abandon 'instruments for rational use' – in Kantian language. Heidegger seems to argue to similar effect on this elusive and yet ubiquitous problem.

> It is important above all that on the way on which we set out when we learn to think, we do not deceive ourselves and rashly bypass the pressing questions. On the contrary, we must allow ourselves to become involved in questions that seek what no inventiveness can find. Especially we moderns can learn only if we always unlearn at the same time. Applied to the matter before us: we can learn thinking only if we radically unlearn what thinking has been traditionally. To do that, we must at the same time come to know it.[30]

If we ask ourselves what listening originally means for us then we will be asking something which calls us into question directly, in that it refers to the prime condition of our ontogenetic history as well as to our evolutionary story. What Heidegger reiterates in his 'descriptions' of thinking may, *a fortiori*, be advocated in our search for listening.

> But if the question 'What does call for thinking?' is asking what it is that first of all directs us to think, then we are asking for something that concerns ourselves to whom the question, 'What is called thinking – what does call for thinking?' is directly addressed. The question 'What calls us to think?' has already drawn us into the substance of the inquiry. We ourselves are, in the strict sense of the word, put in question by the question. The question 'What calls on us to think?' strikes us directly, like a lightning bolt.[31]

It is a matter of being available, and corresponding, even to the immediacy of the 'lightning bolt' in order to persist and succeed in the maieutic method. And to make himself more clearly understood Heidegger insists that it is not very important to propose a new concept of language. The only thing that counts is to learn to 'dwell' in the saying of language. And this cohabitation represents a radically different philosophical method from any cognitive approach which is primarily intended to control, use, shape and analyse. In order that this should be possible, we need continuous self-examination to ascertain if, and up to what point, we are capable of genuine correspondence. It could be contended that it is almost futile that a philosophy should derive from the greater or lesser capacity for genuine correspondence. And yet we are confronting a much more laborious and risky enterprise than the fulfilment of any form of logocratic task.

Knowledge which is primarily logocentric could be likened to the intricacy of a traditional labyrinth. Although there are a few types of labyrinth, the classical type, that of Knossos, has one course only: when we enter we cannot do anything other than reach the centre (and at the centre we can only find the way out). If this one-way labyrinth was 'unrolled' we would find a single thread in our hands. The legend presents Ariadne's thread to us as the means for getting out of the labyrinth – whereas it is in fact nothing else than the labyrinth itself.[32]

This remark gravitates toward Heidegger's suggestion that:

> terms are like buckets or kegs out of which we can scoop sense. Our scientifically organised dictionaries list these vessels of sense in alphabetical order, each entered and described according to its constituents, sound-structure and sense-content. When we are especially concerned with what the word tells us, we stay with our dictionaries. This is how things look at first. Indeed, this 'at first' does on the whole, and from the start, determine the idea we have of the usual ways of being concerned with the word. On the strength of this idea, we then judge the procedure of any thinking that is concerned with the word . . . What about this much-invoked 'at-first'? What we encounter at first is never what is near, but always what is common. It possesses the unearthly power to break us of the habit of abiding in what is essential, often so definitively that we never come to abide anywhere.[33]

But if the way of being concerned with a word 'at first' possesses the terrible power to unaccustom us to 'abide in what is essential', it will be desirable to undertake a tireless search for the conditions which make it possible to avoid the initial preclusion with which we are threatened. It is philosophically disturbing that the recourse to the codified sources of meaning to which we turn in a fateful 'first moment' can cause us to deviate from the search for a fuller relationship with language.

The method of listening cannot be learned, in the strict sense, as it is a way of relating that can only function on condition that the 'learning' is continuous, uninterrupted; we are dealing with a concern which is not conducive to an ultimate 'grasp', or mastery of the issue. The whole question, therefore, lies in the constant renewal of our approach to language; in learning and re-learning how to listen to it.

In order to take an overall look at the phylogenetic development of humanity, we might draw upon the work of Vico, who suggests that:

> Men first feel without perceiving, then they perceive with a troubled and agitated spirit, finally they reflect with a clear mind. This axiom is the principle of poetic sentences, which are formed by feelings of passion and emotion, whereas philosophic sentences are formed by reflection and reasoning. The more the latter rise toward universals, the closer they approach the truth; the more the former descend to particulars, the more certain they become.[34]

It is not a question of favouring one polarity or the other (the universal or the particular, reasoning or emotion) – but rather of resisting the temptation to perpetrate exclusions and thus draw boundaries which cannot be redefined. We may thus reserve the opportunity for identifying mediating elements, for moving in both directions in the range of articulations arranged by degrees of cogency or cognitive quality, exploring the rational span which may link the two kinds of 'sentences'. It is not just a matter of polarities, but perhaps also of functions which are interwoven with each other. The cognitive function of listening is shown, for instance, where an embryonic thought is protected from the restrictive interference of over-zealous classification, so that it can move on its way to mature completion. But above all, listening creates a minimal but fertile logical passage which will then allow our minds to move with greater freedom and envisage still further ways of approaching reality. These ways, moreover, do not imply any criticism or rejection of the prevailing and accredited forms of cognitive conduct.

## THE REBIRTH OF THOUGHT PROCESSES

A further characteristic prevailing in culture is shown today in our busy concern with an ever-growing number of details, both in everyday life and in scholarly research. Despite the help of the enormous extensions to our rationality in terms of computer-ized aids, there is an awareness of being constantly swamped by an infinitely expanding tide of detail. This extension may represent the myriads of details in which the advance of knowledge expresses itself; an increase which is constantly prompting us to further expand knowledge, and at the same time tends to make us strangers to our own inner world, which thus becomes ever-shrinking. And the more our basic functions are inclined to retreat into lethargy the more they turn to sizeable elements in the range of expanding knowledge. The sort of knowledge which can offer very little in the absence of a sufficient interior capacity for redefining priorities. We should ask ourselves if this capacity can be reactivated, and how. It is sometimes argued that we are so profoundly affected by our own dullness that we do not know whether there is a way out, or whether we can 'devise' any kind of a re-awakening.

The exercise of listening to oneself and to others, even if only occasionally, may be of help in the attempt to restore the core of inner functions as a premise for the integration of a 'life of thought' which is often too dissipated and devoid of strength. The attitude toward listening implies a basic trust – almost a hope. The assumption that we can approach the optimal use of even the most rudimentary communications and that there is a desire to represent and express oneself is deeply interwoven with this trust. A trust that our interlocutor may convey what is yet unknown, unexpected or even what may actually be necessary for our own constant renovation. The words of Heraclitus come to mind: 'If one does not hope, one will not find the unhoped-for, since there is no trail leading to it, and no path.'[35]

When each instance is transformed into its opposite or into uncertainty, guidelines are perhaps to be found in a renewed capacity for inner listening. We may begin to perceive the main 'connections' even in the midst of the waves and storms of cultural coexistence. In the exercise of listening, the inessentials seem to fall away, and we are also saved from the deformations imposed by the need to promptly conceptualize at all costs. Even when we reach for lucid articulation or try and define something, we are aware that de-finition is not the final concern – an end in itself; one is in search of possible links with virtual and remote possibilities. We are in fact looking for links with the sources of rational life and not just with more 'concepts'. In our culture, the fears usually associated with advanced age are partly amenable to

the more than justified prospect of a 'missed birth' which nevertheless approximates to a concluding phase. On the other hand,
when something interior is born, the 'years which pass' do not
weigh heavily upon us, but may rather serve to enhance qualitative developments in our inner world. And when the transition
does not take place from biological existence to dialogical life[36]
and maturation, even the so-called youth and maturity become
permeated by an irrepressible (although silent) anger at feeling
like humans for stockbreeding – subjects of zootechnology –
perhaps with some success on the socio-biological plane but
virtually 'aborted' in philosophical terms. The Manichaean paradigms of our 'commercial' culture, hinging on the constant counterposition of good and bad, constitute the converse of genuine
philosophical labour. Unable to be born seriously, or to be re-
born maieutically, humans instead struggle *against* something as
a substitutive activity. Manichaean surrogates of the maieutic
process are readily available as their production is avidly
absorbed by our logocratic culture.

If we do not succeed in coping with a tendency to narcissistic
isolation which only leads to perceiving one's own mirror image
in others, it then becomes difficult to accept others as 'real'
persons. To the extent that we do not overcome a sort of deep-
seated dual narcissism, we find ourselves both perceiving and
using others as ever-new ways of reflecting ourselves, by which
we seek to create a wider but stagnant consensus for everything
that we already believe in. And the mirroring reflection of our
own beliefs does not only refer to the realms of subjective life,
but also extends over a whole vast range of 'purely' cognitive
operations which seem even to attain and affect verifiable and
quantifiable levels. Non-listening reflection can be symbolically
indicated as an extension of the myth in which Narcissus binds
himself to Echo, in a 'consenting' relationship by which everything which Narcissus projects is confirmed and handed back to
him. No philosophical midwifery here. It is a sterile relationship,
then, but one which determines our search for ever greater
consensus. If, however, the demand for mirror-consensus leaves
even a minimal opening for our growth potential, it is then
possible to begin to extricate oneself from the sterile game of
reflections. Kant goes even as far as suggesting in his first
Critique that:

It is nothing unusual, in common conversation as well as in written works, by comparing the thoughts which an author has delivered upon a subject, to understand him better than he understood himself – inasmuch as he may not have sufficiently determined his conception, and may thus have spoken, may even have thought, in opposition to his own opinions.[37]

Thus we come to confront the risk – as fruitful as it is disconcerting – of recognizing that we may think in a way contrary to our intentions and that *others* may understand our questions and our true intentions better – that others may help us give birth to our own thoughts. The sort of experience mentioned by Kant also discloses the possibility that the inner growth which derives from it is not due to the articulation of the thought itself or to the specific meaning of what is understood, but rather to the 'informal' force, or life, of thinking given rise to by the quality of dialogic experience. To open ourselves to such a possibility (and thus create a propensity for it), represents a 'decision' on the part of human beings – based on the greater or lesser capacity for decision-making that we may possess – and it is hard to see how it can be 'given' or 'found' in the context of natural evolution. Usually, in the absence of listening, the cultural paradigms of our thinking are perceived as 'necessary' in themselves; this presumed necessity makes it a fact that culture enters into the inner life of individuals with a series of indisputable assumptions, occupying it and grasping it still further. And this conditioning tends to be institutionalized, becoming the impenetrable web of appearances from which humans hunt for an escape in a variety of 'remedies' ranging from bland diversion to the most obscure flights of a destructive nature.

In our contemporary linguistic situation, we could say there is a search going on for two different kinds of reassurance, which would seem to be incompatible with each other. On the one hand, we seek to believe that language is actually what transforms an agglomeration of individuals into a community in the rich and vital sense of the word; on the other hand, there is an ever-growing desire to believe that language does not constitute a barrier which *divides* one culture from another, but in fact provides an instrument of basic connection for the potential 'brotherhood' of mankind.[38] Perhaps the most suitable point of departure to try and break up this 'intractable' dilemma lies in a philosophical shifting of the attention *from a cult of speech to a culture of maieutics* as the process which supports the birth and rebirth of our thinking. This does not entail, of course, that in maieutic listening strict discipline is attenuated, because listening can in fact be more 'sceptical' and rigorous than standard rational discourse. In this interactive domain there is a renewal which both integrates current rationality, and which also conveys apparently contradictory meanings – not because of lack of meaning but because of the abundance of it. A similar resonance can be found in the work of Ricoeur: 'Hope begins with an a-logic', he says:

> It breaks into a closed order . . . A passion for the possible . . . a remitting of the over-abundance of meaning to the abundance of nonsense . . . are signs of a new creation, the novelty of which literally catches us off guard. Hope, when it breaks out, is 'aporetic', not because of deficiency but because of excess of meaning.[39]

Listening is the attitude which can unblock the creative resources immobilized by the rigidity of traditional 'logical' education; the move which frees us from a cognitive context which is opposed to the incoercible search for further horizons; it is the readiness to tear away ideologizing modes of reflection which define and constrict the ways of coexistence.

## THE GROWTH OF THOUGHT

Understanding the body of knowledge that we commonly call 'philosophy' could be considered 'relatively easy' in that it basically requires good functioning of the intellectual capacities. If one is in a condition to move about easily in the complexity of terms and in the processes of conceptualization, one can understand philosophy without encountering the need to transform oneself or to evolve. We can learn philosophy as we are, without the need for inner changes, but perhaps this is less true for the maieutics of thought. In our concern for listening a demand for change is made upon us – indeed, almost a demand for a mutation. Unless we are prepared to become in some way different from what we are, listening cannot be understood properly: the maieutic method is not comparable to the learning of a set of intellectual axioms, theses or paradigms but rather

to an experience – unattainable unless we are to some degree
ready, receptive and vulnerable. In general, we could say that
philosophy involves our minds and therefore our 'head' is sufficient – there is no need for the 'totality' of us to become
involved. But listening is a far more profound challenge in the
sense that it needs the person as a whole. Absorbed in the use
of his enlightened power, the 'philosopher king' no longer seems
sufficient – however well-disposed he may be to give a hearing
at the appropriate times and places. The Socratic philosopher
seems in fact to be more suited to the processes of maieutics
and growth, for he makes no question of time in the exercise
of patience, irony, tenacity and assiduity. 'The strangest of mortals' is what he is called in the *Theaetetus*. Paradoxically, in
order to create a doctrine it seems that experience is only
partially necessary, and perhaps the less we know the more
easily and unhesitatingly we may put together a theoretical
construction. Knowledge which is more rigorous than exact,
more vital than measurable, is often hesitant. In the domain of
human sciences, the more we know the more we feel that the
'object of knowledge' slowly dissolves or escapes – but in a very
particular fashion: we do not remain inert and dumbfounded;
we actually become anxious to deepen the experience. There is
something acroamatic rather than axiomatic about the saying of
Heraclitus: 'The soul has its own law (logos) which increases
itself (i.e. grows according to its needs).'[40]

The 'advantages' of a concern for listening are obviously not
linked to a 'Why?' understood in one of the logical or causal
senses; they can be more associated with an ironical 'Why not?'.
We may reply with a further question in which we state that we
see no reasons to hold back from a pursuit which shows a
potential for fertility and growth. And although we recognize
that listening is one of the most unexplored and risky of all
processes, for that same reason its desirability and growth value
are not to be underestimated. 'The man who is understood is
misunderstood', Canetti remarks ironically. 'Everything only
keeps operating in misunderstandings. It is nevertheless crucial
that one lives to be truly understood.'[41] It is the crucial nature
of this propensity that deserves philosophical scrutiny.

If we cannot listen properly, it seems that we can no longer
share in 'creative thinking', and that we must confine ourselves
more and more to circulating within a given repertory, or arsenal,

of terms and standard articulations, which can be summoned up each time in mnemonic fashion; almost a pledge to comply with standard ways of mirroring and with reproductive thinking.[42] The inhibition of growth begins to make itself felt, however unhalting the progress of knowledge, when thought rigidifies into the imitative reflection of current epistemological metastructures. This eventually burdens us with images of life that are sadly lifeless. It is the 'de-animation' of our thinking which projects the world into an abstract 'objectivity', obviously very weak in the face of the incursions of the deeper, archaic components of the knowing subject. When we are at the mercy of our more destructive dynamics, it seems almost as if only the *semblance* of growth remains, and that what we had regarded as rational growth turns out to be somewhat illusory and unusable. Harris reports that on the cover of a book entitled *Hermes*, the god is portrayed in the form of a head placed upon a quadrangular base; the author explains how it is that the god of language is represented without a body: only the head, and no other part of the human figure is considered necessary for the cognitive functioning of language.[43] The figure of a decapitated Mercury, Harris suggests, may serve to indicate the deviant attitude which so heavily impinges upon certain views of linguistic theory.[44] This attitude can be summed up in the idea that language is in some way separable from other functions of the whole person and of growth; the idea that a linguistic community can be reduced to an aggregation of 'talking heads', and that the capacity to comply with and use the dominating language is the principal characteristic of mankind; in fact, so Harris maintains, the capacity to *create* and *produce* language is far more significant. Languages and tongues cannot be thought of as available prefabricated objects imposed for consumption. As a generator of language, the person needs far more than a head to speak with in an uprooted, unrelated fashion. The maieutics of listening serves to enhance the *creation* of language and the growth of the speaking person, thus freeing humans in the making from the forced role of users and imitators of whatever language happens to be most effectively propagated in the market. A maieutics rooted in listening – which is always listening to the person, and not just to the skeletal utterances he produces – can make possible the growth of a truly speaking person, rather than the assembling of someone 'spoken' by the dominant rational language he adheres to. And in spite of such adhesion the individual may remain isolated and deprived of dialogue.

It is likely that in the wanderings of solitude a person will construct a special view of the world derived from the meagre links established with a few parts of objects and with a few aspects of oneself. In solitude, that complexity of relationship which includes the recognition of oneself as a genuine generator of messages is not to be found. If we suppose that every link generates some 'power', then even a link with the most uninteresting stereotype or with the most unreal 'objects' will represent something to be safeguarded at all costs. But the links established in 'isolation' and in the absence of growth, so to speak, are detached from a more extensive network of options in which it may be possible to deliberate acceptance and refusal.

The logical roots underlying western tradition lay down that two contradictory assertions cannot be valid at the same time: one of the dominant criteria of our culture, which in fact imposes ostracism on all contradiction. And these cognitive co-ordinates are so rooted in our mentality that we are easily inclined to believe that to demonstrate the falsity of an opposing viewpoint must be the logical equivalent of a guarantee that validates our own conviction. The rare propensity to handle contradictory experiences in fact renders our cognitive structure unsuited to face up to the riskiness of growth. Listening can be a support to the hermeneutic effort whereby we seek to establish a relationship between our world and a different 'world', between our own attitude and a different attitude which seems to be pursuing 'unthinkable' aims and using an untranslatable language. No formative discourse can be 'normal' in the sense that only the force of something which is 'alien' to us, and to which we choose to expose ourselves receptively can draw us out of a restrictive paradigm.

# Chapter 11

# Paths of listening

## LISTENING TO 'SYMBOLIC' LANGUAGE

With the intent of outlining more adequate and efficient listening methods I shall attempt to identify some specific *types* of communication. These typologies are obviously not 'pure', since we are dealing rather with the *prevalence* of one or another expressive style within varied communicative contexts. Provisionally I shall try to 'experiment' with at least three different types of language, which might be named *symbolic, concrete* and *pseudo-symbolic* discourse.[1] 'What is left for us to do', suggests Heidegger:

> is to point out ways that bring us face to face with a possibility of undergoing an experience with language. Such ways have long existed. But they are seldom used in such a manner that the possible experience with language is itself given voice and put into language.[2]

Adopting a dialogic outlook on language we should be better able to discern the levels of discourse that are expressed in it and try to identify – beyond a genuinely 'symbolic' type of language – two other kinds of expression: *concrete* (intent upon eliminating inner events which can not be contained) and *pseudo-symbolic* (whose purpose is actually to pervert language by reducing it to an instrument of non-communication): thus a language that is neither *sym*-bolic, nor *meta*-bolic but rather *dia*-bolic.

We might think of *symbolic* discourse as oriented toward communication, constructive symbolic games and the deepening of self-awareness. In the area of this expressive style, verbal and non-verbal communications function as vehicles for the derivatives of rational processes, as well as of affective and imaginative dynanmics, in a form that allows them to be interpreted with reference to symbolic language itself. *Concrete* language might be characterized as an 'acting out' intended to alleviate inner tensions which can no longer be handled in a purely symbolic form. The negation of reality and the projection into the interlocutor of aspects of one's own ratiocination predominate in this type of 'language' in which, evidently, the tendency to transform discourse into emotional discharge tends to prevail. As to *pseudo-symbolic* discourse, it could be described as a 'static' linguistic style virtually devoid of communication; we might say that this discourse is specifically intended to not-communicate, and to annul the potential for meaningful expression and for the construction of a bipersonal interactive field. Pseudo-symbolic discourse represents a significant means of interaction only if viewed in its negative and circumscribed sense. Recognizing the prevalence of a certain communicative style in a particular context may enable us to revise, and adapt, our disposition toward vigilant listening. Even though we are dealing with provisional and approximate modes of description they can, nevertheless, facilitate a more participatory and accurate listening. And of course any effort to articulate differentiations or classifications may accomplish no more than rudimentary attempts to improve the capacity to be conversant with the language we want to heed.

Invoking the hypothesis of a dialogic field and patiently adhering to it, we can also make use of a conceptual space suitable for distinguishing whether the prevalent motivation of a message lies within a single interlocutor or whether it is determined by a collusive interaction. We can thus better heed the other's messages in the sense, at least, of discerning whether they are expressions of his own inner motivation or responses related to a *dual* situation; in such a way messages which are apparently contradictory or indecipherable if construed as originating from a single inner world may acquire a new, more practicable dimension. Many more messages thus become no longer vulnerable to obscurity – which is tantamount to the preclusion of dialogue. It is a question of understanding whether what a speaker says represents primarily the expression of *his* inner world or primarily a response to the *other's* message. Methodological attention

to the interactive field of listening thus involves a tension toward
otherness, since all communicative levels inevitably allude to
both the 'I' and the 'Thou' of the situation. And in every
situation one can glimpse an enigmatic depth as even the most
enlightened partner in a dialogue not only constantly refers to
himself and to his interlocutor but also does so both 'objectively'
and 'subjectively'. Socrates questions in this way: 'Then you will
be obliged to me if I help you to *unearth* the "hidden" truth of
a famous man or school?' And Theaetetus: 'To be sure, I shall
be very much obliged.'[3]

The eminently philosophical quality of integral listening
becomes clearly evident when we juxtapose it with degraded
ways of being interested in something:

> Interest, *interesse*, means to be among and in the midst of
> things, or to be at the center of a thing and to stay with it.
> But today's interest accepts as valid only what is interesting.
> And interesting is the sort of thing that can freely be regarded
> as indifferent the next moment, and be displaced by something
> else, which then concerns us just as little as what went before.
> Many people today take the view that they are doing great
> honor to something by finding it interesting. The truth is that
> *such an opinion has already relegated the interesting thing to
> the ranks of what is indifferent and soon boring.*[4]

Thus Heidegger warns us of the danger of perverting our interactive abilities, and of consenting to the illusion that we do not
form part of the interactive field. 'Interest' might be reduced to
a propensity that is not concerned with the inexhaustible 'truth'
of the object but with the furtive gain that is illusively derived
from it. The symbolic fruition of the message, on the other
hand, allows for the emergence of something authentically and
unthinkably interesting that is not to be found *already* waiting
in the object – text or message: it is disclosed because radical
and dedicated listening engenders the resonances, recombi-
nations and developments that only derive from a condition of
germinal acceptance. The search for what is interesting, on the
contrary, seems to reproduce on the cognitive level the monotony
of archaic predatory dynamics.

In a culture determined by the technology of information the
human condition is ever more scrutinized and exposed, as if the
dominant tendency were to seek out ever more 'interesting'

material, with the result that we are increasingly immunized
through exposure to human suffering as it is passed to us by the
media. Thus humans seem to reconcile themselves to indifference
while they are induced to constantly say: 'We know everything
and we can't do anything about it.' Paradoxically, listening can
be a way of avoiding passivity and getting lost in the labyrinths
of our time, a way of coming along without capitulating or being
squeezed out of the vast language game. It is a question of
hiding and of avoiding the blunting mechanisms in our cultural
machinery in order to be able to heed something, and to 'dwell'
with it. And simply by avoiding the most resounding cultural
waves we might perhaps be able to inaugurate philosophical
attitudes both innovative and conservative.

In the process of heeding symbolic discourse we begin to draw
upon the unusual, without aspiring to consume it as 'interesting':
and, through the same concern, we familiarize ourselves ever
more with that which is ordinary until it actually becomes disconcerting. And so we find ourselves committed to the posture of
reciprocal listening which alone is capable of generating genuine
intellectual wonder. 'For wonder is the feeling of a philosopher,
and philosophy begins in wonder', we read in *Theaetetus*.[5] The
insatiable search for the 'interesting', as outlined by Heidegger,
conceals the temptation to desert symbolic language by deviating
toward the interactive style of a concrete language likely to
degenerate into collusive, detrimental exchanges, or even of a
pseudo-symbolic language intent upon non-communication and
upon the meaningless turning of our great linguistic machinery.
We want interesting things: we do not want to listen patiently
waiting for wonder to be born. And even our philosophical
assumptions or epistemic paradigms can be used to endorse the
linguistic style we most need in order to find something 'interesting'. A need that is linked to the presumed 'advantages' that
are glimpsed in the variants of our expressive styles. Even the
interactions in which one person officially has the role of the
one who carries more responsibility[6] can be moulded by 'communicative' inclinations aiming at the 'innocent' search for something interesting. And the dominant propensity can be triggered
off in spite of the deliberate intention to achieve communications
that are authentically symbolic and metabolic.

A symbolic discourse that has been sufficiently listened to
reveals in fact an abundance of meaning that would otherwise

be squandered and extinguished. We should not forget, for instance, that an activity that:

> leads the addressee to extract from the text that which the text does not say (but presupposes, promises, and implies), to fill in empty spaces, to connect that which is in the text with the intertextual fabric from which it originates and into which it will flow once more[7]

is a *co-operative* activity. But the problem of co-operation is far more complex and promising when the 'text' to be read is the living expression through which the inner world of the speakers is revealed. The activity of listening in fact has nothing cogent about it but simply indicates an opportunity for co-operative creativity. From the point of view of listening, for example, it does not seem possible to regard as sufficient the psychoanalytic tradition of empathy, containment and interpretation originating from a person who is 'superior' by definition, precisely on account of his ability to empathize, contain and interpret. The suggestion that it is not worth his while to seriously listen to the other might actually be concealed by such an imbalance, or accentuated asymmetry. The most promising features of the analysis may thus be vulnerable to obscurity.

'Language sets everyone the same traps,' warns Wittgenstein;

> it is an immense network of easily accessible wrong turnings. And so we watch one man after another walking down the same paths and we know in advance where he will branch off, where walk straight on without noticing the side turning, etc. etc. What I have to do then is to erect signposts at all the junctions where there are wrong turnings so as to help people past the danger points.[8]

If we were better able to co-operate in genuinely heeding language, we might avoid falling into the traps ourselves and even offer a hand to those who are entangled. Otherwise we have no choice but to debate with one another from within our respective traps. In his constant formulation of the value of a listening attitude Heidegger seems to be 'responding' to Wittgenstein's wise concern:

> Is it playing with words when we attempt to give heed to this game of language and to hear what language really says when

it speaks? If we succeed in hearing that, then it may happen – provided we proceed carefully – that we get more truly to the matter that is expressed in any telling and asking.[9]

If the person who actually assumes a larger share of responsibility (irrespective of his official role) can 'correct' alterations in the linguistic game, he is then using an opportunity of opting for a re-affirmation of symbolic dialogue, as the style most suited to noticing and dissolving traps. And when excessive imbalances are produced in a potentially symbolic dialogue the interaction inevitably degrades to the concrete or pseudo-symbolic level. If these imbalances are not monitored and conceptualized it will not be possible to correct them, and we will tacitly collude with a thickening of linguistic traps. In this sense listening plays a vital role in as much as it is a disposition to capture the elusive moments in which a perversion of symbolic dialogue is perpetrated. And if that initial moment escapes us, correction becomes increasingly difficult. And even the person who actually assumes the larger share of responsibility in a dialogic interaction can induce the use of expressive styles that tend to make the regressive vortices of concrete and pseudo-symbolic language prevail. Both an inappropriate verbalization or a gross silence can motivate relapses that are ultimately conducive to a degradation of dialogue.

In a sense it is precisely these 'errors' that can reveal a maieutic immaturity in the person who is 'first in responsibility' within a dialogic context: the creativity of the open exchange is repressively deflected into the area of narcissism and then used to restore one's inner balance at the expense of the interlocutor. Almost inevitably the second in responsibility will tend to pay with the same coin, so to speak, with an instantaneous change of direction away from the use of symbolic instruments and toward collusive barter or retaliation. The second in responsibility, however, can assume the role of *first*, by summoning all of his inner resources in order to avert the danger of total dialogic degrade. A further risk of deterioration lies in the setting up on either side of pseudo-symbolic positions, intent upon non-communication and on the annulment of any possible symbolic link. This danger is exacerbated by inadequacies in the less responsible interlocutors: already prone to concrete or pseudo-symbolic levels of language they find themselves even more constrained to a regressive style and will certainly be resistant to any sort of symbolic solicitation.

In philosophical endeavours as well as the dialogic contexts, one of the major problems can always be recognized in the presumption that we truly know how to listen. Even among those who dedicate themselves to understanding for teaching purposes or for therapeutic reasons we could see a fluctuation of inner attitudes ranging from a conscious conviction that one knows how to listen (linked to a latent fear of not knowing) to an explicit doubt of one's capacity (linked to a tacit conviction of being more than capable). In the latter oscillation – a conscious conviction of uncertain capacity and an unconscious certainty of knowing how to listen – we might notice one of the many cultural stereotypes available as defences against the impact of potentially over-disturbing questions. In this outlook it is perhaps easier to understand those internal agreements of the 'intellectual groups' whereby they reassure one another of their openness, unaware of clinging to the underlying assumption: 'Of course we know how to listen.' Publicly and consciously, however, they aptly display the philosophical virtue of humility and are always ready to admit that in the field of listening they still have much to learn.

## LISTENING TO 'CONCRETE' LANGUAGE

The insufficiently heeded calls of the maturational potential in the individual can transform themselves into atrophied, 'avenging' functions, a similar process to that which seems to occur in social contexts: the least heeded or actually excommunicated instances tend to dictate their own forms of intransigent and archaic rule. It is almost as though there were a pride in the seemingly 'philosophical' posture of renouncing being heard and of reorganizing oneself in an alternative way. Those renunciations that are consolidated in absolutist and 'primitive' modes thus tell us that effectively *we can not* possibly do without being heard. The aspiration, or *right*, to language possibly represents a part of us that can not remain unknown; vulnerable to obscurity, it reclaims its rights and ultimately makes itself heard through a 'language' composed of illness, aggression and staticity.

Heidegger suggest that 'when we are explicitly hearing the discourse of another, we proximally understand what is said, or

– to put it more exactly – we are already with him, in advance, alongside the entity which the discourse is about'.[10] An awareness of concrete 'language' thus seems to be based upon the gradual discernment of those specific interactive conditions in which the word *can* speak. The word which is 'heard' is not truly able to speak to us to the extent that it is lacerated by our premature questioning or mutilated by our deafness. In these cases it becomes degraded to the anonymity of noise: a distorted word that nevertheless arises once more and comes across in intrusive and deteriorated expressions that are only suited to elicit retaliation.

If we widened our philosophical perspective we could perhaps attempt to concern ourselves with the *margins* that surround the 'sanity' of our intellectual rationality. We might begin, for instance, to compare closely the manifestations of the 'sane' intellect with the 'illnesses' of thought – and vice versa; in any case it would seem that such comparison as well as the concession of a reciprocal hearing between the two can no longer be postponed. Wittgenstein, for example, insists that: ' "It is high time for us to compare these phenomena with something *different*" – one may say. – I am thinking, e.g., of mental illnesses.'[11] When a listening interlocutor re-emerges, or distances himself, from a 'pathological', concrete discourse, he does so in order to be able to enter the discourse more successfully at a deeper level; and, conversely, the deeper he hopes to arrive the more he aspires to a liberating exit. Conceptual abstractions as well as efforts to articulate and describe such 'language' are thus not presented as values in themselves but as auxiliary instruments used to improve our awareness of that which is *different*.

'Look at human beings; one is poison to the other', remarks Wittgenstein.

> A mother to her son, and vice versa, etc. But the mother is blind and so is her son. Perhaps they have guilty consciences, but what good does that do them? The child is wicked, but nobody teaches it to be different and its parents spoil it with their stupid affection; and how are they supposed to understand this and how is their child supposed to understand it? It is as though they were *all* wicked and *all* innocent.[12]

The corroboration of a listening propensity could act as an antidote to this 'poison'; and yet a culture, that in some respects has by now rendered itself torpid, can generate a vast 'philosophical' production concerning expression and, comparatively, very little work on the process of authentic listening. But this should not surprise us if we are only capable of regarding ourselves as producers-consumers of a stupefying and benumbing culture that is unaware of any 'poison' (and thus incapable of neutralizing it), a culture in which one 'interest' is replaced by another in an alternation that is merely apparent since it is determined by an underlying stasis.

Like writing, saying might also go from right to left, or even from bottom to top, from forwards backwards, or in still other directions that we are not even able to envisage: the paradigms of normal rationality might impede the discovery of further paths, trajectories, depths. And as far as our capacity for picking up the irrepressible projections of the speaker is concerned, it would appear that a 'contractual' agreement is tacitly established: the speaker will be able to utter something genuinely better on condition that what is most unacceptable in him is first listened to and contained. It is therefore not uncommon to discover the existence of a terror of listening due to the imbalances and damages that some heeded expressions can cause. A legitimate fear of the lacerations and contamination of our own inner world can arise: 'Do not try to weaken the meaning of the dialogue,' affirms Buber, 'it is a confrontation.'[13] But if this is the most common and fearsome of dangers and if, at the same time, the expulsion by the interlocutor of that which is most difficult to bear constitutes the condition for the development and pursuit of a dialogic event, it is obvious that sufficient awareness of the *extremely exacting* nature of the interaction in prospect is more necessary than ever. It is necessary to postulate situations of emergency, or of dialogic danger, that we are not even capable of describing sufficiently or of 'metabolizing'. We usually safeguard ourselves from this formless danger by ways of *doing* that extend from the most concretely brutal stances to those considered most 'philosophically' elevated. Such states of danger, however, can offer the cue for more enlightened and correct formulations in the sense that they are derived from hypotheses with which we can more fruitfully approach those riddles of coexistence that we can no longer elude.

These vicissitudes point ever more in the direction of the 'dialectic' relevance of the listening process; and the simple term 'listening' appears hopelessly inadequate when we want to refer to those authentic, crucial interactive-dialogical confrontations which are burdened by the risk that our most enlightened capacity for thinking and our ability for constructive argument may be shattered. In these confrontations a significant line of discrimination is also revealed: if the inner obscuration of our thinking induced by a 'wave' of danger impedes the efficient working of reason, the author of an un-thinkable utterance will be legitimated, so to speak, in his unopposed diffusion of destructive contents; this occurs because the interpersonal structure confirms him in his belief that the presumed representative of the dialogic process – he who claims to adhere to the strength of thinking – can not measure up to an authentic confrontation. In this fleeting kind of dialogue, unfeasible inasmuch as we are unaware of the more crucial passages in the listening process, there is nothing left but to relegate the exercise of rationality to the more circumscribed and tranquil situations: possibly the least relevant. In this restricting perspective the moment defined by Heidegger as 'being with him in advance' is clearly undermined as is that advocated by Wittgenstein when he talks of comparing ourselves finally with 'something "different" '.

'Anyone who listens to a child's crying', continues Wittgenstein, 'and understands what he hears will know that it harbours dormant psychic forces, terrible forces different from anything commonly assumed. Profound rage, pain and lust for destruction.'[14] But anyone who hears the child cry and *can not* listen to him is only struck by a sound that will prevent him from arriving at an understanding of what is 'harboured' in those cries; he will no longer be able to recognize a language that is too different from his own, an inarticulate and menacing 'gurgling' that prevents him from 'discerning the *humanity* in a man'.[15] As a result of an attention restricted to symbolic levels of discourse one can let listening to a 'concrete' language slide away and thus risk losing the chance for an authentic dialogic confrontation.[16] But how can we dare *not* to abandon listening if the intrusions of the interlocutor can damage the functioning of our ratiocination? Perhaps the actual block on thought might be revealed as an appropriate defence in an interaction that is too threatening. At the extreme limits of the difficulties of listening, however, one can discern the – virtual – possibility of a temporary dis-identification with our own reasoning functions, as though one took refuge 'elsewhere' in order to avert the double danger of annulling dialogue or benumbing reason.

## LISTENING TO 'PSEUDO-SYMBOLIC' LANGUAGE

If there is a risk of letting the quality of our culture deteriorate in spite of technological advances, this might be connected to the increasing diffusion of pseudo-symbolic styles of language. Although it is a resounding and highly imposing 'language' it does not embody the more authentic functions of our symbolic capacity. Having deserted the genuine nature of communicative language it is simply a 'sick language' turned toward the search for expansionist effects. The devaluation of the word has invisibly and ubiquitously infiltrated into the multimedia of our culture while, at the same time, it seems to affect those who cultivate the symbolic-metabolic function in the form, so to speak, of indifference. The degradation of language can influence all disciplines, even taking the disguise of impressive productivity. Bewildered by pseudo-symbolic contamination we can also pretend to deny it, deny the fiction and so on, in an ever more devaluing spiral. When 'saying' is no longer vigilant and essential, when respect for language is no longer advocated, it almost seems as though the artificial languages of informatics and technology might begin to vacillate as a result of a lack of validity in the basic symbolic function that sustains coexistence.

Evidence of our uncertain capacity for discerning diverse linguistic levels can be found in the indifference with which we passively don the most devitalized language. Just as at work we may make use of a jargon closely resembling a dehumanized mask, so we experience our daily lives in a 'saddened' language that we do not even heed, a language that is neither chosen, nor inherited but simply undergone through lack of attention. The 'ideas' that we claim to think or refute do not really seem to be thought by us; perhaps they are merely mirrorings of the dominant forms of rationality in which we operate; reflections that are responsible for the institution of our internalized referents or referees. Nor is it really true that we desire or detest something if we hypothesize a subjection to, or dependence on, those innumerable reference agents reflected within us.

Our philosophical interest in language might be shown above all by the growing attention it devotes to the listening of language, to the most variegated and even disturbing aspects of our language. And thus even a non-language, whose imitations of language are merely expressed in overwhelming waves of sound, should be recognized and watched over. It is a question of monitoring a discourse that expresses itself as an invasive power from which we ought to escape through lucid awareness rather than flight. In *Euthydemus* Socrates says: 'Seeing that I was on the point of shipwreck, I lifted up my voice, and earnestly entreated and called upon the strangers to save me . . . from the whirlpool of the argument.'[17] Recognizing a certain expression as something pseudo-symbolic involves the adoption of a serious and dangerous position: whereas on the one hand there is the risk of remaining overwhelmed by the most sterile and invasive pseudo-symbolic circuits, on the other hand there is the risk of a diagnostic error. One might in fact give up the laborious attempt of understanding and thus abandon the listening confrontation not so much because one has come up against a pseudo-symbol formation, but because one has run into a misleading . differential evaluation due to a limited diagnostic capacity. If it is philosophically necessary to distinguish speaking from speaking-in-order-to-say-nothing, it is no less necessary to be made aware of the risk of regarding as pseudo-symbolic that which we are simply unable to use properly.

The pseudo-symbolic degradation of language can only be conceptualized in terms of a potentially ubiquitous and interminable perversion. It is a question of being aware of the ineliminable presence of an 'inner sophist', constantly waiting in ambush. But at the very moment in which we try to define the sophist – construed as a mystifying inclination to which we may be vulnerable – the figure takes on a form that is already too definite and thus misleading. Jaspers in fact suggests that the sophist is never present according to ostensibly recognizable modes: capable of moving in all directions, he can assume radically different orientations and goals according to the needs of the moment.[18] The only exorcizing cue, so to speak, is to train ourselves for this 'impossible' cohabitation with something falsifying that can activate itself either 'automatically' or in collusion with external pseudo-symbolic transmitters.

In our extenuating logomachies the argumentative articulations that are enunciated may advance and proliferate as a result of their linguistic *appearance*; and yet, their only purpose is that of reproducing indefinitely. Although such linguistic customs can only be diagnosed with enormous difficulty, humans seem to be stupefied by their prevalence. A language incapable of listening not only reflects and reproduces the error to which it is subjected but also conceals it permanently in the deployment of further elocution. In this obscurity the relationship between ends and means is upset. To the extent that the purpose of language is erroneously identified with expression, its evolutionary strength becomes severely restricted; our modern age thus degrades language to the production of ever more sophisticated discourses. Through the control of language and the use of it as a commodity we may actually lose its innovative force. Although vulnerable to obscurity there is in fact the danger of environmental degradation within our own symbolic domain. In order to realize the threat of such perversion perhaps we may have to engage in a linguistic fasting or in a cultivation of silence intended to disintoxicate a resounding language that renders us cognitively torpid. 'If anyone challenges the least particular of their speech, then they (great orators) spin out a long harangue in answer to a short question, like brazen pots, which when they are struck ring loud and go on ringing', we read in *Protagoras*.[19] And a simple illustration can be seen in the exponential growth of technological means of reproducing language – a growth, however, that moves dangerously away from the purposes of genuine communication.

One of the reasons for entering into collusion with a pseudo-symbolic language is undoubtedly the difficulty of recognizing (intuiting, or suspecting) that any linguistic vehicle or level of discourse *can* in fact be both symbolic and pseudo-symbolic. It is almost as though the first rule of falsification (in individual or group terms) is to ensure that the functions of language are not questioned, to make sure that one does not ask (and the question is rendered unthinkable) whether language is there to allow us to speak or to annul dialogue, to create communication or isolation, order or confusion. It is a question of excluding the possibility that a semantically and formally valid linguistic vehicle be suspected of a role that is contrary to its declared function; in this dangerous condition we hardly have logical spaces for asking if our linguistic means are genuinely at the service of the inexhaustible complexity of reality or whether, on the contrary, they are used to suppress and distort.

The silence that we sometimes create, and in which we try to learn to live philosophically, demands a temporary and laborious abandonment of our familiar ways of reasoning. It is the most difficult of interlocutors that teach us to make this passage: if we consciously accept their devious and grave challenge, they may brusquely impose upon us the urgent need to drop our usual 'strategies'. The 'impossible' interlocutors exhibit themselves in their ability to unsaddle and confuse: with articulations that are suitably seductive, intrusive or concealing they undermine dialogue itself. The risk of damaging the *quality* of one's own arguments arises: 'You ought not to discuss with everybody or exercise yourself against any casual person; *for against some people argument is sure to deteriorate*', advises Aristotle.[20] 'You should not, therefore, readily join issue with casual persons; *this can only result in a debased kind of discussion.*'[21]

The naturalist Aristotle – the philosopher – speaks to us of deterioration. The survival of dialogue, thus, can even rest upon temporary surrender, an abandonment of our obstinate determination to understand according to our logical paradigms in order ultimately to 'share' the avoiding and confusing motivations underlying the pseudo-symbolic discourse of the 'opponent': only thus will we be able to reorient ourselves toward an unsuspected and qualitatively different form of understanding. Of course, in order to try out these methods of listening one must be able to keep a part of oneself alert to play the role of imperturbable spectator: he who keeps silent, not he who is silenced because he can no longer speak; he who remains silent because he chooses to surrender his own instruments of reasoning in order to freely opt for a more radical and implacable listening. And even though it may happen in the most difficult confrontations, the path of listening does not in fact imply either capitulation or a dispersive flaking away.

Passively receiving the pseudo-symbolic waves to which Socrates refers, almost as a result of inertia we might begin to correspond at the same level and thus sanction the diffusion of the most 'debased' expressive mode. The incapacity to identify pseudo-symbolic communication can thus induce a confusion in quality whereby we become bound to the most degraded or mystifying levels. On both the individual and group level it is always possible that this non-language ally itself to archaic phylogenetic derivatives, thus drawing up an inertial power that makes it even more rigid.

It should be reaffirmed that the propensity for listening has nothing to do with a tendency to assent, consent or submit, since this dangerous inclination becomes virulent only in the absence of genuine heeding. Traditional wisdom warns us 'not to listen to evil ones' in the sense of not consenting. But 'consent' is extorted in the degree to which we are incapable of monitoring, probing and heeding wisely. The pseudo-symbolic dimension of language may invade and contaminate situations without even striking a blow whenever there is no awareness of it. The incapacity for listening thus becomes an amorphous, unselective receptivity which precludes not only the fruition of ulterior philosophical work but also exposes us to the crudest of pseudo-symbolic incursions.

# Chapter 12

# The philosophy of listening: an evolutionary approach

## PHYLOGENETIC PERSPECTIVES

To the extent that we cultivate an awareness of belonging to the biological history of the planet we might be able to develop the sort of openness that allows us to reconnect our biological and dialogical dimensions. Whenever our phylogenetic depth is not taken into sufficient account as an inseparable aspect of the human condition we are restricted to an 'abstract' sort of philosophical knowledge that does not measure up to the task of encompassing our own biological nature.[1]

If however we are disposed to look back at the stratified and archaic 'components' of our inner world we may no longer perceive them as fossilized vestiges, but as functioning structures that somehow contribute to determining the present moment of hominization. And the very *propensity* that allows us to recognize the involvement with phylogenetic history can, in the same way, be conducive to a constructive openness toward our future.

As is well known, in the period of time that extends from the Palaeozoic to the Mesozoic era various forms of reptiles lived on the planet earth, and the ancestral memory of these animals is usually epitomized with a generic reference to 'dinosaurs'. Present on earth for a period of approximately one hundred and thirty million years, their cerebral mass was 'disproportionately' small when compared to the dimensions of their bodies and only able to guarantee elementary forms of adaptation on the basis of automatic responses to fundamental instinctive needs. Even though these archaic saurian animals have disappeared from the face of the earth they have 'found' a way of surviving by 'insinuating themselves into the human brain', in the language of Valzelli.[2]

> Through millions of years, in fact, the anthropomorphic primate brain has been structured in three basic and successive directions: reptilian, palaeomammalian and neomammalian. These three lines have been integrated and have taken on a single function. In contributing to this result, the role of the 'fifth column' responsible for the process of infiltrating the reptilian brain into that of humans must be ascribed to theromorph saurians, the distant but direct ancestors of mammals.[3]

In an evolutionary outlook involving the awareness of our historical and biological depth, we might regard the practice of listening as a progressive self-acceptance that in fact makes it possible for us to acknowledge ourselves as rational *animals*. As the rational component is normally focused upon and privileged in intellectual traditions, we are faced with a rationality that tends to be split off from biological history. Connections between behavioural attitudes usually called 'rational' and 'instinctual', 'digital' and 'analogic', 'analytic' and 'synthetic', constitute in fact an area of major concern. And yet, we can not possibly deny that we are *also* animals. But as soon as we recognize our 'animalness' we have made the first step toward overcoming our animal condition, even without denying it. We can not go beyond our animal state by denying it or by refusing to auscultate the ancient history that beats within us: acceptance is possibly the only method that allows us to do so.[4] A progressive self-acceptance makes it easier for us to orient ourselves toward our own centre, so to speak. If however we opt for a doctrinal orientation that involves us 'peripherally', we no longer need to aim for the whole of ourselves. Those processes of self-awareness that include the phylogenetic history of the species can also be eluded in the cultivation of the most rigorous forms of philosophical endeavour. Such potential awareness, however, seems to be inseparable from a listening propensity. In the cultivation of 'peripheral' areas we decentralize ourselves in ways that might be detrimental to our genuine philosophical potential. Outlooks that allow for the avoidance of centring upon the self in depth also appear to be more inclined to emit despising judgements directed toward the outside: saurian dynamics are not *here*, but *there*. Such strategies, moreover, are the prerequisite for tacitly transferring belligerent practices into the domain of knowledge.

It is generally believed that listening involves assent or subjection, and that it consequently consolidates the acceptance of a territorial conquest achieved by any originator of discourse. This fear might be the reflection of archaic territorial structures that have been phylogenetically preserved in the vestiges of our reptilian brain. Refusing to recognize these latent dynamics and opting for a starting point based on logical rather than biological grounds it is possible that we *inadvertently* (unknowingly) allow the most archaic mechanisms to infiltrate into the domain of rationality. We may thus find our cognitive efforts deflected into an illusive and dogmatic dimension that might even turn into a 'nightmare', or rather a 'daymare': the lucid rationality in which humanity glories, vulnerable to archaic saurian mechanisms of territorial control. If we entertained even a tiny 'suspicion' about the influence of the reptilian structures that cohabit within our brains, we would perhaps gain a salutary fear of those cultural expressions that are capable of triggering the most primitive interactions. In order to surpass these archaic mechanisms we should first pay sufficient attention to them: disavowed, they might dominate the whole cultural scene.

Whereas in many ways human activity adapts to the standards of its own culture, in several other aspects (and even in the realm of the most elevated cognitive processes) it reproposes the behavioural engrams of cerebral structures dating back millions of years.[5] Even though it is reclothed in logical and ideological discourses the ancient saurian brain behaves according to rigid biological laws and even *obtains* previously unthought-of power from the creative strength of humans.

## LISTENING AND HOMINIZATION

The evolutionary relevance of a complete maturation of language stands out clearly if we take a brief look at the process of hominization.

It is generally claimed that the most salient element in the history of human evolution is represented by the exceptional development of the brain in the course of the last three million years. From the earliest Palaeolithic times – millions of years ago – to the last stages of the Upper Palaeolithic era, the

trajectory of the hominization process appears to be characterized by the development of a specifically human *communicative*
language.[6] It has been hypothesized that an efficient form of
linguistic communication represented survival value for humans
and thus determined the enormous selective pressure which
would 'explain' the rapid development of the brain, whose mass
has trebled during the last three million years. The most enigmatic aspect, however, is the enormous lapse in time between
the full biological evolution of man – the completely developed
brain – and its consequences in terms of cultural evolution. As
far as we know, in fact, in the course of the extremely long arc
of time comprising the Palaeolithic era – over two million years
– we have nothing but a slow development of small tools that
range from simple flints to stones made to be gripped. Like
other scholars Eccles believes that 'this almost unimaginable
slowness demonstrates that man was greatly handicapped by not
yet having effective communication through speech'.[7] It is not
until we arrive at the Upper Palaeolithic era that humans seem
to have achieved a new awareness and a new sense of purpose.
This evolutionary flowering is silhouetted against a relatively
static temporal background if we only think of the thousands of
years in which the Palaeolithic era unfolded. Eccles believes that
'man was lifted to a new level of creativity by a language that
gave clear identification of objects and descriptions of actions
and, even more importantly, the opportunity of discussing and
arguing'.[8] In an evolutionary approach we may regard 'the world
of culture as *essentially a world of storage*'.[9] Thus a development
of capacities to receive, keep and remember appears to be
motivated by an underlying potential for listening. And it is
possible that evolving humans tend to speak out at their best
because they are listened to – and not vice versa.

A rapid historical glance at the process of hominization *also*
reveals that one of the major forces behind cultural evolution
can be linked to the 'fateful' invention of a written language.
The complexity of life in an agricultural community may have
been the incentive that induced the Sumerians to develop a
written language – perhaps the greatest contribution to the course
of cultural evolution. All archaeological evidence demonstrates,
according to Wolley,[10] that writing was in fact born in Mesopotamia. Even though pictograms already existed, the most they
could do was enumerate objects or depict situations: they could

certainly not be used to communicate utterances, evaluations or thoughts. Representation by pictograms came to an end and the written language was born when the human mind became capable of achieving a surprising and unhoped-for 'wedding', genuinely exogamous and revolutionary: the linking between signs and sounds, between two entities that do not resemble each other in the least.

A proper written language can be recognized only when the signs acquire a phonetic value: the hiatus that separates the pictogram and hieroglyph from phonetic signs is in fact so great that we can legitimately consider the linking of graphic signs and sound vibrations as one of the dizziest springs forward in human history. It is in fact a conjunction, a union, at which humans arrived after a journey of thousands of years, during which they could be regarded as fully evolved humans on the neuro-physiological level since their brains were completely developed. Possibly, the all too human Mesopotamians heeded the surrounding concert of nature and listened carefully to different sounds: the devoted, coexistential attention of a farming and pastoral community to the singularity of individual sounds. The capacity to hear a sound so well that it can be distinguished and differentiated sufficiently may constitute the pre-condition for linking it to a sign and thus inaugurate the immense perspectives of written tradition. Canetti actually writes in a note: 'The ear, not the brain, as the seat of the mind (Mesopotamia).'[11]

This linkage of sign and sound released the specifically human joy that comes from supplementing biological reproduction with cultural fertility, from transplanting our symbolic young shoots in the most varied places, times and domains of knowledge. The 'wedding' that gave rise to a literate culture represents a radical junction with regard to our biological history since it distinguishes human biological evolution from the intentional and inner-directed evolution of civilization. From the invention of written language (in which utterances and thoughts can be transmitted) we arrive, in the span of a few thousand years, at a telematic civilization. And 'Perhaps one day this civilisation will produce a culture', comments Wittgenstein.[12]

Thus language (as well as its constitutive listening dimension) is not something static and open to definition. It is a basic, and possibly the most basic, human function, as susceptible to degradation and illness as it is to evolution and growth.

## PROSPECTS OF COMMUNICATION

Communicative insufficiency is a consuming truth that we recognize in as much as it is a shortcoming rooted within our inner
world: anything which 'absolutely' does not concern us is possibly
dismissed as irrelevant.

In our detached and objective style of knowing, although we
distance ourselves from those ways of understanding humans
geared to attain greater contractual far-sightedness, we nonetheless run the risk of creating a philosophy of listening that is not
really *philo*-sophical because it is substantially colonizing. This
form of 'listening' establishes at the outset that one of the two
interlocutors dominates the interaction in terms of being able to
better understand the other and the relationship itself. And even
if the colonizing mode were to be overturned in the cultural
transformation of the 'colonizers' by the 'colonized', at the very
most these vicissitudes might induce no more than a temporary
ethological relief: an understanding stance which emanates from
a reduced-by-half rationality (only capable of speaking) can do
no more than mirror itself or ignore the relationship with the
other.

Heidegger insistently uses the expression 'to dwell' when referring to a genuine attempt to listen. From this notion of 'dwelling'
one might derive the suggestion of 'getting settled' in a state of
shared destiny, and not simply of staging exploratory visits:
'The claim to understand the other person *in advance*', remarks
Gadamer, 'performs the function of keeping the claim of the
other person at a distance.'[13] But this understanding 'in advance'
shows that the emissary of rationality mistakenly believes himself
capable of 'speaking' (at least in terms of thinking or reasoning),
even before he is prepared to listen.

In authentically *philo*-sophical moments a part of our mind
seems to remain suspended, 'passively' waiting for whatever
expression might originate from a source that seems to be playing
a more 'active' role. This *seeming* is due to our epistemic dislo-
cation: it is in fact the 'passive' attitude of waiting that attracts
and promotes the emergence of thought in the other. And it is
in this demanding interaction of opposites that the process of
genuine listening may unfold.

The constant interaction between the 'first' and the 'second in
responsibility' within any dialogic situation reveals alternating

impulses toward the search for truth conditions or for collusive falsifications. The hypothesis of an interactive field of listening suggests that any communication, exchange, or event that occurs is inevitably related to the initiative of the individual and to the creativity of the bipersonal field.[14] Any communication originated by the 'first in responsibility' is influenced by the 'second in responsibility', and vice versa. And any communication that is made in a dialogue ought to be auscultated, and not simply photographed or dissected according to the devitalizing style of our debating tradition. In the act of auscultation we are genuinely open to heed the array of levels extending from the hypothetical poles of truth and distortion. We attempt in fact to examine each message for its truthfulness as well as for its inclination toward distortion and concealment. In recognizing the deeply interactive nature of every dialogue we discover that we share in both the problem and the solution without being able to escape into neutral and unrelated spaces. An opportunity for discerning which elements may originate from internal dynamics within the single person, or from linked behavioural expressions of the interlocutors, corroborates the dialogic nature of our 'object' of investigation. New perspectives can derive from the hypothesis that a large part of what is said by the person who carries a lesser responsibility refers to the verbal interventions of the one who is committed to a greater responsibility and that even the verbalizations of the latter are a product composed of both objective notations and distorting resonances. Once more then we are led to recognize that listening to oneself and listening to others are synchronic processes that form part of the same interactive function.

In varying degrees of awareness one can oblige the interlocutor to exclude certain levels of expression and to confine himself to those areas which, presumably, the person who is in a 'listening' position will regard as acceptable. And yet the interlocutor inevitably continues to maintain a certain margin of dialogic autonomy and will try to extend his range of expression in order to make himself understood. In every sequence that lacks an authentic reciprocity, in fact, the interlocutor is induced to form a negative alliance with the other and ultimately collude with his areas of defensive blindness. The expression of one's own evolving inner world is thus postponed and one ultimately gives up all dialogic aspiration whenever attempts to communicate in depth are systematically prevented. Conversely, it is possible to make use of a 'validating process', so to speak: when the reply to a communication becomes the source for further dialogic events – unexpected, meaningful and revealing – we are committed to an authentic listening event. Whenever we believe that we can avoid the laborious involvement of listening and interact without some degree of commitment, we can only appeal to a repertoire of conventional verbal exchanges which inevitably degrade the quality of dialogue and even trigger off ambushing mechanisms of projective and controlling interactions. Resorting to stereotypes from our repertory of verbal skirmishing can only contribute to the expansion of a pseudo-symbolic (dia-bolic, rather than meta-bolic) language that perverts communication and keeps the defeated interlocutors obscurely bound to that which most constrains them.

It is perhaps relatively easy to achieve some mastery of philosophical systems and traditions as the essential prerequisite for this purpose is that the intellect works well. Sufficient familiarity with the meta-descriptive languages combined with a capacity to be conversant with different epistemologies may allow one to philosophize. Since there is no need to transform oneself it is primarily a question of perfecting the accuracy and lucidity of the articulations for which the mind is most suited. One can 'study' philosophy with relative ease but it is more difficult to experiment in listening. It is almost as though in order to listen one had to 'become' different, since it is not so much a question of grasping concepts or propositions as of attempting an experience. Unless we are ready, receptive – and also, possibly, vulnerable – the experience of listening appears to be impossible.

*Philosophy demands our entire mind: listening our totality.* Experiential participation does not seem that necessary in seizing a theoretical construct. Possible responses to significant questions are lucidly articulated and when they are sufficiently satisfying they are accepted without any personal transformation being implied. Conversely, the more one listens the more one is absorbed by an awareness of the fragility of our doctrines and of the fertility of a Socratic 'wonder'.

## PROSPECTS OF COEXISTENCE

In a coexistential perspective of humanity in the making we might regard political thinking as one of the 'tangible' manifestations of the hominization process. And in order to approach this concern in philosophical terms we could start out by invoking Kant's political writings: the *Secret Article of a Perpetual Peace* can in fact be placed in a markedly evolutionary outlook. In this celebrated text, reference is made to a 'unique' article, clearly expressed in a principle whereby 'The maxims of the philosophers on the conditions under which public peace is possible shall be consulted by states which are armed for war.'[15] In its broadest sense the notion of a 'state armed for war' might be regarded as comparable to a cognitive or interactive 'state' similarly 'prepared for war'. Thus the need for an article – a 'secret' one – suggested by certain philosophers would appear as even more paradoxical and illuminating: these philosophers might even 'recommend' a change in strategy, no longer aimed at establishing some new kind of argumentative logic so much as at advocating a listening attitude. As a 'strategy' it would in itself be unbeatable in that no state, political or cognitive, armed for war would ever be able to conceive of the existence of a live and genuine listening disposition; it would also be an innovative strategy inasmuch as the war-like games that constantly unfold in both the ethological and epistemic domains, exhibit an extenuating monotony as a result of which they gravitate down toward ever more banal and potentially destructive levels.

There even seems to be a certain humour in these passages from Kant:

> In transactions involving public right, a secret article (regarded objectively or in terms of its context) is a contradiction. But in subjective terms, i.e. in relation to the sort of person who dictates it, an article may well contain a secret element, for the person concerned may consider it prejudicial to his own dignity to name himself publicly as its originator.[16]

And later:

> It is not to be expected that Kings will philosophise or that philosophers will become Kings; nor is it to be desired, however, since the possession of power inevitably corrupts the free judgement of reason. Kings or sovereign peoples . . .

should not, however, force the class of philosophers to disappear or to remain silent, but should allow them to speak publicly.[17]

But a constituted authority can not degrade itself to the point of asking for advice from its subjects, even when they are philosophers: 'The state will therefore . . . invite their help *silently*, making a secret of it. In other words, it will *allow them to speak* . . . The philosopher should be given a *hearing*.'[18]

Transferring the terms of this relation between philosophers and authority into one that can be envisaged between a discursive and a listening rationality, it is evident that official thinking, constantly and monotonously armed for territorial purposes, will never be able to openly seek instruction from 'subjects', the 'beneficiaries' of normal ratiocination. And yet, to the extent it shares in a coexistential outlook, official thinking 'will . . . invite their help *silently*, making a secret of it. In other words, it will *allow them to speak* freely on . . . warfare and peacemaking.'[19]

Allowing them to speak, however, involves the innovative risk of hypothesizing some form of listening. In seeking instruction they can in fact become exposed to those basic questions that authorities (even scientific or philosophical) tend to avoid. Kant thus seems to be suggesting that in the extent to which a legislating authority, both in social and cognitive domains, aspires to free itself from the warlike style of its vicissitudes, it can 'tacitly' make room for profoundly different voices. A difference that is worthy of the most rigorous attention. 'War – the securing of peace; and peace – the elimination of war. How is peace to be secured by what it eliminates? Something is fundamentally out of joint here, or perhaps it has never yet been in joint', remarks Heidegger in *What Is Called Thinking?*.[20] Out of joint in the same way as a reduced-by-half way of thinking: capable of being assertive but unable to listen.

The editor of Kant's text, considering the irony of its title, remarks that the secret articles that are the delight of diplomats, the ace in their hand and the weapon that decides their success, are considered as morally unconfessable pacts; here, however the secret article becomes a secret and it can not be confessed, not for ethical reasons but to safeguard image and prestige. To take into consideration the maxims and suggestions of philosophers is nothing but naivety: this article must therefore remain secret in order to maintain the dignity of diplomats and politicians.[21] And this 'ingenuousness' can be linked to the question, as radical as it is unavoidable, of the germinal silliness of listening. The path of listening, therefore, can only be connected with a *'secret'* article, because otherwise it would inevitably appear too silly to be proposed in the realm of public rationality. 'Never stay up on the barren heights of cleverness, but come down into the green valleys of silliness', suggests the (subject) philosopher Wittgenstein.[22] The green valleys probably hold a promise of fertility and life. And again: 'For a philosopher there is more grass growing down in the valleys of silliness than up on the barren heights of cleverness';[23] a philosophy of silliness that is able to survive even in the accumulation of 'states' ever more armed in the monotony of belligerent rituals.

Kant also tells us that 'A legal constitution of long standing' – such as the constitution of the rationality underlying the power of our culture –

> gradually makes the people accustomed to judging both their happiness and their rights in terms of the . . . *status quo*. Conversely, it does not encourage them to value the existing state of affairs in the light of those concepts of happiness and right which reason provides. It rather makes them prefer this passive state to the dangerous task of looking for a better one . . . [24]

But in exactly what sense can it be true that reason *provides* 'concepts of happiness and right'? These concepts might only be provided by a 'reason' that has lucidly torn itself away from 'judging . . . in terms of the . . . *status quo*'. And whatever human 'reason' may be, it does not simply *provide*, not unless we become patient and tenacious listeners capable of isolating ourselves from the incessant pseudo-symbolic din that speaks and dictates to us; listeners capable of that minimum of inner silence in which 'reason' could tell us something.

In the extent to which reason tells us something we would find ourselves being driven toward the problem of somehow linking, connecting and articulating the voice of reason with the tough dictates of our daily experience. 'It is obvious that no matter how complete the theory may be, a middle term is required between theory and practice, providing a link and a transition from one to the other', Kant also remarks.[25] A fertile philosophical endeavour might thus be the development of a middle term that provides such a link and transition. A mediating term is not striking, generally discredited and almost impossible to propose – ('silly'?) – and yet essential for a *life* of thought unbound to the banality of warlike arguments that infiltrate every aspect of culture. One of the functions of listening can be seen in the effort to link the word received to the word that is issued; and the innovations that sustain coexistence are derived from links of this kind. Conversing in this way we can constantly recast our propensity for a genuine coexistential relationship; and every link re-enters into the relationship as a new word, to be said and heard in view of further developments.

It is a question of developing those intermediate spaces between the extreme poles of an array that stretches from 'a legal constitution of long standing' to the springing to life of opportunities and novelties. 'For the idea that something which has hitherto been unsuccessful will therefore never be successful does not justify anyone in abandoning even a pragmatic or technical aim (for example, that of flights with aerostatic balloons)', insists Kant. 'This applies even more to moral aims, which, so long as it is not demonstrably *impossible* to fulfil them, amount to duties.'[26] And what superior rationality (political, scientific or even philosophical) could demonstrate such a thing? In this sense therefore it seems eminently 'reasonable' to make an effort to remeditate and cultivate Wittgenstein's green 'valleys of silliness' or the unpresentable 'secret articles' suggested by the philosophers.

'And since the class of philosophers is by nature incapable to forming seditious factions or clubs, they cannot incur suspicion of disseminating propaganda.'[27] But our history of philosophy indicates that philosophers are not more free than anyone else from the inclination to form 'seditious factions', and this would render vain the immense value of the 'secret article' suggested by Kant.

How then does Kant arrive at the point of envisaging a class of philosophers 'by nature incapable of forming seditious factions'? The power of ratiocination is such that it is difficult to avoid the temptation to establish ourselves in an optimal stance that tends to dominate the scene by eclipsing other positions. The answer might lie in surmising that Kant, here, wants us to share some kind of *secret* philosophy, publicly inadmissible because undignified and 'silly'. And possibly the 'philosopher' Kant who argues that his colleagues be given a hearing is referring to the Socratic philosophers rather than to the 'kingly' ones, more disposed to listen than to demonstrate; he is probably not alluding to the emissaries of a dominant epistemology. Should they be entirely motivated by the power of western ratiocination, it would be difficult for them to achieve the sort of laborious awareness that frees them from divisive, partisan inclinations: the entire value of the 'secret article' is anchored in fact to the presence of immune philosophers, 'incapable of forming seditious . . . clubs'.

We might understand the 'philosopher' ('incapable of forming . . . clubs') in an almost emblematic sense, as a figure that is distinguished from the 'sophist' (who argues skilfully in order to always win). And we might also regard the 'philosopher' less as a figure in a cultural context and more as the representation of an aspect, or moment in human evolution. As if the 'philosopher' and the 'sophist' symbolized an alternation taking place even within a single person. We might perhaps seek these 'philosophers' far away from the 'heights of cleverness', where language appears less brilliant and where efforts are made to 'dwell with' and listen in a spirit of tenacity and patience.

Philosophically therefore it is a question of identifying any 'silly' or 'secret' point of departure in order to integrate our outlooks and climb up the slope once more. Buber suggests that when an individual:

> draws a lifeless thing into his passionate longing for dialogue, lending it independence and as it were a soul, then there may dawn in him the presentiment of a world-wide dialogue, a dialogue with the world-happening that steps up to him even in his environment.[28]

It is a question of cultivating a capacity to learn from the 'mediocre' philosophers of our environment and not only from the stars as a far more serious listening commitment is required in the former case. It is a question moreover of developing a dialogue whose 'greatness' has nothing to do with triumph. For example: 'Socrates keeps reducing the sophist to silence,' says Wittgenstein:

> but does he have *right* on his side when he does this? Well,

it is true that the sophist does not know what he thinks he knows; but that is no triumph for Socrates. It can't be a case of 'You see! You don't know it!' – nor yet, triumphantly, of 'So none of us knows anything!'[29]

An integrated rationality, capable of listening and speaking, sometimes seems to be submerged by the resounding discourses that fill an age of ever new successes. And humans who 'logically' always aspire to 'be right', no longer have the strength to free themselves from a contaminated language that may become hypertrophic and misleading: a language that is no longer an instrument of communicative coexistence. The path can thus begin from a non-mitigated experience of our cultural predicament. Through faithfully heeding culture, almost auscultating it, we can avoid the temptation of suggesting how it ought to be. In this case we would relapse into the same coercive style of a rationality that can not listen (although it can prescribe) as if we were in search of further triumphs simply because 'the sophist does not know what he thinks he knows'. A cogent and victorious style is the specific driving force behind the 'sophist' and it would be futile and illusive to discard that style just to resume it once again. The 'sophist' in fact is aiming for success whereas the 'philosopher', perhaps secretly, is aspiring towards progress.

In the paths of coexistence and daily experience we often seem to be confronted by thoughts that can be bent either toward the power of discourse, or in the direction of a listening and coexistential outlook. We may recognize that listening, even in its modesty or silliness, might not merely be able to avoid succumbing to the hegemony of normal rationality but actually might absorb it and dwell with it in an 'impossible' cohabitation that opens up previously unsuspected horizons.

We are in fact seeking a coexistential language that safeguards both proximity and distance. Heidegger reminds us more than once that calling brings near that which is called.[30] This does not mean that the 'calling of language' aims at transferring something within the circle of the immediately present, that is within a domain that expressive language controls as a possession.

The historical unfolding of the axioms of rationality may thus induce linguistic developments primarily suited to controlling reality. Axioms by now no longer suitable for coexistence or even for survival. Our powerful (technological) language leads humans to become the actual or potential masters of the world: this makes it necessary for us to consider whether we are dealing with the achievement of a goal or, on the contrary, with a condition of extreme danger. From a listening point of view it would be sterile to restrict our concern to the revelation of a hypertrophic, ill logos, too involved by now in masterful games from which it is incapable of withdrawing. We might, rather, value such a state as a passage involving risk, a passage comparable to the challenge of any freedom. Certain cultural structures appear to us, in fact, as excessively outmoded paradigms. And yet, precisely in situations of extreme danger we might be able to perceive and possibly ignore those rules that prevent us from seeing the rules which govern the vicissitudes of our relationship with language. At this point the opportunity is offered for becoming aware that the compulsion to win is due less to the intrinsic difficulty of the situation than to inhibitions induced by a non-listening language that prevents us from seeing that which would otherwise be clear.

For those of us who are to live through this challenging philosophical moment it is a question of understanding the passage that is drawing near, and of glimpsing its evolutionary potential.

# Notes

## 1 Towards a fuller understanding of *logos*

1 On the meaning of the term see *A Greek-English Lexicon*, compiled by G. Liddell and R. Scott, Oxford, Clarendon Press, 1968, p. 1057. The word 'logos' is presented as a verbal noun, common in all periods in prose and verse. Possible meanings of this term are grouped in the following ways: (1) computation, reckoning, account of money handled; (2) relation, correspondence; (3) explanation, plea, pretext, ground, statement of a theory, argument, law, rule of conduct, thesis, hypothesis, provisional ground, reason, formula, law; (4) narrative, fable, tale, oration, legend, speech; (5) verbal expression or utterance, word; (6) common talk, report, tradition; (7) divine utterance, oracle, proverb, maxim; (8) assertion; (9) word of command, behest; (10) thing spoken of, subject matter, the truth of the matter.

2 In reference to this word the following meanings are indicated in the same lexicon: pick up, gather, count, tell, say, speak; op. cit., pp. 1033–4.

3 M. Heidegger, *Early Greek Thinking*, p. 67.

4 On this issue see G. Corradi Fiumara, *Funzione simbolica e filosofia di linguaggio*, especially chapter 10, 'Genesi della funzione simbolica', pp. 185–206, and chapter 11, 'Mondo biologico e orizzonte dialogico', pp. 207–33.

5 M. Heidegger, see the chapter entitled 'Logos (Heraclitus, Fragment B.50)', in op. cit., p. 77. This chapter was originally a contribution to the *Festschrift für Hans Jantzen*, edited by Kurt Bauch (Berlin 1951), pp. 7 and following; presented as a lecture to the Bremen Club on May 4 1951; fully discussed in an unpublished lecture course entitled 'Logic'.

6 On this issue see M. Foucault, *Microfisica del potere. Interventi politici*, p. 185.

7 M. Heidegger, *What Is Called Thinking?*, part II, p. 155.

8 Heraclitus, fragment 50. See K. Freeman, *Ancilla to the Pre-Socratic Philosophers. Complete Translation of the Fragments in Diels 'Fragmente der Vorsokratiker'*, p. 28. This is the translation that appears

in M. Heidegger's *Early Greek Thinking*, p. 59: 'When you have listened not to me but to the Meaning, it is wise within the same Meaning to say: *One* is All.'

9  M. Heidegger, *Early Greek Thinking*, p. 60.

10  Heraclitus, fragment 19, see K. Freeman, op cit., p.26.

11  A listening approach which allows for the development of language in the individual may also be regarded as a precondition for creating conventions. 'Beliefs, desires and intentions are a condition of language, but language is also a condition for them . . . Language is a condition for having conventions.' D. Davidson, 'Communication and Convention' in *Inquiries into Truth and Interpretation*, p. 280.

12  M. Heidegger, *Early Greek Thinking*, p. 61.

13  ibid., pp. 61–2, italics added.

14  ibid., p. 62.

15  ibid., p. 63.

16  Buber reminds us that the Greeks distinguished between a powerful world-begetting Eros and one which is weak. 'Those who are loyal to the strong-winged Eros of dialogue know the beloved being. They experience his particular life in simple presence . . . The kingdom of the lame-winged Eros is a world of mirrors and mirrorings. But when the winged one holds sway there is no mirroring.' M. Buber, *The Writings of Martin Buber*, p. 29.

17  G. Vico, *The New Science of Giambattista Vico*, paragraph 151, p. 65.

18  M Heidegger, *Early Greek Thinking*, p. 62.

19  J. Derrida suggests that much could be said on the 'fact' that the primal unity of voice and writing is prescriptive; the superword, *archi-parole*, thus becomes a command. *De la grammatologie*, p. 30.

20  M. Heidegger, *Early Greek Thinking*, p. 64.

21  L. Wittgenstein, *Culture and Value*, p. 30e.

22  ibid., p. 30e.

23  M. Heidegger, *Early Greek Thinking* p. 65.

24  E. Canetti, *The Human Province*, p. 265.

25  H. G. Gadamer, *Truth and Method*, p. 324.

26  G. Vico, op. cit., Section II, p. 60, italics added.

27  op. cit. paragraph IV, p. 61.

28  M. Heidegger, *Early Greek Thinking*, p. 66, italics added.

29  ibid., p. 63.

30  Concerning this issue see E. M. Barth and E. C. W. Krabbe, *From Axiom to Dialogue. A Philosophical Study of Logics and Argumentation*. In this and in other works by Barth there is an endeavour to propagate a more communicative outlook on formal and informal logic, language and semantics as different from a purely deductively defined logic and as different from a purely objective attitude toward language and as against a purely referential or (at least) demonstrational view of semantics.

31  The notion of 'rules of good manners' is derived from P. K. Feyerabend, *Science in a Free Society*.

32  I. Kant, *Political Writings*, 'Perpetual Peace. A Philosophical

Sketch', Appendix I,'On the disagreement between morals and politics in relation to perpetual peace', p. 123.
33 P. K. Feyerabend, *La scienza in una società libera*, p. 112.
34 M. Heidegger, *What is Called Thinking?*, part II, pp. 154–5.
35 P. K. Feyerabend, *La scienza in una società libera*, p. 113.
36 G. Vattimo, preface to M. Heidegger, *Che cosa significa pensare?*,
Vol. I, Milano, Sugar Edizioni, 1979, p.15.
37 J. Derrida, *Margins of Philosophy*, pp. XIV-XV.
38 De la grammatologie, p. 39.
39 Heraclitus, fragment 50, in K. Freeman, p. 28.
40 M. Heidegger, *Early Greek Thinking*, p. 67.
41 ibid., p.68.
42 ibid., p.66.
43 ibid., p.66.
44 ibid., p.67.
45 M. Heidegger, *What is Called Thinking?*, pp. 150–1.
46 M. Heidegger, *Early Greek Thinking*, p. 64.
47 G. W. F. Hegel, *The Phenomenology of Mind*, p. 18.
48 R. Poole, *Towards Deep Subjectivity*, p. 14.

## 2 The logocentric system of culture

1 Xenophanes of Colophon, fragment 16, in K. Freeman, *Ancilla to
the Pre-Socratic Philosophers. Complete Translation of the Fragments
in Diels 'Fragmente der Vorsokratiker'*, p. 22.
2 Xenophanes of Colophon, fragment 14, ibid., p. 22.
3 Xenophanes of Colophon, fragments 23, 24, 25 and 26; ibid., p. 23.
4 P. K. Feyerabend, *La scienza in una società libera*, p. 114, italics
added. With regard to this passage and the chapter as a whole, also
see Feyerabend's *Science in a Free Society*, especially the part entitled
'The Spectre of Relativism', pp. 79–86.
5 E. Severino, *La struttura originaria*, p. 14.
6 L. Wittgenstein, *Culture and Value*, p. 40.
7 In this connection we should once again resort to Heraclitus: 'One
should quench arrogance rather than a conflagration', fragment B43,
in K. Freeman, op. cit., p. 27.
8 L. Wittgenstein, op. cit., p, 40.
9 G. H. von Wright, discussion of the paper 'Action, Psycho-Physical
Parallelism and Freedom'.
10 M. Heidegger, *In cammino verso il Linguaggio*, Milano, Mursia,
1973, p. 30. In reference to this passage and to the chapter as a
whole, see M. Heidegger, *On the Way to Language*, chapter II 'The
Nature of Language', pp. 57–108. One of Wittgenstein's remarks
seems related to this issue: 'The power language has to make
everything look the same, which is most glaringly evident in the
*dictionary* and which makes the personification of *time* possible:
something no less remarkable than would have been making divinit-
ies of the logical constants.' *Culture and Value*, p. 22.

11 I. Kant, *Political Writings*, 'Perpetual Peace. A Philosophical Sketch', Appendix I. 'On the disagreement between morals and politics in relation to perpetual peace', p. 120.

12 P. K. Feyerabend, *La scienza in una società libera*, p. 123.

13 G. Vico, *The New Science of Giambattista Vico*, paragraph XXXII, p. 70, italics added.

14 See G. Corradi Fiumara, *Funzione simbolica e filosofia del linguaggio*, especially chapters 5, 9, 10 and 11.

15 H. G. Gadamer, *Truth and Method*, p. 429.

16 ibid., p. 429.

17 I. Prigogine and I. Stengers, *La nuova alleanza. Metamorfosi della scienza*, pp. 43–4.

18 I. Prigogine and I. Stengers, ibid., p. 44, italics added. Perhaps J. F. Lyotard argues to a similar effect where he says: 'The question of the legitimacy of science has been indissociably linked to that of the legitimation of the legislator since the time of Plato. From this point of view the right to decide what is true is not independent of the right to decide what is just, even if the statements consigned to these two authorities differ in nature. The point is that there is a strict interlinkage between the kind of language called science and the kind called ethics and politics: they both stem from the same perspective, the same "choice" if you will – the choice called the Occident.' *The Postmodern Condition: A Report on Knowledge*, p. 8.

19 P. K. Feyerabend, *La scienza in una società libera*, p. 107.

20 I. Kant, *Political Writings*, 'On the Common Saying: "This May Be True in Theory but it Does not Apply in Practice" ', Section II, 'On the Relationship of Theory and Practice in Political Right', p. 74.

21 ibid., p. 74.

22 P. K. Feyerabend, *La scienza in una società libera*, p. 16.

23 ibid., p. 16.

## 3 A philosophy of listening within a tradition of questioning

1 H. G. Gadamer, *Truth and Method*, p.325, italics added.

2 ibid., p. 324, italics added.

3 N. Tommaseo, *Della bellezza educatrice. Pensieri*, p. 296, italics added.

4 P. Ricoeur, *L'ermeneutica del sublime. Saggi per una critica dell'illusione*, p. 7, italics added.

5 M. Heidegger, *Early Greek Thinking*, p. 65.

6 L. Wittgenstein, *Culture and Value*, p. 63.

7 H. G. Gadamer, op. cit., p. 326, italics added.

8 ibid., p. 326.

9 ibid., p. 326.

10 ibid., p. 327.

11 G. Vico, *The New Science of Giambattista Vico*, p. 88, italics added.

12 H. G. Gadamer, op cit., p. 325, italics added.

13 ibid., p. 325.

14 J. F. Lyotard, *The Postmodern Condition. A Report on Knowledge*, p. 15.

15 S. K. Langer, *Philosophy in a New Key. A Study in the Symbolism of Reason, Rite and Art*, p. 4, italics added.
   The following quotation is connected with this passage in Langer's book: 'A question is really an ambiguous proposition; the answer is its determination.' F. Cohen, 'What is a Question?', pp. 350–64.

16 Heraclitus, fragment B43, quoted in M. Heidegger, *Early Greek Thinking*, p. 75. The other version appears in K. Freeman, *Ancilla to the Pre-Socratic Philosophers. Complete translation of the Fragments in Diels 'Fragmente der Vorsokratiker'*, p. 27.

17 M. Heidegger, op. cit., p. 76.

18 H. G. Gadamer, op. cit., p. 330, italics added.

19 I. Prigogine and I. Stengers, *La nuova alleanza. Metamorfosi della scienza*, p. 44.

20 H. G. Gadamer, op. cit., pp. 330–1.

21 ibid., p. 327. The point at issue could be related to Wittgenstein's recommendation: 'Don't, for *heaven's sake*, be afraid of talking nonsense! But you must pay attention to your nonsense.' *Culture and Value*, p. 56.

22 H. G. Gadamer, op. cit., pp. 336–7.

23. ibid., p. 333.

24 M. Heidegger, *On the Way to Language*, p. 58.

25 ibid., p. 71.

26 M. Heidegger, *What is Called Thinking?*, p. 138.

27 ibid., pp. 175–6.

28 A pseudo-symbolic process, which has the appearance of symbolism but is not conducive to object formation and object use, is 'diabolic' in the etymological sense of the word: the Greek verb *diaballo* is a compound of the word *dia* (across) and the verb *ballo*. Hence a 'diabol' is something that flings things across and, as a consequence, jumbles them up. I suggest, therefore – trying to stay close to the vital complexities of the symbolic function – that communication is symbolic when we have activities which lead to a fuller appreciation of 'reality' and that, in so far as this is carried out, the activity is also a truly metabolic one, a vital one. Pseudo-symbols are diabolic in the sense that they can not possibly be metabolic. On this topic see my article 'The Symbolic Function, Transference and Psychic Reality', *The International Review of Psycho-Analysis*, 1977, pp. 171–80, and also my book *Funzione simbolica e filosofia del linguaggio*.

29 R. Rorty, *Philosophy and the Mirror of Nature*, p. 322.

30 ibid., p.320.

31 Heraclitus, fragment 101a, in K. Freeman, p. 31.

32 R. Rorty, op. cit., p. 320.

33 With regard to the notion of 'commensurability' see the paragraph

entitled 'Commensuration and Conversation' in Rorty, op. cit., pp. 315–22.
34 ibid., p. 321.
35 ibid., p. 321.
36 ibid., p. 318.
37 ibid., p. 316.
38 ibid., p. 316.
39 I. Prigogine and I. Stengers, op. cit., pp. 286–7.
40 R. Rorty, op. cit., pp. 363–5.
41 Heraclitus, fragment B43, in M. Heidegger, *Early Greek Thinking*, p. 75, and in K. Freeman, op. cit., p. 27.
42 L. Wittgenstein, op. cit., p. 73.
43 ibid., p. 72.
44 H. G. Gadamer, op. cit., p. 329.
45 ibid., p. 329.
46 C. Taylor, 'Interpretation in the Sciences of Man', pp. 48–65.
47 T. S. Kuhn, 'The Essential Tension: Tradition and Innovation in Scientific Research', p. XXII.
48 E. Canetti, *The Human Province*, pp. 280–1.

## 4 The power of discourse and the strength of listening

1 Concerning the notion of speech acts, see J. R. Searle, *Speech Acts. An Essay in the Philosophy of Language*.
2 E. Canetti, *The Human Province*, p. 256.
3 S. Freud, Lecture XXXIII, 'Femininity', in *New Introductory Lectures on Psycho-Analysis and Other Works*.
4 G. Vattimo, *Le avventure della differenza*, p. 10.
5 E. Canetti, op. cit., p. 248.
6 ibid., p. 231.
7 J. F. Lyotard, *The Postmodern Condition. A Report on Knowledge*, p. 4.
8 M. Foucault, *Microfisica del potere. Interventi Politici*, p. 20.
9 E. Severino, *Téchne. Le radici della violenza*, p. 91.
10 E. Canetti, op. cit., p. 275.
11 J. F. Lyotard, p. 15. He also suggests that 'Knowledge in the form of an informational commodity indispensable to productive power is already, and will continue to be, a major – perhaps *the* major – stake in the world wide competition for power', p. 5.
12 E. Severino, op. cit., pp. 92–3.
13 F. Rella, *Il silenzio e le parole. Il pensiero nel tempo della crisi*, p. 192.
14 O. Spengler, *Le déclin de l'Occident*.
15 E. Canetti, op. cit., p. 249. He also says: 'They are wise, but their diction is vehement', p. 270. Perhaps the medium is more instructive than the contents.
16 P. A. Rovatti and G. Vattimo, preface to G. Vattimo and P. A. Rovatti, *Il pensiero debole*, p. 7.

17 E. Canetti, op. cit., p. 242.
18 F. Nietzsche, *The Complete Works*, Volume Nine – XIV – *The Will to Power*, Books one and two, paragraph 110, in section entitled 'Signs of Increasing Strength', p. 91. With regard to this topic also see F. Nietzsche, 'The Strong and the Weak', Section II, Part I, Book IV, Volume XV, *The Will to Power*, paragraphs 298–350.
19 Aristotle, *The Metaphysics*, Book IX, paragraph II, 4, p. 435, italics added.

## 5 Listening to philosophical tradition

1 K. Jaspers, *La mia filosofia*, Torino, Einaudi, 1981, p. 6, italics added.
2 M. Sgalambro, *La morte del sole*, p. 13.
3 M. Heidegger, *What Is Called Thinking?*, p. 176, italics added.
4 M. Heidegger, *Early Greek Thinking*, p. 105, italics added.
5 ibid., p. 106, italics added.
6 R. Musil, *L'uomo senza qualità*, Volume 1, Torino, Einaudi, 1979, p. 630.
7 K. Jaspers, op. cit., pp. 6–7.
8 G. Corradi Fiumara, Chapter 9, 'Epistemophily and Knowledge' ('Epistemofilia e conoscenza') in *Funzione simbolica e filosofia del linguaggio*.
9 L. Wittgenstein, *Culture and Value*, p. 83.
10 K. Jaspers, op. cit., pp. 7–8.
11 'For scientific knowledge the world lies in fragments, the more so the more precise our scientific knowledge becomes.' K. Jaspers, *Philosophy Is for Everyman. A Short Course in Philosophical Thinking*, p. 8.
12 H. G. Gadamer, *Truth and Method*, p. 337.
13 G. Vico, *The New Science of Giambattista Vico*, paragraphs 138, X, 139, XI, and 140, p. 63.
14 E. Canetti, *The Human Province*, p. 17.
15 P. Ricoeur, *L'ermeneutica del sublime. Saggi per una critica dell'illusione*, p. 154.
16 G. Vico, op. cit., paragraph 169, p. 68.
17 M. Heidegger, *What Is Called Thinking?*, p. 5.
18 Regarding the interpretation of 'weakness' as freedom, see F. Nietzsche, *The Genealogy of Morals*, Volume XIII, paragraph 47. *The Complete Works*.
19 M. Heidegger, *What Is Called Thinking?*, pp. 238–39.
20 H. G. Gadamer, op. cit., p. 321.

## 6 The philosophical problem of benumbment

1 M. Heidegger, *What Is Called Thinking?*, p. 30.
2 K. Jaspers, *La mia filosofia*, Torino, Einaudi, 1981, p. 236.
3 Regarding the notion of 'forms of life' see L. Wittgenstein, *Philo-

*sophical Investigations*: 'What has to be accepted, the given, is – so one could say – *forms of life.*' p. 226. And also: ' "So you are saying that human agreement decides about what is true and what is false?" – It is what human beings *say* that is true and false; and they agree in the *language* they use. That is not agreement in opinions but in forms of life.' Paragraph 241, p. 88e.

4  R. Musil, *L'uomo senza qualità*, Torino, Einaudi, 1974, Volume I, p. 295.

5  M. Heidegger, op. cit., p. 29.

6  'Philosophy is a battle against the bewitchment of our intelligence by means of language', L. Wittgenstein, *Philosophical Investigations*, paragraph 109, p. 47e.

7  M. Heidegger, op. cit., p. 29.

8  G. Corradi Fiumara, Chapter 7, 'Linguaggio pseudonimbolico' ('Pseudo-symbolic Language'), in *Funzione simbolica e filosofia del linguaggio*.

9  Heraclitus, fragment 34, in K. Freeman, *Ancilla to the Pre-Socratic Philosophers. Complete Translation of the Fragments in Diels 'Fragmente der Vorsokratiker'*, p. 27.

10  K. Jaspers, op. cit., p. 230–1.

11  For an eloquent discussion of 'trembling' see G. W. F. Hegel, *The Phenomenology of Mind*, Section A, 'Lordship and Bondage', pp. 228–40.

12  L. Wittgenstein, *Culture and Value*, p. 37.

13  ibid., p. 54.

14  ibid., p. 52.

In a letter to Goethe, Schopenhauer says: 'Almost all the errors and unutterable follies of which doctrines and philosophies are so full seem to me to spring from a lack of . . . probity. The truth was not found, not because it was unsought, but because the intention always was to find again instead some preconceived opinion or other or at least not to wound some favourite idea, and with this aim in view subterfuges had to be employed against both other people and the thinker himself. It is the courage of making a clean breast of it in face of every question that makes the philosopher. He must be like Sophocles' Oedipus, who seeking enlightenment concerning his terrible fate, pursues the indefatigable enquiry, even when he divines that appalling horror awaits for him in the answer. But most of us carry in our hearts the Jocasta, who begs Oedipus for God's sake not to enquire further; and we give way to her, and that is the reason why philosophy stands where it does.' Letter of Schopenhauer to Goethe, dated 11 November 1815; quoted in S. Ferenczi, *First Contributions to Psycho-Analysis*, London, The Hogarth Press, 1952 (Authorized translation by E. Jones); 'The Symbolic Representation of the Pleasure and Reality principles in the Oedipus Myth', Chapter X, Part 1, pp. 253–4.

15  H. G. Gadamer, *Truth and Method*, p. 319.

16  L. Wittgenstein, Culture and Value, p. 62.

17 ibid., p. 44.
18 E. Canetti, *The Human Province*, p. 276, italics added.

## 7 Silence and listening

1 M. Heidegger, *What Is Called Thinking?*, pp. 191–2.
2 G. Durand, *Le strutture antropologiche dell'immaginario. Introduzione all'archetipologia generale*, Bari, Dedalo Libri, 1972, pp. 157–8.
3 M. F. Sciacca, *Come si vince a Waterloo*, p. 100.
4 Augustine, *De Libero Arbitrio*, Patrologia Latina, Part III, 13, 35, '*Mentibus nostris sine ullo strepitu, ut ita dicam, canorum et facundum quoddam silentium veritatis illabitur*'.
5 L. Wittgenstein, *Tractatus Logico-Philosophicus*, paragraph 7, p. 89.
6 M. Heidegger, *Being and Time*, paragraph 34, p. 208, italics added.
7 G. Corradi Fiumara, 'The symbolic function, transference and psychic reality', pp. 171–80.
8 M. F. Sciacca, op. cit., p. 129.
9 ibid., p. 183.
10 Lao Tze, *Tao Teh Ching. The Way and Its Power* (translated by A. Waley), Boston, Houghton Mifflin, 1934, p. 155. Also reported in L. Wieger, *Les pères du système taoiste. Texte et traduction de Lao-Tzeu, Lie-Tzeu, Tchoang-Tzeu.*
11 M. F. Sciacca, op. cit., p. 26.
12 L. Wittgenstein, *Culture and Value*, p. 77.
13 M. F. Sciacca, op. cit., p. 102.
14 B. McGuinness, 'Freud and Wittgenstein', pp. 32–3.
15 ibid., p. 42, italics added.
16 G. Lakoff and M. Johnson, *Metaphors We Live By*, p. 4.
17 M. F. Sciacca, op. cit., p. 131.
18 The 'battle' metaphor is reflected in our everyday language by a wide variety of expressions suggested by G. Lakoff and M. Johnson: 'Your claims are *indefensible*. – He *attacked every weak point* in my argument. – His criticism was *right on target*. – I *demolished* his argument. – I have never *won* an argument with him. – You disagree? Okay, *shoot*! – If you use that *strategy*, he'll *wipe you out*. – He *shot down* all of my arguments.' op. cit., p. 4.
19 G. Lakoff and M. Johnson, op. cit., p. 5.
20 L. Wittgenstein, Big Typescript MS 213, 423, in G. H. von Wright, 'The Wittgenstein Papers', pp. 483–503. Quoted by A. Kenny, 'Wittgenstein on the Nature of Philosophy', p. 16.
21 L. Wittgenstein, MS 219, 11, quoted in A. Kenny, op. cit., p. 13.
22 L. Wittgenstein, MS 213, 406, quoted in A. Kenny, op. cit., p. 16.
23 G. Ryle, quoted by A. Kenny, op. cit., p. 12.
24 L. Wittgenstein, MS 219, 11, quoted in A. Kenny, op. cit., p. 13, italics added.
25 L. Wittgenstein, *Culture and Value*, p. 2.
26 L. Wittgenstein, MS 213, 431f, quoted in A. Kenny, op. cit., p. 10.
27 A. Kenny, op. cit., pp. 10–11.

28 K. Jaspers, *La mia filosofia*, Torino, Einaudi, 1980, p. 239, italics added.
29 M. F. Sciacca, op. cit., p. 60.
30 ibid., p. 61.

## 8 Dialogic interaction and listening

1 L. Wittgenstein, *Culture and Value*, p. 55.
2 G. Mazzacurati, 'Robert Musil e la crisi della verità', preface to R. Musil, *Discorso sulla stupidità*, Milano, Shakespeare and Company, 1980, p. 9.
3 K. Jaspers, *La mia filosofia*, Torino, Einaudi, 1980, p. 17.
4 I. Kant, *Political Writings*, 'Idea for a universal history with a cosmopolitan purpose', Seventh Proposition, pp. 47–9.
5 ibid., p. 47, italics added.
6 M. Heidegger, *On the Way to Language*, p. 123.
7 F. Halbwachs, 'Causalità lineare e causalità circolare in fisica', pp. 112–3.
8 ibid., p. 113.
9 ibid., p. 71.
10 ibid., p. 72.
11 ibid., p. 72.
12 ibid., p. 73.
13 J. A. Wheeler, 'Genesis and observership', quoted in J. C. Eccles, *The Human Mystery*, p. 29. See also J. A. Wheeler, *Frontiers of Time. Enrico Fermi Course.*
14 L. Wittgenstein, op. cit., p. 62.
15 M. Heidegger, op. cit., p. 57.
16 ibid., p. 71.
17 M. Heidegger, *Early Greek Thinking*, p. 78.
18 E. Canetti, *The Human Province*, p. 243, italics added.
19 M. Heidegger, *On the Way to Language*, p. 66.
20 ibid., p. 66.
21 ibid., p. 59.
22 ibid., p. 142.
23 ibid., p. 65.
24 P. Ricoeur, *L'ermeneutica del sublime. Saggi per una critica dell'illusione*, p. 103.
25 H. G. Gadamer, *Truth and Method*, p. 329.

## 9 On inner listening

1 Plato writes of the '*daimon*' in the *Apology* (31a and 40a), in the *Euthyphro* (3b) and in the *Theaetetus* (151a). Socrates says: 'The truants often return to me, and beg that I would consort with them again – they are ready to go to me on their knees – and then, if my divine sign allows, which is not always the case, I receive them, and they begin to improve again.' Plato, *Theaetetus, The Dialogues*

*of Plato*, Volume III, 151a, p. 245.

In this connection also see J. Jaines, *The Origin of Consciousness and the Breakdown of the Bicameral Mind*.

2 P. Friedlaender, *Plato I. An Introduction*, p. 137.
3 ibid., p. 32, italics added.
4 J. Hillman, *Il mito dell'analisi*, Milano, Adelphi, 1979, p. 85, italics added.
5 P. Friedlaender, op. cit., p. 33.
6 ibid., p. 36, italics added.
7 ibid., p. 37.
8 Heraclitus, fragment 45. K. Freeman, *Ancilla to the Pre-Socratic Philsophers. Complete Translation of the Fragments in Diels 'Fragmente der Vorsokratiker'*, p. 27.
9 P. Friedlaender, op. cit., p. 39.
10 Buber reminds us that the Greeks distinguished between a powerful world-begetting Eros and one which is weak. 'Those who are loyal to the strong-winged Eros of dialogue know the beloved being . . . The kingdom of the lame-winged Eros is a world of mirrors and mirrorings.' M. Buber, *The Writings of Martin Buber*, p. 29.
11 G. Vico, *The New Science of Giambattista Vico*, paragraph 869-XXX, p. 322.
12 ibid., paragraph 870-XXXI, p. 322.
13 P. Friedlaender, op. cit., p. 40.
14 ibid., p. 43.
15 Plato, *Phaedo, The Dialogues of Plato*, 89d, p. 445.
16 M. Heidegger, *Kant and the Problem of Metaphysics*.
17 M. Buber, op. cit., p. 29.
18 L. Wittgenstein, *Culture and Value*, p. 57, italics added.
19 ibid., p. 68, italics added.
20 M. Heidegger, *Che cos'é la metafisica?*, p. 46.
21 ibid., p. 47.
22 M. Heidegger, *Kant and the Problem of Metaphysics*, p. 195.
23 M. Riedel, 'Logik und Akroamatik. Vom zweifachen Anfang der Philosophie', 'Logica e acroamatica. Sul duplice inizio della filosofia', pp. 125–42, italics added.
24 ibid., pp. 125–42, italics added.
25 I. Kant, *Critique of Pure Reason*, Chapter I, The Discipline of Pure Reason, Section I, The Discipline of Pure Reason in the Sphere of Dogmatism, Paragraph 3, Of Demonstrations, p. 420.
26 ibid., p. 420.
27 ibid., p. 421.
28 M. Heidegger, *Kant and the Problem of Metaphysics*, p. XXV.
29 L. Pareyson, *Veritá e interpretazione*, p. 207, italics added..
30 M. Heidegger, *Kant and the Problem of Metaphysics*, p. 194.
31 V. Verra, 'Introduzione' in M. Heidegger, *Kant e il problema della metafisica*, p. XIX.
32 M. Heidegger, *Kant and the Problem of Metaphysics*, p. 194.
33 V. Verra, op. cit., p. II.
34 M. Heidegger, *Aus der Erfahrung des Denkens*, Pfullingen, Gunther

Neske, 1954, p. 17; quoted in L. Pareyson, *Verità e interpretazione*, p. 244.
35 M. Heidegger, *Kant and the Problem of Metaphysics*, pp. 194–5.
36 M. Heidegger, *On the Way to Language*.
37 V. Verra, op. cit., p. X.
38 M. Heidegger, *Kant and the Problem of Metaphysics*, p. 252.
39 ibid., pp. 196–7, italics added.

## 10 Midwifery and philosophy

1 Plato, *Theaetetus, The Dialogues of Plato*, Volume III, 148d, 148e, 149, p. 243.
2 'Si tu veux réussir à ce que vive un arbre projette autour de lui cet espace intérieur qui réside en toi . . . Ce n'est que en prenant forme dans ton renoncement qu'il devient reéllement arbre.' R. M. Rilke, 'Vision intérieure et perspective inversée', translation by L. Brion-Guerry from *Aestetik und Kunstwissenschaft*, Band XI–2, reported in J. C. Chevalier (ed.), *Dictionnaire des Symboles*, Paris, Robert Laffont, 1969, p. XXIII.
3 M. Heidegger, *Che cos'é la metafisica?*, p. 54.
4 ibid., p. 54.
5 Plato, *Theaetetus, The Dialogues of Plato*, 149d, 149e, 150, p. 244, italics added.
6 M. Heidegger, *On the Way to Language*, p. 68.
7 P. Ricoeur, *L'ermeneutica del sublime. Saggi per una critica dell'illusione*, pp. 106–7.
8 M. Heidegger, *Being and Time*, p. 206.
9 P. Ricoeur, op. cit., pp. 103.
10 G. H. von Wright, 'Action, Psycho-Physical Parallelism and Freedom', p. 26 in the typescript.
11 L. Wittgenstein, *Philosophical Grammar*, pp. 381–82; quoted in A. Kenny, 'Wittgenstein on the Nature of Philosophy', p. 3.
12 M. Heidegger, *On the Way to Language*; the expression is used a few times in the volume.
13 M. Heidegger, *What Is Called Thinking?*, p. 131.
14 ibid., p. 131.
15 E. Fox Keller, *A Feeling for the Organism. The Life and Work of Barbara McKlintock*, New York, Freeman, 1983; quoted in E. Fox Keller, *Sul genere e la scienza*, Milano, Garzanti, 1987, p. 165; a translation of the volume *Reflections on Gender and Science*.
16 Plato, *Theaetetus, The Dialogues of Plato*, 151, p. 245 and 131c, p. 246.
17 K. Jaspers, *Philosophy is for Everyman. A Short Course in Philosophical Thinking*, p. 11.
18 M. Heidegger, *On the Way to Language*, pp. 68–9, italics added. He also says 'Why does he tell precisely of renunciation? . . . Because this renunciation is a genuine renunciation, not just a question of Saying, not a mere lapse into silence. As self-denial,

renunciation remains Saying. It thus preserves the relation to the word. But because the word is shown in a different, higher rule, the relation to the word must also undergo a transformation. Saying attains to a different articulation.'¹, p. 147.

19 There must be problems in listening to something new, even if it is as 'simple' as heart beats. William Harvey has had serious difficulties in propagating his observations. In the Epistle Dedicatory to Dr Argent, President of the College of Physicians, he says: 'But, my loving colleagues . . . I do not profess either to learn or to teach . . . from books or from the maxims of philosophers . . .', p. 7. And later on in his essay: 'The heart rises up and lifts itself upward into a point, so that at that moment it strikes the chest and the beat can be felt outside.', p. 32. William Harvey, 'Exercitatio anatomica de motu cordis et sanguinis in animalibus', first translated into English in 1653; *An Anatomical Disputation Concerning the Movement of the Heart and Blood in Living Creatures*.

20 I. Kant, *Political Writings*, 'An Answer to the Question: "What is Enlightenment?" ', p. 54.

21 ibid., p. 54.

22 ibid., p. 54–5.

23 L. Wittgenstein, *Culture and Value*, p. 52. He also says: 'Sometimes a sentence can be understood only if it is read at the right *tempo*. My sentences are all supposed to be read *slowly*.', p. 57. Italics in the text.

24 Concerning the problem, Habermas suggests that 'I understand myself only in the "sphere of what is common" in which I simultaneously understand the other in his objectivations. For our two expressions of life are articulated in the same language, which for us has intersubjectively binding validity.' J. Habermas, *Knowledge and Human Interests*, p. 156.

25 M. Heidegger, *In cammino verso il Linguaggio*, Milano, Mursia, 1973, p. 28.

26 In *On the Way to Language* this notion is expressed several times. He also reiterates: 'To let ourselves be told what is worthy of thinking means – to think.', p. 155.

27 M. Heidegger, *In cammino verso il Linguaggio*, p. 42.

28 L. Wittgenstein, *Culture and Value*, p. 77.

29 M. Heidegger, *What Is Called Thinking?*, p. 130.

30 ibid., p. 8.

31 ibid., pp. 115–16.

32 U. Eco, 'L'antiporfirio', in G. Vattimo and P. A. Rovatti (eds), *Il pensiero debole*, Feltrinelli, Milano 1984, p. 76.

33 M. Heidegger, *What Is Called Thinking?*, p. 129.

34 G. Vico, *The New Science of Giambattista Vico*, p. 75, paragraphs 218–19.

35 Heraclitus, fragment 34, in K. Freeman, *Ancilla to the Pre-Socratic Philosophers. Complete Translation of the Fragments in Diels 'Fragments der Vorsokratiker'*, p. 26.

36 See G. Corradi Fiumara, chapter 11, 'Dal mondo biologico all'

orizzonte dialogico' ('From biological reality to dialogic life'), in *Funzione simbolica e filosofia del linguaggio*.

37 I. Kant, *Critique of Pure Reason*, 'Transcendental Dialectic', Book I, Section I, 'Of Ideas in General', p. 219.

38 R. Harris, *The Language Makers*, p. 187.

39 P. Ricoeur, op. cit., p. 153.

40 Heraclitus, fragment 115, in K. Freeman, op. cit., p. 32.

41 E. Canetti, *The Human Province*, p. 268.

42 'Thinking habits will develop because other possibilities have not even emerged. Contents enter into me unquestioned; I have turned into something before asking myself what I want to be.' K. Jaspers, *Philosophy. Volume I* (translated by E. B. Ashton), Chicago, University of Chicago Press, 1969, p. 287.

43 R. Harris, op. cit., p. 11.

44 ibid., p. 11.

## 11 Paths of listening

1 See G. Corradi Fiumara, *Funzione simbolica e filosofia del linguaggio*, especially in reference to the discussion of pseudo-symbolic language and of the normative function of expression.

2 M. Heidegger, *On the Way to Language*, p. 59.

3 Plato, *Theaetetus, The Dialogues of Plato*, Volume III, 155d, p. 251, italics added.

4 M. Heidegger, *What Is Called Thinking?*, part I, p. 5, italics added.

5 Plato, *Theaetetus, The Dialogues of Plato*, 155d, p. 251.

6 In a variety of dialogic confrontations it is possible to identify the person who, at least in theory, should carry more responsibility than the other. This is obvious in situations such as interactions between a doctor and a patient, a teacher and a student, a parent and a child. And quite apart from official roles which can often be reversed, one of the two actually takes up more responsibility than the other in view of the overall development of the situation; and this may be the case for a number of reasons such as maturity, intelligence, patience, willingness to survive, etc.

7 U. Eco, *Lector in fabula. La cooperazione interpretativa nei testi narrativi*, p. 3.

8 L. Wittgenstein, *Culture and Value*, p. 18.

9 M. Heidegger, *What Is Called Thinking?*, p. 119.

10 M. Heidegger, *Being and Time*, part I, paragraph 34, 'Being-there and discourse. Language', p. 207.

11 L. Wittgenstein, op. cit., p. 55.

12 ibid., p. 86.

13 M. Buber, *Il principio dialogico*, p. 13.

14 L. Wittgenstein, op. cit., p. 2.

15 ibid., p. 1, italics in the text.

16 E. Canetti, *The Human Province*, p. 253.

17 Plato, *Euthydemus, The Dialogues of Plato*, 293, p. 230.

18  K. Jaspers, *Man in the Modern Age*, p. 182.

19  Plato, *Protagoras, The Dialogues of Plato*, 239, pp. 153–4.

20  Aristotle, *Posterior Analytics, Topica*, book VIII, XIV, 164b 10, p. 739, italics added.

21  ibid., p. 739, italics added.

## 12  The philosophy of listening: an evolutionary approach

1  On this problem see P. Filiasi Carcano, *Epistemologia delle scienze umane e rinnovamento filosofico*.

2  L. Valzelli, *L'uomo e il rettile*, p. 14.

3  ibid., p. 15.

4  Regarding the evolutionary potential of the human brain, see R. Fiumara, 'Il cervello come macchina darwiniana', pp. 63–6.

5  'If we now ask what means there are of maintaining and indeed accelerating . . . progress toward a better state, we soon realise that the success of this immeasurably long undertaking will depend not so much upon *what* we do (e.g. the education we impart to younger generations) and upon what methods *we* use to further it; it will rather depend upon what human *nature* may do in and through us, to compel us to follow a course which we would not readily adopt by choice.' I. Kant, *Political Writings*, 'On the Common Saying: "This may be True in Theory, but it Does not Apply in Practice" ', III, 'On the relationship of theory to practice in international right', p. 90.

6  On this problem see, for instance; H. F. Blum, *Time's Arrow and Evolution*; T. Dobzhanski, *Mankind Evolving. The Evolution of the Human Species*; J. Hawkes, *Prehistory in the History of Mankind. Cultural and Scientific Development*; H. J. Jerison, *Evolution of the Brain and Intelligence*; P. V. Tobias, *The Brain in Hominid Evolution*.

7  J. C. Eccles, *The Human Mystery*, p. 103.

8  ibid., p. 103.

9  ibid., p. 100, italics added.

10  L. Woolley, *The Beginnings of Civilization*, quoted in J. C. Eccles, op. cit., p. 110. See also J. Jaines, *The Origin of Consciousness and the Breakdown of the Bicameral Mind*.

11  E. Canetti, *The Human Province*, p. 200.

12  L. Wittgenstein, *Culture and Value*, p. 64.

13  H. G. Gadamer, *Truth and Method*, p. 323, italics added.

14  The term 'bipersonal field' is taken from R. Langs, *The Listening Process*.

15  I. Kant, *Political Writings*, 'Perpetual Peace. A Philosophical Sketch', 'Second Supplement: Secret Article of a Perpetual Peace', p. 115.

16  ibid., p. 114.

17  ibid., p. 115.

18  ibid., p. 115, italics added.

19 ibid., p. 115, italics added.
20 M. Heidegger, *What Is Called Thinking?*, p. 83.
21 D. Fauci, 'Introduzione', pp. VII-XLIV, in I. Kant, *Scritti di filosofia politica. Per la pace perpetua e altri saggi*, footnote on p. 131.
22 L. Wittgenstein, op. cit., p. 76.
23 ibid., p. 80.
24 I. Kant, *Political Writings*, 'On the Common Saying: "This may be True in Theory, but it Does not apply in Practice" ', II, 'On the relationship of theory to practice in political thought' – Conclusion, p. 86.
25 ibid., p. 61.
26 ibid., p. 89, italics added.
27 ibid., p. 115.
28 M. Buber, *The Writings of Martin Buber*, p. 38.
29 L. Wittgenstein, op. cit., p. 56.
30 M. Heidegger, *On the Way to Language*, Chapter II, 'The nature of language', pp. 57–108.

# Bibliography

Antiseri, D. *Teoria unificata del metodo*, Padova: Liviana, 1981.

Apel, K. O. *Comunità e comunicazione*, Torino: Rosemberg e Sellier, 1977.

Aristotle *Posterior Analytics. Topica* (translated by E. S. Forster), Cambridge, Mass.: Harvard University Press, 1960.

Aristotle *The Metaphysics*, Books I-IX (translated by H. Tredennick), Cambridge, Mass.: Harvard University Press, 1980.

Banville, T. *How to Listen: How to Be Heard*, Chicago: Nelson-Hall, 1978.

Barth, E. M. and Krabbe, E. C. W. *From Axiom to Dialogue. A Philsophical Study of Logics and Argumentation*, Berlin-New York: Walter de Gruyter, 1982.

Bartlett, F. *Remembering*, London: Cambridge University Press, 1961.

Bateson, G. *Mind and Nature. A Necessary Unity*, Toronto: Bantam Books, 1979.

Bernstein, B. *Class, Codes and Control*, London: Routledge & Kegan Paul, 1971.

Bespaloff, R. *On the Iliad*, New York: Tudor Press, 1967.

Betti, E. *Teoria generale della interpretazione*, Milano: Giuffré, 1955.

Bettinghaus, E. P. *Persuasive Communication*, New York: Holt, Rinehart & Winston, 1968.

Black, M. *Language and Philosophy*, Ithaca, N.Y.: Cornell University Press, 1952.

Blum, H. F. *Time's Arrow and Evolution*, Princeton: Princeton University Press, 1968.

Bruner, J. *On Knowing: Essays for the Left Hand*, Cambridge, Mass.: Harvard University Press, 1962.

Brunschvicg, L. *Héritage de mots, héritage d'idées*, Paris: Presses Universitaires de France, 1945.

Buber, M. *Between Man and Man* (translated by R. G. Smith), London: Kegan Paul, 1947.

Buber, M. *The Writings of Martin Buber* (selected, edited and introduced by W. Herberg), New York: World Publishing Company, 1956.

Buber, M. *Il principio dialogico*, Milano: Comunitá, 1959.

Buber, M. *The Knowledge of Man* (translated by M. Friedman and R. G. Smith), London: Allen and Unwin, 1965.

Bunge, M., Halbwachs, F., Kuhn, T. S., Piaget, J. and Rosenfeld, L. (eds) *Les théories de la causalité*, Paris: Presses Universitaires de France, 1971.

Canetti, E. *The Human Province* (translated by J. Neugroschel), London: Pan Books, 1986.

Caracciolo, A. Presentazione di M. Heidegger, *In cammino verso il Linguaggio*, Milano: Mursia, 1973.

Chase, S. *The Power of Words*, New York: Harcourt, 1938.

Cohen, F. 'What Is a Question?', *The Monist*, 1929, XXXIX, 3: 350–64.

Corradi, G. *Philosophy and Coexistence*, Leyden: Sijthoff, 1966.

Corradi Fiumara, G. 'Filosofia del linguaggio e costruzione della realtá', in P. Filiasi Carcano *Introduzione alla lettura di 'Ricerche filosofiche' di Wittgenstein*, Roma: Bulzoni, 1976.

Corradi Fiumara, G. 'The symbolic function, transference and psychic reality', *The International Review of Psycho-Analysis*, 1977, 4: 171–80.

Corradi Fiumara, G. *Funzione simbolica e filosofia del linguaggio*, Torino: Boringhieri, 1980.

Davidson, D. *Inquiries into Truth and Interpretation*, Oxford: Clarendon Press, 1985.

Dechend (von), H. and Santillana (de), G. *Hamlet's Mill. An Essay on Myth and the Frame of Time*, London: MacMillan, 1970.

Derrida, J. *La voix et le phénomène*, Paris: Presses Universitaires de France, 1967.

Derrida, J. *De la grammatologie*, Paris: Editions de Minuit, 1967.

Derrida, J. *Margins of Philosophy* (translated by A. Bass), Brighton: The Harvester Press, 1982.

Dobzhanski, T. *Mankind Evolving. The Evolution of the Human Species*, New Haven: Yale University Press, 1962.

Durand, G. *Les structures anthropologiques de l'imaginaire*, Paris: Presses Universitaires de France, 1963.

Eccles, J. C. *The Human Mystery*, Berlin-Heidelberg: Springer International, 1979.

Eco, U. *Lector in fabula. La cooperazione interpretativa nei testi narrativi*, Milano: Bompiani, 1979.

Eco, U. 'L'antiporfirio', in G. Vattimo and P. A. Rovatti (eds), *Il pensiero debole*, Milano: Feltrinelli, 1984.

Egidi, R. *Il linguaggio delle teorie scientifiche. Esperienza ed ipotesi nell'epistemologia contemporanea*, Napoli: Guida Editori, 1979.

Faucci, D. Introduzione e note, in I. Kant *Scritti di filosofia politica. Per la pace perpetua e altri saggi*, Firenze: La Nuova Italia, 1975.

Feyerabend, P. K. *Las scienza in una società libera* (translated by L. Sosio from the modified German edition *Erkenntnis für freie Menschen*, Frankfurt am Main: Suhrkamp Verlag: 1980), Milano: Feltrinelli, 1982.

Feyerabend, P. K. *Science in a Free Society*, London: Verso Editions-NLB, 1987.

Filiasi Carcano, P. *Epistemologia delle scienze umane e rinnovamento filosofico*, Roma: Bulzoni, 1976.

Fiumara, R. 'Il cervello come macchina darwiniana', *Bollettino di Psichiatria Biologica*, 1988, IV, 3:63–6.

Flew, A. *Thinking about Thinking*, London: Fontana, 1975.

Foucault, M. *Microfisica del potere. Interventi politici*, Torino: Einaudi, 1977.

Fox Keller, E. *Reflections on Gender and Science*, New Haven: Yale University Press, 1985.

Freeman, K. *Ancilla to the Pre-Socratic Philosophers. Complete Translation of the Fragments in Diels 'Fragmente der Vorsokratiker'*, Oxford: Basil Blackwell, 1956.

Freud, S. Lecture XXXIII, 'Femininity', *New Introductory Lectures on Psycho-Analysis and Other Works*, The Standard Edition of the Complete Psychological Works of S. Freud, Volume XXII, 1932–6, London: The Hogarth press and The Institute of Psycho-Analysis.

Friedlaender, P. *Plato. I. An Introduction* (translated by H. Meyerhoff), London: Routledge & Kegan Paul, 1958.

Gadamer, H. G. *Kleine Schriften*, Tübingen: J. C. B. Mohr, 1967.

Gadamer, H. G. *Truth and Method* (translated by W. Glen-Doepel, J. Cumming and G. Barden), London: Sheed & Ward, 1979.

Galilei, G. *Dialogo sopra i due massimi sistemi del mondo, tolemaico e copernicano*, Torino: Einaudi, 1975.

Gavuzzo, M. L. *Metafisica e condizione umana*, Roma: Ianua, 1983.

Geach, P. *Reason and Argument*, Oxford: Basil Blackwell, 1976.

Goethe, J. W. 'Vorarbeiten zu einer Physiologie der Pflanzen', *Werke*, II, VI, Stuttgart-Tübingen: Cotta, 1827.

Habermas, J. *Knowledge and Human Interests* (translated by I. Shapiro), London: Heinemann Educational Books, 1978.

Habermas, J. *Communication and the Evolution of Society* (translated by T. McCarthy), Boston: Beacon Press, 1979.

Halbwachs, F. 'Causalità lineare e causalità circolare in fisica', in M. Bunge, F. Halbwachs, T. S. Kuhn, J. Piaget and L. Rosenfeld, (eds) *Le teorie della causalità*, Torino: Einaudi, 1974.

Harris, R. *The Language Makers*, London: Duckworth, 1980.

Harvey, W. *An Anatomical Disputation Concerning the Movement of the Heart and Blood in Living Creatures, (Exercitatio anatomica de motu cordis et sanguinis in animalibus*; translated by G. Whittenridge), Oxford: Blackwell Scientific Publications, 1976.

Hawkes, J. *Prehistory in History of Mankind. Cultural and Scientific Development*, Vol. I, UNESCO, London: New English Library, 1965.

Hegel, G. W. F. *The Phenomenology of Mind* (translated by J. B. Baillie), London: Allen and Unwin, 1966.

Heidegger, M. *Kant and the Problem of Metaphysics* (translated by J. S. Churchill), Bloomington, Indiana: Indiana University Press, 1962.

Heidegger, M. *Being and Time* (translated by J. Macquarrie and E. Robinson), London: SCM Press, 1962.

Heidegger, M. *On the Way to Language* (translated by P. D. Hertz), New York: Harper & Row, 1971.

Heidegger, M. *What Is Called Thinking?* (translated by J. G. Gray and F. D. Wieck), New York: Harper & Row, 1972.

Heidegger, M. *Che cos'é la metafisica? (Con estratti della 'Lettera su l'Umanesimo')*, Firenze: La Nuova Italia, 1974.

Heidegger, M. *Early Greek Thinking* (translated by D. Farrell Krell and F. A. Capuzzi), New York: Harper & Row, 1975.

Hillman, J. *The Myth of Analysis*, Urbana: North Western University Press, 1972.

Hintikka, J. and Vaina, L. (eds) *Cognitive Constraints in Communication. Representations and Processes*, Reidel: Dordrecht, 1983.

Husserl, E. *Die Krisis der europäischen Wissenschaften und die transzendentale Phänomenologie*, Den Haag: Martinus Nijhoff Bookhandel, 1959.

Husserl, E. *Logical Investigations* (translated by J. N. Findlay), Vol. I, London: Routledge & Kegan Paul, 1960.

Jaines, J. *The Origin of Consciousness and the Breakdown of the Bicameral Mind*, Princeton: Princeton University Press, 1976.

Jaspers, K. *Man in the Modern Age*, Garden City, N. J.: Doubleday, 1957.

Jaspers, K. *Philosophy is for Everyman. A Short Course in Philosophical Thinking* (translated by R. F. C. Hull and G. Wels), London: Hutchinson, 1969.

Jaspers, K. *Reason and Anti-Reason in Our Time* (translated by S. Godman), Hamden, Connecticut: Anchor Books, 1971.

Jerison, H. J. *Evolution of the Brain and Intelligence*, London: Academic Press, 1973.

Kant, I. *Critique of Pure Reason* (translated by J. M. D. Meiklejohn), London: J. M. Dent, 1986.

Kant, I. *Political Writings* (translated by H. B. Nisbet; edited by H. Reiss), Cambridge: Cambridge University Press, 1987.

Kenny, A. 'Wittgenstein on the Nature of Philosophy' in B. McGuinness (ed.) *Wittgenstein and his Times*, Oxford: Basil Blackwell, 1982.

Kuhn, T. S. 'The Essential Tension: Tradition and Innovation in Scientific Research', in C. W. Taylor and F. Barron (eds) *Scientific Creativity: Recognition and Development*, New York: Wiley and Sons, 1963.

Lakoff, G. and Johnson, M. *Metaphors We Live By*, Chicago: University of Chicago Press, 1980.

Langer, S. K. *Philosophy in a New Key. A Study in the Symbolism of Reason, Rite and Art*, London: Oxford University Press, 1951.

Langs, R. *The Listening Process*, New York: Jason Aronson, 1978.

Levin, D. M. *The Listening Self*, London: Routledge, 1989.

Lugarini, L. *Critica della ragione e universo della cultura. Gli orizzonti cassireriani della filosofia trascendentale*, Roma: Edizioni dell'Ateneo, 1983.

Lyotard, J. F. *The Postmodern Condition: A Report on Knowledge* (translated by G. Bennington and B. Massumi), Manchester: Manchester University Press, 1987.

McGuinness, B. 'Freud and Wittgenstein', in B. McGuinness (ed.) *Wittgenstein and his Times*, Oxford: Basil Blackwell, 1982.

McLuhan, M. *The Gutenberg Galaxy*, Toronto: The University Press, 1962.

McLuhan, M. *Understanding Media. The Extensions of Man*, London: Ark, 1987.

Morris Engel, S. *Wittgenstein's Doctrine of the Tyranny of Language*, The Hague: Martinus Nijhoff, 1971.

Nietzsche, F. W. *The Complete Works* (edited by O. Levy; translated by P. V. Cohen and A. M. Ludovici; the first complete and authorized English translation; 18 volumes), Edinburgh-London: T. N. Foulis, 1909–13.

Pareyson, L. *Verità e interpretazione*, Milano: Mursia, 1972.

Plato *Thirteen Epistles* (translated by L. A. Post), Oxford: Clarendon Press, 1925.

Plato *The Dialogues of Plato* (translated into English with analyses and introductions by B. Jowett), Oxford: Clarendon Press, 1953.

Poole, R. *Towards Deep Subjectivity*, London: Allan Lane, 1973.

Prigogine, I. and Stengers, I. *La nuova alleanza. Metamorfosi della scienza*, Torino: Einaudi, 1981.

Quine, W. V. O. *The Roots of Reference*, The Paul Carus Lectures, Illinois: La Salle, 1974.

Radnitzky, G. and Andersson, G. (eds) *Progresso e razionalità della scienza*, Roma: Armando, 1984.

Rella, F. *Il silenzio e le parole. Il pensiero nel tempo della crisi*, Milano: Feltrinelli, 1981.

Rescher, N. *The Logic of Commands*, London: Routledge & Kegan Paul, 1966.

Ricoeur, P. *L'ermeneutica del sublime. Saggi per una critica dell'illusione*, Messina: Sortino Editore, 1972.

Ricoeur, P. *Fallible Man* (revised translation by C. A. Kelbley), New York: Fordham University Press, 1980.

Ricoeur, P. *Hermeneutics and the Human Sciences. Essays on Language, Action and Interpretation* (translated by J. Thompson), Cambridge: Cambridge University Press, 1980.

Ricoeur, P. *Time and Narrative* (translated by K. McLaughlin and D. Pellaner), Vol. I, Chicago: University of Chicago Press, 1984.

Riedel, M. 'Logica e acroamatica. Sul duplice inizio della filosofia', *Paradigmi*, 1985, 7:125–42.

Rorty, R. *Philosophy and the Mirror of Nature*, Oxford: Basil Blackwell, 1980.

Rovatti, P. A. 'Trasformazioni nel corso dell'esperienza', in G. Vattimo and P. A. Rovatti (eds) *Il pensiero debole*, Milano: Feltrinelli, 1984.

Rovatti, P. A. and Vattimo, G. 'Premessa', in G. Vattimo and P. A. Rovatti (eds) *Il pensiero debole*, Milano: Feltrinelli, 1984.

Santillana (de), G. and Dechend (von), H. *Hamlet's Mill. An Essay on Myth and the Frame of Time*, London: MacMillan, 1980.

Schilpp, P. A. *Albert Einstein: Philosopher-Scientist*, New York: The Library of Living Philosophers, 1951.

Schwaber, E. 'Psychoanalytic listening and psychic reality', *The International Review of Psycho-Analysis*, 1983, 10, 4:379–92.

Sciacca, M. F. *Come si vince a Waterloo*, Milano: Marzorati, 1963.
Searle, J. R. *Speech Acts. An Essay in the Philosophy of Language*, London: Cambridge University Press, 1969.
Severino, E. *Téchne. Le radici della violenza*, Milano: Rusconi, 1979.
Severino, E. *La struttura originaria*, Milano: Adelphi, 1981.
Sgalambro, M. *La morte del sole*, Milano: Adelphi, 1982.
Spengler, O. *Le déclin de l'Occident* (translated by M. Lazerout), Paris: Gallimard, 1931.
Taylor, C. 'Interpretation in the Sciences of Man', *Review of Metaphysics*, 1971, 25:48–65.
Thalberg, I. 'Mental Activity and Passivity', *Mind*, 1978, LXXXVII, 347:376–95.
Tobias, P. V. *The Brain in Hominid Evolution*, New York: Columbia University Press, 1971.
Tomellini, P. *Linguaggio e percezione*, Roma: Ianua, 1983.
Tommaseo, N. *Della bellezza educatrice. Pensieri*, Napoli: Giovanni Pedone Lauriel Editore, 1855.
Vaina, L. and Hintikka, J. (eds) *Cognitive Constraints in Communication. Representations and Processes*, Dordrecht: Reidel, 1983.
Valzelli, L. *L'uomo e il retille*, Torino: Edizioni Medico Scientifiche, 1976.
Vattimo, G. *Le avventure della differenza*, Milano: Garzanti, 1980.
Vattimo, G. and Rovatti, P. A. (eds) *Il pensiero debole*, Milano: Feltrinelli, 1984.
Verra, V. 'Introduzione', in M. Heidegger *Kant e il problema della metafisica*, Roma-Bari: Laterza, 1981.
Vico, G. *The New Science of Giambattista Vico* (revised translation of the third edition of 1744; translated by I. G. Bergin and M. H. Fisch), Ithaca, N.Y.: Cornell University Press, 1968.
Wheeler, J. A. *Frontiers of Time. Enrico Fermi Course*, Amsterdam: North Holland Publishing Company, 1979.
Wieger, L. *Les pères du système taoiste. Texte et traduction de Lao-Tzeu, Lie-Tzeu, Tchoang-Tzeu*, Paris: Belles Lettres, 1950.
Wisdom, J. *Philosophy and Psychoanalysis*, Oxford: Basil Blackwell, 1953.
Wittgenstein, L. *Philosophical Grammar* (edited by A. Kenny), Oxford: Basil Blackwell, 1974.
Wittgenstein, L. *Remarks on the Philosophy of Psychology* (edited by G. E. M. Anscombe, G. H. von Wright and H. Nyman), Oxford: Basil Blackwell, 1980.
Wittgenstein, L. *Tractatus Logico-Philosophicus* (translated by P. F. Pears and B. McGuinness), London: Routledge & Kegan Paul, 1981.
Wittgenstein, L. *Philosophical Investigations*, (translated by G. E. M. Anscombe), Oxford: Basil Blackwell, 1988.
Wittgenstein, L. *Culture and Value* (translated by P. Winch; edited by G. V. von Wright in collaboration with H. Nyman), Oxford: Basil Blackwell, 1988.
Woolley, L. *The Beginnings of Civilization*, New York: Mentor Books, 1963.

Wright (von), G. H. 'The Wittgenstein Papers', *Philosophical Review*, 1969, 79:483–503.

Wright (von), G. H. 'Action, Psycho-Physical Parallelism and Freedom', paper presented at the Institute of Philosophy, Facoltà di Magistero, of the First University of Rome on 17 November 1988.

Zappella, M. *Non vedo, non sento, non parlo*, Milano: Mondadori, 1984.

# Subject index

acroamatic proofs 136–7
activity, philosophical 92, 126
affection 148
*Amicus Plato sed magis amica veritas* 77
annihilation 89
anomalies, philosophical use of 49–51
answer/s 32, 38, 39, 126
argument/s 129, 182; importance of 133; philosophical 136–7; and reflections 93; in terms of war 108–10
arrogance 45
articles, secret 193–4, 195; unique 192
articulation, capacity for 61
attention, contextual circle of 135
authority, philosophical 193

battle, metaphor of 108, 110, 207 (18n)
benumbment 76, 127; awareness of 82–6; description of 86–90; passion for 84, 86, 91
boredom 140–1; problem 133

Cartesian stance 117
causal logic 66
casual point of view 91
casuality, circular 75, 118, 119; classical 66; linear 119; simple 119; transformed conception of 118
cause and effect 118, 120

coexistence, and integration 16; prospects of 192–8
coexistential space, creation of 99–100
cognitive boredom 85
cognitive function 24
cognitive interactions 46
cognitive models 107
cognizance-taking 74
communication, defined 111–12; prospects of 189–91; responsibility in 88; and silence 101
computers 55
continuity, need for 129
courage, philosophical 94
creative endeavours 141–2
crying, of a child 178
cultural structures, as outmoded paradigms 198
culture, western, ambiguity and misunderstanding in 69; conceit of 9–10; as constraining and limiting 60, 120–1; decline of 65; full of detail 161–2; humanistic approach to 97; as incomplete 121; as logical 26–7; logocentric 19; and military devices 68; as (non)-listening 47, 150; and notions of power and strength 62–4; and perfection of language 107–8; tribal limits of rationalism and 18; underlying *logos* of 7–8

# Name index